# THE
# TOURIST

W9-BZO-645

SCHOCKEN BOOKS · NEW YORK

# THE TOURIST

A new theory of the leisure class

## DEAN MacCANNELL

With a New
Introduction
by the Author

New Introduction Copyright © 1989 by Dean MacCannell

Copyright © 1976 by Schocken Books Inc.

All rights reserved under International and Pan-American Copyright Conventions. Published in the United States by Schocken Books Inc., New York, and simultaneously in Canada by Random House of Canada Limited, Toronto. Distributed by Pantheon Books, a division of Random House, Inc., New York.

Material quoted from the *The New York Times* and *New York Times Magazine* copyright © 1967, 1968, 1969, 1970, 1972 by the New York Times Company. Reprinted by permission.

Chapter 5, "Staged Authenticity," originally appeared in the *American Journal of Sociology*, vol. 79, n. 3 (November 1973), copyright © 1973 by The University of Chicago, and is published here by permission.

Library of Congress Cataloging in Publication Data

MacCannell, Dean.
  The tourist.

  Includes bibliographical references and index.
  1. Travelers. 2. Tourist trade. 3. Civilization,
Modern. 4. Leisure. I. Title.
G155.A1M17    338.4'7'91    75-7770
ISBN 0-8052-0895-x

Display typography by Archie Ferguson

Manufactured in the United States of America

Revised Edition

987654

# CONTENTS

# Introduction to the 1989 Edition

If the founding claim of postmodernism is taken seriously, the social arrangements I described more than a dozen years ago passed out of existence almost exactly coincident with the original publication date of *The Tourist*. I wanted the book to serve as a new kind of ethnographic report on *modern* society, as a demonstration that ethnography could be redirected away from primitive and peasant societies, that it could come home. My approach was to undertake a study of tourists, to follow and observe them with seriousness and respect, as a method of gaining access to the process by which modernity, modernization, modern *culture* was establishing its empire on a global basis. Now, according to the postmodern thesis, the edge of sociocultural change is no longer the province of modernity. Lyotard, Jameson, Kroker, and others whose thought deserves respect combine a kind of Marxism (without the labor theory of value) with a recently developed, powerful method of esthetic analysis, deconstruction, for purposes of describing current cultural phenomena. Their approach teaches us that the rise of multinational corporations and the corresponding global extension of American economic and military domination fundamentally altered the substance and behavior of classic capitalism. Esthetic production, which in an earlier time might have provided a critique of capitalism, has become fully integral with commodity production. This integration disrupts the dialectic of surface and depth on which we could once depend for alteration of social and economic relations from within; the simmering or explosion of revolutionary sentiments from the depths of capitalist civilization (modernity) are fully neutralized (postmodernity). Now we have all surface and no depth, the death of the critical, revolutionary, and free subject, and the end of "history."

Postmodernism is not to be dismissed as mere leisure of the theory class. Photorealist painting, the valorization of surfaces in art, architecture, and human relationships, pastiche and the recycling of cultural elements, etc., are fully empirical and susceptible to ethnographic investigation concerning their cultural significance. Much of the material that would eventually be analyzed under the heading "postmodern" already put in an appearance in *The Tourist*. So if I could accept the critical theory of postmodernism, I would want to identify *The Tourist* with its prestige and smooth over the embarrassment of republishing a book about something that no longer exists. Perhaps "the tourist" was really an early postmodern figure, alienated but seeking fulfillment in his own alienation—nomadic, placeless, a kind of subjectivity without spirit, a "dead subject." There is even textual evidence for this: for example, the term "postindustrial modernity," is used throughout the book. The sights and spectacles of tourism were specifically described as a concrete form of the internationalization of culture and as a system of esthetic surfaces which are comprehensive and coercive. Even the figure of the "revolutionary" has a cameo role on the first pages of *The Tourist* and then, as if on cue, disappears.

But the interpretation I gave these matters is not the same as that which would eventually be provided by theorists of the postmodern condition. The difference in treatment has to do with the validity of claims on behalf of the postmodern for its extraordinary historical privilege and ethnographic salience.[1] In

1. For example, Fredric Jameson (p. 68) has commented: "This mesmerizing new aesthetic mode itself emerged as an elaborated symptom of the waning of historicity, of our lived possibility of experiencing history in some active way" ("Postmodernism, or The Cultural Logic of Late Capitalism, *The New Left Review* vol. 146, July–August, 1984, pp. 53–93). And Umberto Eco: "There is a constant in the average American imagination and taste, for which the past must be preserved and elabo-

the context of current research and scholarship I would want to be held accountable in *ethnographic* terms. There are grounds (about which more later) for theoretical disagreement. But I would hope that any student who enters this arena will hold to the principle of holism on a methodological level even as we recognize that our subject matter is not classically "bounded"; that observation be detailed and based on living with the people we write about, even if we don't identify with them; that descriptions are perspicacious from the double perspective of objective specialists (e.g., social scientists, critics) *and* those whose lives are touched by the conditions described, in this case, the tourists and especially those the tourists come to see; and finally that concern for observation of real people in real situations always precede the development of socio-cultural theory.

On the basis of my own observations, and my reading of the work of other students who have done research on tourism and modernity, I am not prepared to argue that the accumulation of materials called "postmodern" constitute the end of history, or even a distinct historical epoch, nor can I say that I believe they touch humanity in its tenderest parts. They are more a repression and denial necessary to the dirty work of modernity so it can continue to elaborate its forms while seeming to have passed out of existence or to have changed into something "new" and "different." I could not personally undertake the task of explaining to an assembly line worker that industrial society "no longer exists." And while there are strong historical grounds for the claim that the United States' invasion of Grenada was devised in the first place to serve as a kind of "text," I would not undertake to explain Vietnam as a "textual effect," certainly not to someone who was there.[2]

Much of our current critical and political project appears to me as a kind of unrealized mourning in which all of life has become

rated in full-scale authentic copy; a philosophy of immortality as duplication. It dominates the relation with the self, with the past, not infrequently with the present, always with History . . ." (*Travels in Hyperreality* [San Diego: Harcourt Brace Jovanovich, 1986] p. 6).

2. See, for example, Jameson's discussion of Michael Herr's *Dispatches*, in "Postmodernism," p. 84.

reorganized around something that "died," bestowing upon the purportedly dead subject, dead epoch, dead values, etc.—honors, privilege, and prestige denied them in life. With all the goodwill in the world, current criticism is a self-conflicted exercise. There is no way to prevent pronouncements concerning "the death of the subject" or the "crisis of historicity" from being readable as expressions of an anticreative ethos, nostalgia for the bourgeois or Cartesian subject, and a Eurocentric past—the very institutions and concepts which the critics seek to deconstruct. The rhetoric of postmodernity virtually assures that all thought, not merely "critical" thought, will be compromised in this way. Ronald Reagan rose to power on the Berkeley Free Speech Movement. He was ostensibly opposed to the movement, but now it is clear that no one listened more attentively to what the student revolutionaries were actually saying, and no one would eventually benefit more, even directly, from the rhetorical power of their statements. Recall that he called it "The Reagan Revolution" and that it was the students, not he, who first enunciated the demand to "get bureaucracy off our backs." Reagan's recycling of 1960s politics is a postmodern gesture *par excellence,* as if the recycling of *any* form, even one which was originally antipathetic to current political goals, is automatically superior to the creation of something new. His politics were not technically of the political right. They established the "center" as a place of political indifference by means of a violent trivialization of political and historical distinction. This absolute commitment to the process of recycling political positions, no longer as positions but as pure form, is a kind of death at the cultural level. It makes the idea of the "end of history," if not quite a self-fulfilling prophesy, at least a self-propelling fallacy.

A main procedure employed by tourism precisely parallels the founding theoretical gesture of postmodernism: an arbitrary line is drawn across the path of history—postmodernists jump across the line in one direction, into the historyless void, and tourists jump in the other, to "where the action was."[3] The

3. Louis Marin has suggested language for both destinations in his concept of a "degenerate utopia"; See his essay on Disneyland in *Utopics: Spatial Play* (New Jersey: Humanities Press, 1984).

doctrine of historylessness has been articulated at least twice before. It was developed during the neolithic by our ancestors for reasons that remain obscure, and it was developed in the early 1950s by strategic nuclear planners who believed that after the stockpiling of nuclear weapons we must never again have history. Lévi-Strauss has made a methodological point of the difference between types of society which operate in "reversible time," that although "surrounded by the substance of history . . . try to remain impervious to it," versus societies that turn history into the "motive power of their development."[4] Of course, for Lévi-Strauss, these two types of society are unambiguously "primitive" and "modern" respectively. He does not remark on the possibility, increasingly real after Hiroshima and Nagasaki, that modern peoples might attempt to enter "reversible time," to join with primitives in deciding not to have a history. When a major postmodernist writes about the *modern* world,[5] he speaks of such things as monumental architecture and abstract expressionism: a combination of which could be *real*ized only in a nuclear holocaust. But he does not address the nuclear or even its declaration in modern art and architecture. It is suppressed as primitives suppress from their narratives anything that might qualify as historical. One is reminded that among the most popular types of tourist attractions are memorials and tombs, and primitive and peasant peoples.

The need to be *post* modern can thus be read as the same as the desire to be a tourist: both seek to empower *modern* culture and its conscience by neutralizing everything that might destroy it from within. Postmodernism and tourism are only the positive form of our collective inarticulateness in the face of the horrors of modernity: of mustard gas and machine guns, Hiroshima and Nagasaki, Dachau, Buchenwald, Dresden. Tourism is an alternate strategy for conserving and prolonging the modern and protecting it from its own tendencies toward self-destruction.

4. G. Charbonnier, *Conversations With Claude Lévi-Strauss* (London: Cape, 1969) p. 39. Cited by Anthony Giddens in a helpful chapter on "Structuralism and the Theory of the Subject," pp. 9–48 in his *Central Problems in Sociological Theory* (Berkeley: University of California Press, 1979).

5. E.g., Jameson, "Postmodernism," pp. 56ff.

Ground zero at Hiroshima, the Kennedy assassination site, the ovens at Dachau, the Berlin Wall—all figure in *The Tourist* as important attractions. Sightseeing, rather than suppressing these things from consciousness, brings them to our consciousness, "as if" we might assimilate them.

All of this raises a question which a reader might want answered: Does tourism and/or postmodernity, conceived in the most positive possible way as a (perhaps final) celebration of distance, difference, or differentiation, ultimately liberate consciousness or enslave it? Is modernity, as constituted in the system of attractions and the mind of the tourist, a "utopia of difference," to use Van den Abbeele's energetic phrase?[6] Or does it trap consciousness in a seductive pseudo-empowerment, a prison house of signs? *The Tourist* does not give an answer. When this question arises in the text (and it does about every ten pages) the language becomes evasive and patently annoying, for which I now apologize.[7] It is really a question for Professor Derrida. Philosophy need not await the results of ethnographic investigations, an answer is always only a pen-stroke away; it need only be written. But current philosophical writing, to the extent that I am familiar with it, exhibits deep ambivalence on the matter of the historical arrangement, and especially the rearrangement of human differences, as between men and women, or the First and Third Worlds. Is it not possible that any celebration of "difference" is something insidious: that is, the sucking of difference out of difference, a movement to the

6. Georges Van den Abbeele, "Sightseers: The Tourist as Theorist," *Diacritics* vol. 10, December 1980, pp. 2–14.

7. A few examples: "Sightseeing is a kind of collective striving for a transcendence of the modern totality, a way of attempting to overcome the discontinuity of modernity, of incorporating its fragments into unified experience" (p. 13). "This craziness of mere distinctions forces the modern consciousness to explore beyond the frontiers of traditional prejudice and bigotry in its search for a moral identity" (p. 41). "Modernity is staggering right now, not so much as a result of its 'internal contradictions' as of plenitude and stagnation. . . . It is not now possible to describe the end of this particular development of culture. If our consciousness fails to transcend this, it will resolve itself in a paroxysm of differentiation and collapse" (p. 86).

still higher ground of the old arrogant Western Ego that wants to see it all, know it all, and take it all in, an Ego that is isolated by its belief in its own superiority.

Here, I can only comment in personal terms on the *conditions* for an answer. While I abhor any tendency to belittle the motives or competencies of the people we study, I still doubt that a "utopia of difference" has been established anywhere. The tourist may be involved in the production of culture by his movements, markings, deployment of souvenirs, and, of course, the creation of entire environments for his pleasure. But this does not insure against the tourist building his own prison house of signs even, or especially, if he is on the leading edge of the social construction of reality. Whether or not tourism, on a practical level (or philosophy at the level of theory), can ever be a "utopia of difference," ultimately depends on its capacity to recognize and accept *otherness* as radically other. To me, this means the possibility of recognizing and attempting to enter into a dialogue, on an equal footing, with forms of intelligence absolutely different from my own.

The system of attractions as signs that mediate between the consciousness of the tourist and the other is treated in *The Tourist* as an enormous deferral of the question of the acceptance of otherness. If the tourist simply collects experiences of difference (different peoples, different places, etc.), he will emerge as a miniature clone of the old Western philosophical Subject, thinking itself unified, central, in control, universal, etc., mastering otherness and profiting from it. But if the various attractions force themselves on consciousness as obstacles and barriers between tourist and other, that is, as objects of analysis, if the deconstruction of the attraction is the same as the reconstruction of authentic otherness (another person, another culture, another epoch) as having an intelligence that is not our intelligence, then tourism might contribute to the establishment of a utopia of difference. Of course, this is only a *theoretical* possibility which, given the dialectics of authenticity, someone will claim to have achieved on a practical level at the moment of its enunciation. In short, I suspect a pseudo-reconstruction of "authentic otherness" is the most probable historical outcome of this particular development of culture.

As I have already suggested, if it were being written now, I would not much modify the position of *The Tourist* on the question of modernity, except to incorporate a specific criticism of the postmodernist thesis. But several changes *would* be necessary, foremost among these a modification dictated by historical events. Twenty-five years ago the dominant activity shaping world culture was the movement of institutional capital and tourists to the remote regions, and the preparation of the periphery for their arrival.[8] This, of course, followed on three hundred years of foreplay by explorers, soldiers, missionaries, and anthropologists. Today, the dominant force—if not numerically, at least in terms of its potential to re-shape culture—is the movement of refugees, "boat people," agricultural laborers, displaced peasants, and others from the periphery to the centers of power and affluence. Entire villages of Hmong peasants and hunters, recently from the highlands of Laos, have been relocated and now live in apartment complexes in Madison, Wisconsin. Refugees from El Salvador work in Manhattan, repackaging cosmetics, removing perfume from Christmas gift boxes, rewrapping it in Valentine gift boxes. Legal and illegal "aliens" weed the agricultural fields of California. The rapid implosion of the "Third World" into the First constitutes a reversal and transformation of the structure of tourism, and in many ways it is more interest-

8. *The Tourist* might be read as a study of the cultural forms associated with the historical forces described in organizational and economic terms by Immanual Wallerstein in his *Capitalist World Economy* (Cambridge: Cambridge University Press, 1979), except that touristic apparatus often exhibits a peculiar capacity to transcend the capitalist/socialist distinction, reminding us that this might not be an ultimate kind of distinction from the standpoint of history. Recently, Ernesto Laclau and Chantal Mouffe have made a theoretical move on the left that similarly questions the capitalist/socialist opposition, an attempt to pull the revolutionary struggle for economic equality out from between these two aging giants as they collapse into each other's arms. See their *Hegemony and Socialist Strategy: Toward a Radical Democratic Politics* (London: Verso, 1985).

ing than the first phase of the globalization of culture.[9] The test of the integrity of current research on tourism and modernity will be its contribution to our understanding of these new historical cases. For example, I would hope soon to see a clarification of the application of the Deleuzian concept of "nomadism" which is now in fashion. No doubt someone will be tempted to squeeze the homeless and the impoverished for symbolism even after their last dollars are gone. But it would be theoretically and morally wrong to equate the forced nomadism and homelessness of the refugee and the impoverished with the supercilious voluntaristic Abercrombie and Fitch tourist or other soldiers of fortune.

A second new concern, if *The Tourist* had just been written, would be its relationship to feminist theory. There has been much progress in the last dozen or so years in our understanding of the myths and ideologies of gender, or the ways gender is used to shape other aspects of culture. This progress has not been so much in biological and social-psychological areas as in semiotics and psychoanalysis, specifying the *modus operandi* of the hegemonic drive at the cultural level, something I was also trying to accomplish in *The Tourist*. A discovery of feminist scholarship has to do with the way power hides itself in order to operate more universally and effectively. "Hides itself" is actually incorrect. It would be better to say that "it pretends to be hiding something" that, if exposed, would justify control of culture, as in "this might be a gun in my pocket." Thus, the maintenance of the generative principle of culture under a male sign (e.g., the name of the father, the phallus, etc.) requires the covering of the male "member," the urinary segregation of the sexes noted by Lacan and Goffman, and a corresponding public exposure of women as proof that they, unlike men, have "nothing to hide." The most common procedure used to accomplish this hiding is to shield it behind the principle of the genderlessness of power which is

9. A recent special issue of *The Annals of Tourism Research* (vol. 16, 1989), on the "Semiotics of Tourism," is devoted almost entirely to ethnographic and historical accounts of the effects of repositioning the periphery.

always really male: e.g., "the president" is categorically gender-less but always male—"the surgeon," "the millionaire," etc. The cultural forces at work here are so strong that even if the surgeon happens to be biologically female she is still culturally a "he." "The tourist" may be the most frivolous of these putatively gender-less but masculine figures, so beside the point of gender poli-tics that I doubt feminists would think it worthwhile to attack him. Yet we can note a certain realization on the current fron-tiers of tourism: e.g., the sex tours of Bangkok. Masculism and modernism are still making effective use of nameless, faceless, "genderless," seemingly "minor" armies: What is an expedition-ary force without guns? Tourists. A combination of feminist theory and tourism research could yield needed descriptions of the self-destructive elements found at the end of a hegemonic drive.

Certain other events and experiences which might have modi-fied my thinking on tourism did not. My travels in the course of gathering observations for the book were restricted to an area of the earth extending along the Pacific coast of North America: from Vancouver, British Columbia, in Canada to Baja California, then across the United States and Western and Eastern Europe to Istanbul. After I finished *The Tourist,* I was able to visit Mexico, Africa, and Asia. Nothing that I found in my subsequent travels has caused me to want to change the overall thesis of the book, though I admit to having been surprised to discover villages in Nigeria and India where (although *I* was there) there is no insti-tutionalized tourism.

In the last decade, tourism research has established itself as a virtual field of study. By a peculiar twist of fate, I have not directed any of the numerous dissertations that clarify *The Tourist* and correct for its shortcomings. But I owe a tremendous debt of gratitude to those who have been involved in this work, and I apologize that circumstances do not permit the incorporation of their new findings in this edition. I am especially grateful to Professor Bennetta Jules-Rosette and her students at the Univer-sity of California at San Diego for finding sociological applications, and to Professor Nelson Graburn and his students in anthropology at Berkeley. Professor Jean-Paul Dumont of the University of Washington has brought together anthropological studies, Lévi-Straussian theory, and tourism research. The late Donald Appleyard of the University of California at Berkeley (city planning), was an early reader and developed the critique of modernity for the design professions. Professors Richard Baumann and Beverly Stoeltje and their students in folklore at Indiana University have done interesting case studies on the rodeo and on tour guide speeches. Professor Dan Rose and his students and colleagues in architecture and anthropology at the University of Pennsylvania have made discoveries at the juncture of these fields, especially in their ethnographic studies of Chadds Ford. There are also applications that are beginning to appear in the field of American studies. Everyone with an interest in tourism is indebted to Professor Jafar Jafari of the University of Wisconsin for founding the *Annals of Tourism Research*. Many of the articles appearing in the *Annals* involve interesting empirical tests of hypotheses derived from *The Tourist*. Others who may have been more energetic than I in developing the thesis and implications of *The Tourist* include Professor Erik Cohen in Israel, Marie-Françoise Lanfant and Didier Urbain in France, and Marc Laplante in Canada. Several reviews of the book, in which I was able to recognize my aims in writing it, came from scholars outside the social sciences. I learned some things from Georges Van den Abbeele's review in *Diacritics* (cited above), for example, and Jonathan Culler's in *The American Journal of Semiotics*.

Perhaps this is an appropriate place to note that while I may seem to have overlooked or neglected to report the sources of support for my research on tourism and travel, this is not the case. I have never received any institutional funding for this work. This was certainly not my intention at first. I applied for support from Social Science Research Council in 1967, and from the National Science Foundation in 1971. Now I admit to a certain perverse pleasure in the knowledge that none of this work is on anyone else's balance sheet or ledger. There is an element of willfulness here, of course, but mainly I have Juliet Flower MacCannell, our sons, Daniel and Jason, and my publishers to thank for freely extending to me a level of confidence that I could not imagine demanding. Nor have I taken any fees for consultation on matters of travel and tourism. I *did*, however, once give several days of free advice to a group of elderly retired Chinese farm laborers who asked me how they might fight against the plans of a land developer and the State of California to turn their entire town into a "living museum," a "monument" recognizing the "important contribution of Asian Americans to California agriculture." So far, they have succeeded in their resistance.

D. MacC.
Lafayette, California
February, 1989

# ACKNOWLEDGMENTS

I think a book of this kind would not have been written without the assistance of a specialist in one of the "cultural sciences." I have discussed every aspect of this work with my wife, Dr. Juliet Flower MacCannell, an active literary scholar, and she has given freely of her admirable insight.

Barbara Sirota, who teaches English in the Humanities Program at MIT, read the first draft and gave me an interpretation that helped pave the way for the second.

I have benefited from many conversations with Robert J. Maxwell, and with Ruth C. Young who shares my interest in the relationship of tourism and modern society. It was Paul de Man who first suggested to me the need for a study of modernity.

Professors Jack V. Buerkle, Lewis Coser, Erving Goffman, A. Paul Hare, John A. Hostetler, Everett C. Hughes, John M. Roberts, and Frank W. Young have given me both encouragement and assistance of a specific kind with this project.

More thanks are owed Frank Young who first taught me how to analyze complex social structures. Young's own research is so scientifically clear-cut and sound that I hesitate to acknowledge his influence on this work which is often speculative and probably raises more questions than it settles.

Many friends and colleagues, many more than are mentioned here by name, have brought me observations from their own travels. I have been helped most in this regard by my mother, Dr. Frances M. MacCannell, who taught me never to pass an historical marker without reading it. Pat Arnold made some excellent video tapes of sightseers for me which I was able to use to check some of my ideas.

LeGrace Benson, David Flower, Leslie Burlingame, and Judith Adler helped me by making diaries, or by letting me "de-brief" them on tape after their travels.

My friend, Ron Nordheimer, of Delaware Travel Agency, Inc., of Wilmington, was my travel agent and consultant on technical aspects of the travel business for the duration of this study. He never gave me a bad piece of information.

Janet Walters gave me money which made it possible for me to continue working on the book at a time when its future was in doubt.

All unattributed quotes and descriptions are from my own field notes and are based on first-hand observation.

D. MacC.
September 1975

The University of California, Davis

LIFE is a hospital where each patient is dying to change beds. One of them would like to suffer in front of the heater; another thinks he could get better next to the window.

It seems to me that I would always be better off where I am not, and this question of moving is one of those I discuss incessantly with my soul.

"Tell me, my soul, poor chilled soul, what would you think of going to live in Lisbon? It must be warm there, and you would be renewed, happy as a lizard. This city is near the water; they say it's built of marble, and that the people there have such a hatred of vegetation, they rip out all the trees. Here is a country to your taste; a landscape of light and mineral, and liquid to reflect them."

My soul does not answer.

"Since you love to relax so much, watching the spectacle of movement, do you want to live in Holland, that beatifying land? Perhaps you would be amused in this country whose image you have so often admired in museums. What would you think of Rotterdam, you who love forests of masts, and ships anchored at the steps of houses?"

My soul remains mute.

"Batavia, would it be more amenable? We would find there, besides, the spirit of Europe married to tropical beauty."

Not a word. My soul, could it be dead?

"Have you then come to the point of such torpor, paralysis, that you are not happy except in your pain? If it is so, let us flee toward countries that are analogous to Death. I have it, poor soul! We shall pack our trunks for Torneo, the North of Sweden. Let's go further still, to the extreme end of the Baltic; still further than life, if this is possible; let's install ourselves at the pole. There the sun grazes the earth obliquely, and the slow alternatives of light and night suppress variety and augment monotony, this half of nothingness. There we could take long baths of shadow, while, to give us diversion, the aurora borealis would send us from time to time their pink sheaves, like reflections of fireworks from Hell.

Finally, my soul explodes, and wisely cries to me: "Anywhere! Anywhere! Only let it be out of this world."

CHARLES BAUDELAIRE

"Anywhere out of this world—N'importe où hors du monde," *Petits Poèmes en Prose (Le Spleen de Paris)* (Paris: Editions Garnier Frères, 1962), pp. 211-13. Translated by Juliet Flower MacCannell.

# THE
# TOURIST

# INTRODUCTION

"TOURIST" is used to mean two things in this book. It designates actual tourists: sightseers, mainly middle-class, who are at this moment deployed throughout the entire world in search of experience. I want the book to serve as a sociological study of this group. But I should make it known that, from the beginning, I intended something more. The tourist is an actual person, or real people are actually tourists. At the same time, "the tourist" is one of the best models available for modern-man-in-general. I am equally interested in "the tourist" in this second, metasociological sense of the term. Our first apprehension of modern civilization, it seems to me, emerges in the mind of the tourist.

I began work on this project in Paris in 1968 with much disregard for theory. Shortly after my arrival, I found myself at a reception given for some American scholars by the wife of the owner of Maxim's Restaurant. We were presented to Professor Claude Lévi-Strauss. Lévi-Strauss gave us a brief statement on some recent developments in the structural analysis of society and then he invited questions. It was not possible, he said, to do an ethnography of modernity. Modern society is just too complex; history has intervened and smashed its structure. No matter how hard one searched, one would never find a coherent system of relations in modern society. (I did not bring up this matter which was so important to me. Someone else did. I just sat there listening.) Perhaps it would be possible, Lévi-Strauss concluded, to do a structural analysis of a detail of modern etiquette, something like "table manners in modern society." I admit to having

1

been somewhat put off by his remarks, so much so, in fact, that I turned away from French Structuralism at that point, seeking refuge in my small but growing inventory of observations of tourists. I would try to understand the place of the tourist in the modern world, I thought, outside of existing theoretical frameworks.

When I returned to Paris in 1970-71 to analyze my field notes and observations, I was surprised to discover that my interpretations kept integrating themselves with a line of inquiry begun by Émile Durkheim in his study of primitive religion. I was not surprised to discover that the existing theory that best fit my facts originated in another field: structural anthropology. This kind of theoretical transfer is commonplace. Nor was I surprised that a theory devised to account for primitive religious phenomena could be adapted to an aspect of modern secular life. I do not believe that all men are essentially the same "underneath," but I do believe that all cultures are composed of the same elements in different combinations. I was surprised because the most recent important contribution to this line of research is, of course, Lévi-Strauss's own studies of the *Savage Mind* and of primitive classification. I admit that I am still somewhat concerned about the implications of his admonition that one cannot do an ethnography of modernity, but I shall go ahead anyway, confident at least that I did not *try* to do a structural analysis of the tourist and modern society. It forced itself upon me.

The more I examined my data, the more inescapable became my conclusion that tourist attractions are an unplanned typology of structure that provides direct access to the modern consciousness or "world view," that tourist attractions are precisely analogous to the religious symbolism of primitive peoples.

Modernity first appears to everyone as it did to Lévi-Strauss, as disorganized fragments, alienating, wasteful, violent, superficial, unplanned, unstable and inauthentic. On second examination, however, this appearance seems almost a mask, for beneath the disorderly exterior, modern society hides a firm resolve to establish itself on a worldwide base.

Modern values are transcending the old divisions between the Communist East and the Capitalist West and between the "de-

veloped" and "third" worlds. The progress of modernity ("modernization") depends on its very sense of instability and inauthenticity.
For moderns, reality and authenticity are thought to be elsewhere: in
other historical periods and other cultures, in purer, simpler life-
styles. In other words, the concern of moderns for "naturalness,"
their nostalgia and their search for authenticity are not merely casual
and somewhat decadent, though harmless, attachments to the
souvenirs of destroyed cultures and dead epochs. They are also
components of the conquering spirit of modernity—the grounds of its
unifying consciousness.

The central thesis of this book holds the empirical and ideological
expansion of modern society to be intimately linked in diverse ways to
modern mass leisure, especially to international tourism and sightseeing. Originally, I had planned to study tourism and revolution, which
seemed to me to name the two poles of modern consciousness—a
willingness to accept, even venerate, things as they are on the one
hand, a desire to transform things on the other. While my work on
revolution continues, it is necessary for several reasons to present the
tourist materials now. This book may also serve as an introduction to
the structural analysis of modern society.

A structural approach to society departs somewhat from traditional sociological approaches, and I should attempt to characterize
that difference. Academic sociology has broken modern society into
several researchable subelements (classes, the city, the rural community, ethnic groups, criminal behavior, complex organization, etc.)
before having attempted to determine the ways these fit together.
This procedure has led to careful empirical research and "theories of
the middle range," but it has not resulted in a sociology that can keep
pace with the evolution of its subject. Now, it seems to me that
sociology will not progress much beyond its current glut of unrelated
findings and ideas until we begin to develop methods of approaching
the total design of society and models that link the findings of the
subfields together in a single framework.

This task is difficult because of the complexity of modern society
and because its boundaries do not fit neatly with some other boundary
system such as those circumscribing a religion, language or nation.
There are pockets of traditional society in modern areas and outposts

of modernity in the most remote places. Modernity cannot, therefore, be defined from without; it must be defined from within via documentation of the particular values it assigns to qualities and relations.

## The Method of the Study

The method for this study began with a search for an existing institution or activity with goals very similar to my own: an explication of modern social structure. This approach enables me to draw upon the collective experiences of entire groups, that is, to adopt the "natural standpoint" and detour around the arbitrary limits sociology has imposed upon itself. The organized activities of international sightseeing seemed reasonably adapted to my purposes. The method is similar to the way Erving Goffman reconstructs everyday life in our society by following the contours of face-to-face interaction— interaction itself being a naturally occurring collective effort to understand, or at least to cope with, everyday life. It is also similar to the method Lévi-Strauss uses to arrive at *la pensée sauvage* via an analysis of myths—myths being the masterworks of "untamed" minds.

I saw in the collective expeditions of tourists a multibillion dollar research project designed, in part, around the same task I set myself: an ethnography of modernity. I never entertained the notion that the old one-man–one-culture approach to ethnography could be adapted to the study of modern social structure, not even at the beginning. Methodological innovations such as those provided by Goffman and Lévi-Strauss, far from being exemplary, are minimally adequate. So I undertook to follow the tourists, sometimes joining their groups, sometimes watching them from afar through writings by, for and about them. Suddenly, my "professional" perspective which originally kept me away from my problem opened outward. My "colleagues" were everywhere on the face of the earth, searching for peoples, practices and artifacts we might record and relate to our own sociocultural experience. In Harold Garfinkel's terms, it became possible to stop thinking about an ethnography of modernity and to start *accomplishing* it.

Perhaps I am guilty of presenting an ancient phenomenon as if we moderns just invented it. If, as a matter of fact, I am guilty of this, I can only say that such an act is a commonplace of social science, and is almost to be expected. Actually, self-discovery through a complex and sometimes arduous search for an Absolute Other is a basic theme of our civilization, a theme supporting an enormous literature: Odysseus, Aeneas, the Diaspora, Chaucer, Christopher Columbus, *Pilgrim's Progress*, Gulliver, Jules Verne, Western ethnography, Mao's Long March. This theme does not just thread its way through our literature and our history. It grows and develops, arriving at a kind of final flowering in modernity. What begins as the proper activity of a *hero* (Alexander the Great) develops into the goal of a socially organized *group* (the Crusaders), into the mark of status of an entire social *class* (the Grand Tour of the British "gentleman"), eventually becoming *universal experience* (the tourist). I will have occasion to draw upon this tradition and other traditions which are submerging in modernity.

At a time when social science is consolidating its intellectual empire via a colonization of primitive people, poor people and ethnic and other minorities, it might seem paradoxically out of the "mainstream" to be studying the leisure activities of a class of people most favored by modernity, the international middle class, the class the social scientists are serving. Nevertheless, it seems to me that if we are eventually to catch up with the evolution of modern society, we must invent more aggressive strategies to attempt to get closer to the heart of the problem. By following the tourists, we may be able to arrive at a better understanding of ourselves. Tourists are criticized for having a superficial view of the things that interest them—and so are social scientists. Tourists are purveyors of modern values the world over —and so are social scientists. And modern tourists share with social scientists their curiosity about primitive peoples, poor peoples and ethnic and other minorities.

## The Sociology of Leisure

This is, then, a study in the sociology of leisure. This field is relatively undeveloped, but it will develop quite rapidly, I think, as a consequence of the transition of industrial social structure to a "post-industrial" or "modern" type. Leisure is displacing work from the center of modern social arrangements. There is evidence in the movements of the 1960's that the world of work has played out its capacity for regeneration. Experimental forms of social organization are no longer emerging from the factories and offices as they did during the period of mechanization and unionization. Rather, new forms of organization are emerging from a broadly based framework of leisure activities: T-groups, new political involvements, communal living arrangements, organized "dropping out," etc. "Life-style," a generic term for specific combinations of work and leisure, is replacing "occupation" as the basis of social relationship formation, social status and social action.

Wherever industrial society is transformed into modern society, *work* is simultaneously transformed into an object of touristic curiosity. In every corner of the modern world, *labor* and *production* are being presented to sightseers in guided tours of factories and in museums of science and industry. In the developing world, some important attractions are being detached from their original social and religious meanings, now appearing as monumental representations of "abstract, undifferentiated human labor," as Karl Marx used to say. The Egyptian pyramids exemplify this. Sightseeing at such attractions preserves still important values embodied in work-in-general, even as specific work processes and the working class itself are transcended by history.

It is only by making a fetish of the work of others, by transforming it into an "amusement" ("do-it-yourself"), a spectacle (Grand Coulee), or an attraction (the guided tours of Ford Motor Company), that modern workers, on vacation, can apprehend work as a part of a meaningful totality. The Soviet Union, of necessity, is much more developed along these lines than the industrial democracies of the capitalist West. The alienation of the worker stops where the alienation of the sightseer begins.

The destruction of industrial culture is occurring from within as alienation invades the work place, and the same process is bringing about the birth of modernity. Affirmation of basic social values is departing the world of work and seeking refuge in the realm of leisure. "Creativity" is almost exclusively in the province of cultural, not industrial, productions, and "intimacy" and "spontaneity" are preserved in social relations away from work. Working relations are increasingly marred by cold calculation. Tourism is developing the capacity to organize both positive and negative social sentiments. On the negative side, for example, "social problems" figure in the curiosity of tourists: dirt, disease, malnutrition. Couples from the Midwest who visit Manhattan now leave a little disappointed if they do not chance to witness and remark on some of its famous street crime. One is reminded that staged "holdups" are a stable motif in Wild West tourism. And tourists will go out of their way to view such egregious sights as the Berlin Wall, the Kennedy assassination area and even the ovens at Dachau.

The act of sightseeing is uniquely well-suited among leisure alternatives to draw the tourist into a relationship with the modern social totality. As a worker, the individual's relationship to his society is partial and limited, secured by a fragile "work ethic," and restricted to a single position among millions in the division of labor. As a tourist, the individual may step out into the universal drama of modernity. As a tourist, the individual may attempt to grasp the division of labor as a phenomenon *sui generis* and become a moral witness of its masterpieces of virtue and viciousness.

The industrial epoch has biased its sociology in several ways. Our research is concentrated on work, not leisure, and on the working class, not the middle class.[1] Modernity calls into question the necessity of the dirtily industrial version of work, advancing the idea that work should have other than economic rewards and leisure should be productive. New species of commodities (do-it-yourself kits, packaged vacations, entertainments, work-study programs) reflect the modern fragmentation and mutual displacement of work and leisure, and the emergence of new synthetic structures as yet unanalyzed. This recent coming together of work and leisure suggests the need for a sociology of middle-class leisure that can integrate itself with our already established sociology of the working class.

## The Structure of Postindustrial Modernity

The characteristics of modernity examined by social scientists are advanced urbanization, expanded literacy, generalized health care, rationalized work arrangements, geographical and economic mobility and the emergence of the nation-state as the most important sociopolitical unit. These are merely the surface features of modernity. The deep structure of modernity is a totalizing idea, a modern mentality that sets modern society in opposition both to its own past and to those societies of the present that are premodern or un(der)developed.

No other major social structural distinction (certainly not that between the classes) has received such massive reinforcement as the ideological separation of the modern from the nonmodern world. International treaties and doctrines dividing the world into multinational blocs serve to dramatize the distinction between the developed nations and the lesser ones which are not thought to be capable of independent self-defense. Modern nations train development specialists, organizing them into teams and sending them to the underdeveloped areas of the world which are thereby identified as being incapable of solving their own problems. The giving of this and other forms of international aid is a *sine qua non* of full modern status, as dependence on it is a primary indicator of a society trying to modernize itself. The national practice of keeping exact demographic records of infant mortality and literacy rates, per capita income, etc., functions in the same way to separate the modern from the nonmodern world along a variety of dimensions. The domestic version of the distinction is couched in economic terms, the "poverty line" that separates full members of the modern world from their less fortunate fellow citizens who are victims of it, immobilized behind the poverty line in such places as Appalachia and the inner city. The field of ethnology dramatizes a still more radical separation: primitive versus modern. When the underdeveloped world fights back, the distinction is embedded in the structure of conflict, where one side uses "guerrilla" while the other side uses "conventional" warfare.

Interestingly, the best indication of the final victory of modernity over other sociocultural arrangements is not the disappearance of the nonmodern world, but its artificial preservation and reconstruction in modern society. The separation of nonmodern culture traits from their original contexts and their distribution as modern playthings are evident in the various social movements toward naturalism, so much a feature of modern societies: cults of folk music and medicine, adornment and behavior, peasant dress, Early American decor, efforts, in short, to museumize the premodern. A suicidal recreation of guerrilla activities has recently appeared in the American avant-garde. These displaced forms, embedded in modern society, are the spoils of the victory of the modern over the nonmodern world. They establish in consciousness the definition and boundary of modernity by rendering concrete and immediate that which modernity is not.

## The Tourist

It is intellectually chic nowadays to deride tourists. An influential theoretician of modern leisure, Daniel J. Boorstin, approvingly quotes a nineteenth-century writer at length:

> The cities of Italy [are] now deluged with droves of these creatures, for they never separate, and you see them forty in number pouring along a street with their director—now in front, now at the rear, circling round them like a sheep dog—and really the process is as like herding as may be. I have already met three flocks, and anything so uncouth I never saw before, the men, mostly elderly, dreary, sad-looking; the women, somewhat younger, travel-tossed but intensely lively, wide-awake and facetious.[2]

Claude Lévi-Strauss writes simply: Travel and travellers are two things I loathe—and yet here I am, all set to tell the story of my expeditions."[3] A student of mine in Paris, a young man from Iran dedicated to the revolution, half stammering, half shouting, said to me, "Let's face it, we are all tourists!" Then, rising to his feet, his face contorted with what seemed to me to be self-hatred, he concluded dramatically in a hiss: "Even *I* am a tourist."

I think it significant that people who are actually in accord are struggling to distance themselves from themselves via this moral stereotype of the tourist. When I was eighteen years old, I returned a date to her home on a little resort-residential island. As the ferry approached the slip, I reached for the ignition key. She grabbed my hand, saying vehemently, "Don't do that! Only *tourists* start their cars before we dock!"

The rhetoric of moral superiority that comfortably inhabits this talk about tourists was once found in unconsciously prejudicial statements about other "outsiders," Indians, Chicanos, young people, blacks, women. As these peoples organize into groups and find both a collective identity and a place in the modern totality, it is increasingly difficult to manufacture morality out of opposition to them. The modern consciousness appears to be dividing along different lines against itself. Tourists dislike tourists. God is dead, but man's need to appear holier than his fellows lives. And the religious impulse to go beyond one's fellow men can be found not merely in our work ethic, where Max Weber found it, but in some of our leisure acts as well.

The modern critique of tourists is not an analytical reflection on the problem of tourism—it is a part of the problem. Tourists are not criticized by Boorstin and others for leaving home to see sights. They are reproached for being satisfied with superficial experiences of other peoples and other places. An educated respondent told me that he and his wife were "very nervous" when they visited the Winterthur museum because they did not know "the proper names of all the different styles of antiques," and they were afraid their silence would betray their ignorance. In other words, touristic shame is not based on being a tourist but on not being tourist enough, on a failure to see everything the way it "ought" to be seen. The touristic critique of tourism is based on a desire to go beyond the other "mere" tourists to a more profound appreciation of society and culture, and it is by no means limited to intellectual statements. All tourists desire this deeper involvement with society and culture to some degree; it is a basic component of their motivation to travel.

## Some Remarks on Method and Theory

My approach to leisure is *metacritical* or "anthropological" in the technical sense of that term. I do not, that is, treat moral pronouncements on leisure as having the status of scientific statements, even though some might qualify as such. Rather, I have used critical statements such as Boorstin's in the same way that an ethnographer uses the explanations of social life volunteered by his native respondents: as a part of the puzzle to be solved, not as one of its solutions. I assume no one will think me motivated by a desire to debunk my fellow students of leisure. I aim only to understand the role of the tourist in modern society.

I am very much indebted to the other scholars who preceded me. Thorstein Veblen provided the most complete study of leisure in his *Theory of the Leisure Class*. I do not think I have deviated much from the spirit of Veblen's original inquiry, even though, for reasons I will try to give, there is almost no resemblance between our specific findings.

I have adopted Veblen's general thesis that leisure reflects social structure. My work departs significantly from his, however, in the selection of a dimension of structure on which to base the analytic of leisure. Veblen anchors his analysis in the class structure, calling our attention to the uneven distribution of work in society and the status components of leisure: for example, the ways it is consumed conspicuously as a symbol of social status. I am suspicious of research that insists on the primacy and independence of social class, that does not attempt to go beyond class to discover still deeper structures that might render class relations in modern society more intelligible. It is necessary to recall that Marx *derived* his model of social class relations from his analysis of the value of commodities. As new species of commodities appear in the modern world, and as the fundamental nature of the commodity changes (for example, from a pair of pants to a packaged vacation; from a piece of work to a piece of no-work), Marx's deduction must be repeated.

My analysis of sightseeing is based on *social structural differentiation*. Differentiation is roughly the same as societal "development" or "modernization." By "differentiation" I mean to designate the totality of differences between social classes, life-styles, racial and ethnic groups, age grades (the youth, the aged), political and professional groups and the mythic representation of the past to the present. Differentiation is a *systemic variable:* it is not confined to a specific institution of society, nor does it originate in one institution or place and spread to others. It operates independently and simultaneously throughout society. In highly differentiated societies such as those found in Western Europe and North America, social life constantly subdivides and reorganizes itself in ever-increasing complexity. The class structure moves from simple duality (owners vs. workers) to upper-upper/middle-upper/lower-upper/upper-middle/middle-middle/lower-middle/upper-lower/middle-lower/lower-lower. Sexual differentiation progresses beyond its typically peasant, biologically based binary opposition into publicly discriminated third, fourth, fifth and sixth sexes. Differentiation is the origin of alternatives and the feeling of freedom in modern society. It is also the primary ground of the contradiction, conflict, violence, fragmentation, discontinuity and alienation that are such evident features of modern life.

It is structural differentiation, I think, and not some inherent quality of capitalism (its alleged fit with human nature, for example) that confines the revolution to the less developed, agricultural areas of the world. In the modern urban-industrial centers, working-class consciousness is already too differentiated to coordinate itself into a progressive, revolutionary force. In modern society, revolution in the conventional sense awaits the transcendence of sociocultural differentiation. Modern mass leisure contains this transcendence in-itself, but there is as yet no parallel revolutionary consciousness that operates independently and for-itself.

## The Evolution of Modernity

Imagine what no revolutionary party or army has dared to imagine—a revolution so total as to void every written and unwritten constitution and contract. This revolution changes not merely the laws but the norms: no routine, no matter how small, can be accomplished without conscious thought and effort. During this revolution, every book is completely rewritten and, at the same time, every book, in fact, thought itself, is translated into a new kind of language. During this revolution, the cities are leveled and rebuilt on a new model. Every masterpiece is repainted and every unknown shred of the past is dug out of the earth while all known archaeological finds are buried under new meanings. During this revolution, the overthrow of capitalist economies appears as a midterm economic adjustment. This revolution is a true revolution, unlike the regressive, pseudo-revolutions of political and religious movements that make a place for themselves by burning the land and the books of others. This revolution that submerges the most radical consciousness in its plenitude is, of course, unthinkable.

And yet, our laws have undergone total change and our cities have been replaced block by block. Our masterpieces are remade in each new genre. Critical and scientific language that wants to describe these changes always risks seeming to have lost its meaning. This revolution continues. Modern culture is more revolutionary in-itself than the most revolutionary consciousness so far devised. Every major sector of modern society—politics, ethics, science, arts, leisure—is now devoted almost entirely to the problem of keeping pace with this revolution. "The Revolution" in the conventional,

Marxist sense of the term is an emblem of the evolution of modernity. Sociocultural differentiation contains the secret of its own destruction and renewal.

After considerable inductive labor, I discovered that *sightseeing is a ritual performed to the differentiations of society*. Sightseeing is a kind of collective striving for a transcendence of the modern totality, a way of attempting to overcome the discontinuity of modernity, of incorporating its fragments into unified experience. Of course, it is doomed to eventual failure: even as it tries to construct totalities, it celebrates differentiation.

The locus of sightseeing in the middle class is understandable in other than merely economic terms. It is the middle class that systematically scavenges the earth for new experiences to be woven into a collective, touristic version of other peoples and other places. This effort of the international middle class to coordinate the differentiations of the world into a single ideology is intimately linked to its capacity to subordinate other peoples to its values, industry and future designs. The middle class is the most favored now because it has a transcendent consciousness. Tourism, I suggest, is an essential component of that consciousness.

The touristic integration of society resembles a catalogue of displaced forms. In this regard it is empirically accurate. The differentiations of the modern world have the same structure as tourist attractions: elements dislodged from their original natural, historical and cultural contexts fit together with other such displaced or modernized things and people. The differentiations *are* the attractions. Modern battleships are berthed near *Old Ironsides;* highrise apartments stand next to restored eighteenth-century townhouses; "Old Faithful" geyser is surrounded by bleacher seats; all major cities contain wildlife and exotic plant collections; Egyptian obelisks stand at busy intersections in London and Paris and in Central Park in New York City. Modernization simultaneously separates these things from the people and places that made them, breaks up the solidarity of the groups in which they originally figured as cultural elements, and brings the people liberated from traditional attachments into the modern world where, as tourists, they may attempt to discover or reconstruct a cultural heritage or a social identity.

Interestingly enough, the generalized anxiety about the authenticity of interpersonal relationships in modern society is matched by certainty about the authenticity of touristic sights. The rhetoric of tourism is full of manifestations of the importance of the authenticity of the relationship between tourists and what they see: this is a *typical* native house; this is the *very* place the leader fell; this is the *actual* pen used to sign the law; this is the *original* manuscript; this is an *authentic* Tlingit fish club; this is a *real* piece of the *true* Crown of Thorns.[4] The level of authentication can be very low. After the fashion of a doctor with his ear pressed to the chest of a dying patient, a Councilman has suggested that New York City is "alive" because it makes "noise":

> Some see a certain danger in the anti-noise program. On the council floor Bertram A. Gelfand, a Bronx Democrat, said the code raised the possibility not only of a loss of jobs but also of delaying, or raising the cost of, vitally needed facilities such as new housing and rapid transit. Still others see another danger: That the code might rob the city of a certain *je ne sais quoi*. "One of the enjoyable things about New York," said Councilman Michael DeMarco, "is that it's alive, there's a lot of noise."[5]

Some tourist attractions are not merely minimal, they are subminimal or generally regarded as "pseudo" or "tacky":

> A 13-story Fiberglas statue of Jesus Christ is the centerpiece of a new Biblical amusement park called Holyland, being built near Mobile, Ala. The park . . . will include visits to heaven and hell, Noah's ark, gladiator fights, the Tower of Babel and the belly of the whale temporarily occupied by Jonah. All for just $6 a ticket.[6]

But this type of attraction in fact functions to enhance the supposed authenticity of true sights such as the Statue of Liberty or the Liberty Bell. Modern society institutionalizes these authentic attractions and modern life takes on qualities of reality thereby.

In the establishment of modern society, the individual act of sightseeing is probably less important than the ceremonial ratification of authentic attractions as objects of ultimate value, a ratification at once caused by and resulting in a gathering of tourists around an attraction and measurable to a certain degree by the time and distance the tourists travel to reach it. The actual act of communion between tourist and attraction is less important than the *image* or the *idea* of society that the collective act generates. The image of the Statue of Liberty or the Liberty Bell that is the product of visits to them is more enduring than any specific visit, although, of course, the visit is indispensable to the image. A specific act of sightseeing is, in itself, weightless *and*, at the same time, the ultimate reason for the orderly representation of the social structure of modern society in the system of attractions.

This should not be taken to imply that sightseeing is without its importance for individual consciousness. Presumably sightseeing, along with religious fervor and patriotism, can be important for the development of a certain type of mind. It seems that individual thought and comportment add and detract almost nothing in modern society, but this is only an appearance that breeds a necessary sense of danger. It is a source of anxiety that our kind of society has the capacity to develop beyond the point where individuals can continue to have a meaningful place in it. If this development were to progress without a corresponding reconstitution of a place for man in society, modernity would simply collapse at the moment of its greatest expansion. But this collapse is not happening in fact. Tourism and participation in the other modern alternatives to everyday life makes a place for unattached individuals in modern society. The act of sightseeing is a kind of involvement with social appearances that helps the person to construct totalities from his disparate experiences. Thus, his life and his society can appear to him as an orderly series of formal representations, like snapshots in a family album.

Modernity transcends older social boundaries, appearing first in urban industrial centers and spreading rapidly to undeveloped areas. There is no other complex of reflexive behaviors and ideas that follows this development so quickly as tourism and sightseeing. With the possible exceptions of existentialism and science fiction, there is no other widespread movement universally regarded as essentially modern. Advanced technology is found everywhere in modern society, of course, and many students have examined it for clues about modernity, but it is not a reflective structure that expresses the totality of the modern spirit as, for example, a modern religion might if a modern religion existed. On this level, only the system of attractions, including the natural, cultural, and technological attractions, reflects the differentiations of modern society and consciousness.

Existentialism, especially in its popular and Christian versions, attempts to provide moral stability to modern existence by examining the inauthentic origins of self-consciousness. From a critical examination of existentialism (or sightseeing), there arises the question that directs this present study: How can a society that suppresses interpersonal morality (the old, or traditional, morality founded on a separation of truth from lies) be one of the most solidary societies, one of the strongest and most progressive known to history?

Both sightseeing and existentialism provide the beginnings of an answer to this question in their equation of inauthenticity and self-consciousness. Modern society, it is widely believed, has become moral in-itself. It contains its own justification for existence which it maintains as its most closely kept secret. The individual's place in this society, his role in the division of labor, is no longer basic to social structure. Modern man (sociology has contributed to this somewhat) has been forced to become conscious of society as such, not merely of his own "social life." As the division of labor is transformed into social structural differentiation, morality moves up a level, from the individual to society, and so does "self"-consciousness. Entire cities and regions, decades and cultures have become aware of themselves as tourist attractions. The nations of the modern world, for example, are not total structures that situate every aspect of the life and thought of their citizens, the sociologists' "ideal societies." At most, modern societies like France and Japan are relatively solidary subdifferentiations of the modern world: places to be visited, i.e., tourist attractions. Modern interest in science fiction (as well as in existentialism and sightseeing) is motivated by a collective quest for an overarching (solar or galactic) system, a higher moral authority in a godless universe, which makes of the entire world a single solidary unit, a *mere* world with its proper place among worlds.

# 1

## Modernity and the Production of Touristic Experiences

AT the beginning of the industrial age, Karl Marx, basing his ideas on those of Hegel, wrote a theory accurate enough for several revolutionary governments to use as a guide for building new societies. To my knowledge, there is no other sociological thesis which has been so applied, and (by this standard of applicability) Marx's work remains a high point in sociological macrotheory construction.[1]

The industrial epoch is ending, however, and Marx's thought, once at the vanguard, has become separated from the revolution. European intellectuals (Sartre and especially Merleau-Ponty) saw in Stalinization the first signs of the petrifaction of Marxism. The current generation has its own evidence of the phenomenon, including *Pravda*'s denunciation of the student-worker revolution in Paris in May, 1968.

Perhaps the most dramatic evidence of the recent failure of Marxist thought to articulate its content to the revolution is found in the classrooms of community colleges in New Jersey, Kansas, and California. The Marxist perspective is being taught and studied sympathetically in working-class colleges across the U.S.A. with no evident impact—as yet, anyway.[2] It might prove fruitful to reopen the books in search for an alternate path to the end of the industrial age.

Hegel was the first modern thinker to take as his proper task the incorporation into a single system of *all thought*, including the history of each department of thought which, before him, appeared to be

17

discrete and isolated. Hegel treated pure science, fine art, history, morality and politics as but differentiations of consciousness, and he explicates *consciousness* so understood. In his *Phenomenology of Mind*,[3] Hegel grasps intellectual movements and entire epochs of culture history as fragments of a totality. He set as his goal the discovery of the ordering principles interior to the totality which gives rise to seemingly independent ideas and particular historical periods.

Hegel held the natural, material world to be the realm of the contingent and accidental. *Order*, in his view, is a product of consciousness. For example, his analysis of the State made of it the visible, tangible spirit of a people, a reflex of consciousness transcended only by art, philosophy, and religion. These go beyond the State because they are *partial* reflections, not of the spirit of a historically existent people, but of *absolute* spirit.

Hegel was first turned around by Ludwig Feuerbach, who suggested that consciousness originates in the world of things and empirical affairs. Far from being a reflection of absolute spirit, religion, according to Feuerbach, is only a reflex of society: the Holy Family is an image of the earthly one. In his influential *Theses* on Feuerbach, Marx claims that Feuerbach's materialism is an essential reinterpretation of Hegel but degenerate. Because Feuerbach located the universality of meaning in each individual's consciousness, his materialism necessarily leads to a degraded, epicurean sensualism. It was Feuerbach who wrote, *"Man ist, was er isst."*[4]

The difference between Marx and Feuerbach is still reflected in the political left of today in the division between epicurean vs. ascetic communism: hippies on communes vs. the Weather Underground or the Progressive Laborites.[5] Feuerbach conceived of practical everyday activity only in individual personal (social psychological) terms. Marx viewed practical activity, work, in social structural terms. Its immediate referent is whole groups of men classified according to the division of wealth and labor into groups. The activity of Feuerbachian materialism is a sterile kind of individual restlessness. For Marx, change is not merely a change of mind or social position, but a change of the total society.

Karl Marx began his analysis of social structure *not* with the individual but with an examination of the relations between man and his productions. The Holy Family is only a reflex of the family of man, but understanding the fullness of the meaning of the human situation requires going beyond the determination of a parallelism between the (religious) ideal and the empirical world. It is necessary, he says, to demystify the relationship between the material and the nonmaterial, between quantity and quality. The family of man subordinates itself to an image of itself which it creates and then holds to be superior to itself. Marx (unlike Durkheim) read this as a sign of an agonizing alienation resting on a schism in social structure itself. This alienation of man from his creations culminates, according to Marx, in capitalist production.

Marx foresaw the flowering of the importance of *commodities* under industrial capitalism. He saw in the manufacture, exchange and distribution of commodities a novel structure. The relationship between *things*—their relative values, arrangement into hierarchies, their progressive development in production processes—is modeled on social relations in human society. Moreover, Marx found that the relations between the men involved in commodity production were developing in an opposing direction and becoming rational and objectified, or thinglike. The double movement of social relations onto a material base and of the material base into ideology is the main legacy of industrial society and Marx's understanding of it.

## MARX'S SEMIOTIC

In Marx's close analysis of the commodity he finds its *value* is equal to the amount of labor (from the total available labor) required to make it. Its monetary value is only a reflection of the common denominator of all commodities: labor. Every commodity can have a price tag because each one has more or less of the same ingredient: labor. Marxists have drawn moral conclusions about the rightful place of the worker in society from this theory. I want to point out another feature of the theory, an implication of its systemic quality: there is no such thing as a commodity in isolation. Commodities originate in systems of exchanges. These systems are entirely social, entirely "unnatural," and fully capable of generating values in themselves. In other words, in Marx's treatment of it, the system of commodity production under capitalism resembles nothing so much as a language. A language is entirely social, entirely arbitrary and fully capable of generating meanings in itself. In updated terms, Marx wrote a "semiotic" of capitalist production. As Marx himself said: "value . . . converts every product into a social hieroglyphic. . . . We try to decipher the hieroglyphic, to get behind the secret of our own social product; for to stamp an object of utility as a value, is just as much a social product as language."[6]

Of course, Marx only wanted us to see commodities as a sign of the labor invested in them. He attempted to block their interpretations as meaningful elements in other cultural systems, but in a sense he tricked himself. Once the language-like or signifying capabilities of any object or gesture have been exposed, it begins an unstoppable journey between systems of meaning, revealing depths of religious, legal, esthetic and other values alongside the economic. In Marx's analysis of commodities, he was already beginning to draw out their other potential cultural meanings, especially in his discussion of the *fetishism* of commodities. This is the almost automatic result of his willingness to treat the commodity as a bond of objective and subjective values unified via social production processes. In manufacture, each individual's contribution is, in-itself, meaningless, and meaning occurs as the outcome of a collective effort. As such, the industrial production process is an index of the social grounds of all meaning, and the finished commodity is a *symbol*. Capitalism is the form of production that makes the commodity its most important symbol. After Marx, the search for the historical development of social facts and their eventual destruction has passed beyond a concern for the grounds of the value of commodities to a search for the *meaning* of modern social life. This is so even among Marxists as diverse as Sartre and Marcuse and among the anti-Marxists as well.

Marx was the first to discover the symbolic or fetishistic aspect of the commodity: its capacity to organize meaning and to make us want things for reasons that go beyond our material needs. But this realization called forth his antagonism, and (I am tempted to write "and so") he cut short his analysis of the fetishism of commodities. But in the subsequent history of the industrial object, it is just this feature that undergoes the greatest development, transforming the merely industrial world into the modern world: the appeal to the *gourmet* in the processed food, the *fidelity* of the radio. Even such mundane items as automobile parts fall under this principle. An advertisement reads:

> ANTI-SWAY BARS. Don't talk sports action, experience it with positive vehicle control! Enjoy the safety and comfort of taut, flat, balanced cornering. Stop plowing on turns, under or oversteer, wheel hop and spin, boatlike handling. Eliminate dangerous body roll and rear end steering effect. Feel the thrill of a perfectly balanced car.[7]

The other aspects of manufacture are now subordinated to building in the "style," the "feel," the "ambiance." Increasingly, pure experience, which leaves no material trace, is manufactured and sold like a commodity.

I have departed significantly from Marx on the matter of the role of culture in the modern world. I am about to depart even further, but I am accepting a basic tenet of Marx's analysis, perhaps its most controversial point: that the most important relationship in modern society is not between man and man (as in peasant society) but between man and his productions. With the possible exception of life in the family and other similar social arrangements left over from a simpler time, man in our modern society is related to others only through the things he makes. I see little reason to dispute this or its projected economic consequences. There will be revolution so long as men without work are thought to be worthless. This revolution may not be successful from the standpoint of the "undesirables" who wage it, yet there is nothing more damaging to a society than uninterrupted unsuccessful revolution. A short and successful revolution, by comparison, resembles the holiday that marks it. But I have turned away from these troublesome matters, which are deductions, after all, and have pressed the original question further, to continue the examination of our society where the thing that man creates—that is, the "thing" that mediates social relations—is a symbol.

## COMMODITY AND SYMBOL

One of the most striking aspects of modern capitalist societies, not often remarked, is the degree to which the commodity has become integral with culture: language, music, dance, visual arts and literature. This culminates in advertising, film, comic books and highbrow pop art. It was this integration (not the conservatism of the industrial proletariat) that Marx did not predict. There is a certain hostility in Marx's thought toward art and culture. Culture is the original system of signification and the original reflection (Marx would call it a distorted reflection) of the human condition. Marx held that anything merely symbolic could be annihilated to expose the material substratum of society. He hoped for the day when *revolutionary praxis*—action based on critical demystification of inhuman social arrangements—would replace culture as the ultimate expression of human values. But as modern left-wing Marxism (that of Mao Tsetung, and in quite a different way, that of the Frankfurt school of Adorno and others) is trying to teach us, culture prevails and the revolution must learn to operate in and through it.

There are some families here on earth that are modeled as closely as is humanly possible on the Holy Family. In these cases, the symbolic form of social organization is the original, and the "real-life" families are mere copies. As Durkheim wrote, "social life, in all its aspects and in every period of its history, is made possible only by a vast symbolism."[8] The commodity has become an integral part of everyday life in modern society because its original form is a symbolic representation (advertisement) of itself which both promises and guides experience in advance of actual consumption.

I am suggesting that modern materialistic society is probably less materialistic than we have come to believe. We have experienced brief periods of collective guilt. During the 1950's, for example, some intellectuals worried about being too "thing-oriented" and purchased Danish Modern things which are designed to seem a little less thing-like than their traditional counterparts. There is a perennial concern for the "overcommercialization" of Christmas. Marxist planners do not let us forget that *they* are materialists as they cautiously release each new consumer item into the eager hands of Russian and Eastern European workers. But when the final reckoning is over, we see that our modern kinds of society are less wrapped up in their consumer goods than in a somewhat more complex and fuller view of themselves: that is, in the representation of modern social life in the sciences, arts, politics, social movements, lifestyles, sports, the press, motion pictures and television. Modern culture may be divided and marketed after the fashion of a commodity, but the economic and social structure of these bits of modernity is quite different from that of the old industrial commodity.

The value of such things as programs, trips, courses, reports, articles, shows, conferences, parades, opinions, events, sights, spectacles, scenes and situations of modernity is not determined by the amount of labor required for their production. Their value is a function of the quality and quantity of *experience* they promise. Even the value of strictly material goods is increasingly similarly derived from the degree to which they promise to form a part of our modern experience. Phonograph records and pornographic movie superstars are produced and marketed according to principles that defy the labor theory of value. Moreover, the old-style material type of commodity retains an important position in modern society only insofar as it has the capacity to *deliver* an experience: TVs, stereos, cameras, tape recorders, sports cars, vibrators, electric guitars or recreational drugs. The commodity has become a means to an end. The end is an immense accumulation of reflexive experiences which synthesize fiction and reality into a vast symbolism, a modern world.[9]

## THE STRUCTURE OF CULTURAL EXPERIENCES

"Experience" has a quasi-scientific origin, sharing the same root with *experiment*.[10] Like so many words in our language, the term hides a short time span. It implies an original skepticism or an emptiness transformed into a specific belief or feeling through direct, firsthand involvement with some data. The term can have a certain "hip" or "gamy," even sexual, connotation beyond its sterile scientific and occupational meanings.

Here I want to isolate and analyze a subclass of experiences I am calling *cultural experiences*. The data of cultural experiences are somewhat fictionalized, idealized or exaggerated models of social life that are in the public domain, in film, fiction, political rhetoric, small talk, comic strips, expositions, etiquette and spectacles. All tourist attractions are cultural experiences. A cultural experience has two basic parts which must be combined in order for the experience to occur. The first part is the representation of an aspect of life on stage, film, etc. I call this part the *model*, using the term to mean an embodied ideal, very much the same way it is used in the phrase "fashion model." Or, as Goffman has written, "a model for, not a model of."[11] The second part of the experience is the changed, created, intensified belief or feeling that is based on the model. This second part of the experience I call the *influence*. The spectacle of an automobile race is a model; the thrills it provides spectators and their practice of wearing patches and overalls advertising racing tires and oils are its influence. Famous psychoanalytic case histories are models: everyone's analysis is influenced by them. A bathing-suit model is a model; the desire for a real-life girl friend that looks "just like a model" is its influence.

A *medium* is an agency that connects a model and its influence. A social situation of face-to-face interaction, a gathering, is a medium, and so are radio, television, film and tape. The media are accomplices in the construction of cultural experiences, but the moral structure of the medium is such that it takes the stance of being neutral or disinterested.[12] Models for individual "personality," fashion and behavior are conveyed in motion pictures, for example, but if there is any suspicion that mannerisms, affectations, clothing or other artifacts were put before the audience for the purpose of initiating a commercially exploitable fad, the fad will fail. It is a mark of adulthood in modern society that the individual is supposed to be able to see through such tricks. Whatever the facts in the case, the medium must appear to be disinterested if it is to be influential, so that any influence that flows from the model can appear to be both spontaneous and based on genuine feelings. High-pressure appeal in children's advertising on television permits parents to teach their children about these delicate matters, another kind of childhood immunization.

Extending conventional usage somewhat, I will term a cultural model, its influence(s), the medium that links them, the audiences that form around them, and the producers, directors, actors, agents, technicians, and distributors that stand behind them, a *production*. Cultural productions so defined include a wide range of phenomena. Perhaps the smallest are advertising photographs of a small "slice" of life: for example, of "the little woman" at the front door meeting her "man" home from the "rat race" and proffering his martini. The largest cultural productions are the summer-long and year-long festivals that tie up the entire life of a community, even a nation, as occurs in international expositions and centennials. Cultural productions of the middle range include big games, parades, moon shots, mass protests, Christmas, historical monuments, opening nights, elections and rock music festivals.[13] It can be noted that the owners of the means of *these* productions are not as yet organized into a historically distinct class, but it is becoming clear that *governments* at all levels and of all types are becoming increasingly interested in controlling cultural production.

Attending to cultural *productions* avoids, I think, some of the problems we encounter when dealing with the concept of culture. When we talk in terms of *a culture*, we automatically suggest the possibility of *a consensus*. Then, anyone who wishes to point out internal differences in society undercuts the validity of the analysis. This is a good way of perpetuating an academic field, but not a very good approach to society. To suggest, in the first place, that culture rests on a consensus reveals, it seems to me, a profound misunderstanding of culture and society. Social structure *is* differentiation. Consensus is a form of death at the group level. All cultures are a series of models of life. These models are organized in multiples according to every known logical principle, and some that are, so far, unknown: similitude, opposition, contradiction, complement, parallel, analogy. There has never been a cultural totality. Lévi-Strauss has mistakenly attributed totality to primitive cultures in order to contrast them to our own.[14] Primitive cultures achieve the semblance of totality by their small size, acceptance on the part of the entire group of a relatively few models and their isolation. But this "totality" results from demographic and historical accidents, not from any quality of culture itself.

This approach to culture permits the student of society to search for the explanation and logic of his subject in the subject itself, that is, to substitute cultural models for the intellectual and ideologically biased models of sociological theory. Cultural models are "ideal" only from the standpoint of everyday life. They are not ideal from the standpoint of any absolute such as a religion, a philosophy or a sociology. There is no "mother" representation, itself inaccessible, behind all the others copied from it. Each production is assembled

from available cultural elements and it remains somewhat faithful to
the other cultural models for the same experience.

Cultural productions, then, are *signs*. Like the faces of Jesus Christ
on religious calendars, they refer to (resemble) each other but not the
original. Cultural productions are also *rituals*. They are rituals in the
sense that they are based on formulae or models and in the sense that
they carry individuals beyond themselves and the restrictions of
everyday experience. Participation in a cultural production, even at
the level of being influenced by it, can carry the individual to the
frontiers of his being where his emotions may enter into communion
with the emotions of others "under the influence."[15]

In modern societies, the more complex cultural productions are
understood to be divided into types such as world's fairs, epic motion
pictures, moon shots, scandals, etc. Each example of a type is located
in a specific relationship to its forebears. A collective consciousness
relates the bicentennial to the centennial, Watergate to Teapot Dome,
*Around the World in Eighty Days* to *Potemkin*, if not always in the
experience phase, at least at the level of production. Each genre of
production is constructed from basically the same set of cultural
elements, but precise arrangement varies from production to production or the result is perceived as "dated," a "copy," "rerun," "spinoff"
or a "poor man's version" of an original. The space race petered out
from the lack of significant variation on the themes of "countdown,"
"launching" and "moon landing."[16] Of course, once a type of cultural
production has died out, it can be revived by a clever copy which is
said to be a remake of a "classic." Perhaps on the centennial of man's
first trip to the moon, we will send a party up in old-fashioned
equipment as a kind of celebration.

The system of cultural productions is so organized that any given
production automatically serves one of two essential functions: (1) it
may add to the ballast of our modern civilization by sanctifying an
*original* as being a model worthy of copy or an important milestone in
our development, or (2) it may establish a new direction, break new
ground, or otherwise contribute to the progress of modernity by
presenting new combinations of cultural elements and working out
the logic of their relationship. This second, differentiating, function
of cultural productions dominates the other in modern society and is

at the heart of the process that is called "modernization" or "economic development and cultural change." Modern international mass tourism produces in the minds of the tourists juxtapositions of elements from historically separated cultures and thereby speeds up the differentiation and modernization of middle-class consciousness.

Even though a given "experience" (in the less restricted sense of the term) may not be influenced by a cultural model, there are usually several models available for it. For example, one might have a drug experience, a sex experience—some might even go so far as to claim a religious experience—seemingly independent of cultural models and influences. On the other hand, many recipes for very similar kinds of experiences originate on a cultural level. The cultural models are attractive in that they usually contain claims of moral, esthetic and psychological superiority over the idiosyncratic version. The discipline and resources required to organize sexual activities on the model provided by pornographic motion pictures exceed that required by mere individualistic sexual expression. And the cultural version promises greater pleasure to those who would follow it.

Cultural productions, then, are not merely repositories of models for social life; they organize the attitudes we have toward the models and life. *Instant replay* in televised professional sports provides an illustration. The "play" occurs and the sportscaster intervenes (his role similar to that of the priest) to tell the audience what is important about what has happened, what to look for, what to experience. Then, instant replay delivers the exemplar, the model, slowed down, even stopped, so it can be savored. From the stream of action, select bits are framed in this way as cultural experiences.

The structure of cultural productions is adapted to the cultivation of values even on the frontiers where society encounters its own evil and error or undergoes change. The official model of the "drug experience," which moralizes against the use of marijuana, speed, or LSD, nevertheless subversively represents the experience as a powerfully seductive force, so desirable that it is impossible for an individual to resist it on his own without terrifying countermagic. The "uplifting" experience which restores conventional morality can arise from the dramatic representation of the darkest and most threatening of crimes. Christianity stretched the dramatic possibilities here to the limit, perhaps, as Nietzsche suggested, beyond the limit.

Cultural experiences are valued in-themselves and are the ultimate deposit of values, including economic values, in modern society. The value of the labor of a professional football player, for example, is determined by the amount of his playing time that is selected out for instant replay, that is, by the degree to which his work contributes to a cultural production and becomes integral with our modern cultural experience. Motion picture stars were the first to cash in on this structure, the "romantic experience" being among the first to undergo modernization.

Workers of the traditional industrial type are crowded on the margins of the modern economy where there is no relationship between their standard of living and the importance of the work they do. Food producers and field hands are among the lowest-paid workers, while energy producers like coal miners are among our most cruelly treated. The organization of labor into unions serves mainly as an ongoing dramatization of what our collective minimal standards are for the respectable poor. Recently, there have been some bright spots within this bleak panorama, labor movements that seem to have a "natural" understanding of the importance of articulating their programs to the society via cultural productions. Important among these has beeen Cesar Chavez's United Farm Workers with its coordination of unorthodox tactics, including hunger strikes, consumer boycotts and the development and wide promulgation of symbolism for the struggle: the Thunderbird buttons, postcards, etc. Criteria for the success of this movement emerge from an entirely cultural model, involving not merely a mobilization of the workers but of segments of the society socially and geographically distant from the fields and vineyards. Not unexpectedly, this movement (which will be a model for future struggles) faced as much opposition from labor already organized in an industrial framework as it has from the fruit growers.

The economics of cultural production is fundamentally different from that of industrial production. In the place of exploited labor, we find exploited leisure. Unlike industry, the important profits are not made in the production process, but by fringe entrepreneurs, businesses on the edge of the actual production. These can be arranged on a continuum from popcorn and souvenir sales through booking agents and tour agents to the operations that deal in motion picture rights or closed-circuit television hook-ups. The focal point of such action is a cultural production that almost magically generates capital continuously, often without consuming any energy for itself. Greek ruins are an example. Festivals and conventions organize the economic life of entire cities around cultural productions.

On a national level, economic development is linked to the export of cultural products for sale to other countries. The Beatles received the O.B.E. not so much because the Crown liked their music as because their international record sales arrested the disastrous growth of the trade deficit in Great Britain at the time. Underdeveloped countries can "export" their culture without having to package it just by attracting tourists. The foreign consumer journeys to the source. Developed economies pioneer these complex cultural arrangements by experimenting on their own populations: "See America First."

## CULTURAL PRODUCTIONS AND SOCIAL GROUPS

Cultural productions are powerful agents in defining the scope, force and direction of a civilization. It is only in the cultural experience that the data are organized to generate specific feelings and beliefs. Cultural experiences, then, are the opposite of scientific experiments—opposite in the sense of being mirror images of each other. Scientific experiments are designed to control bias, especially that produced by human beings, out of the result, but cultural experiences are designed to build it in. The attitudes, beliefs, opinions and values studied by sociologists are the residues of cultural experiences, separated from their original contexts and decaying (perhaps in the sense of "fermenting") in the minds of individuals.

With the exception of those involved in ethnic studies, where the relationship is obvious, I think sociologists are not attentive enough to the importance of cultural productions in the determination of the groups they study. For example, generational groups are determined by the different influences of rock music and hip fashion, and "bridging the generation gap" usually means an older person has experienced a rock music concert or smoked marijuana.[17] The mechanics of group formation are nicely simplified when cultural productions mediate in-group/out-group distinctions. Almost everyone has had the experience of attending a show with a group and on the way home dividing into subgroups on the basis of being differently influenced by it. When people are getting to know each other (a distinctively modern routine), they will compare the way they feel about several cultural models (Joe Namath, the "California Life-Style," a famous trial, the attitude of Parisians toward tourists, etc.) and move closer together or further away from a relationship on the basis of their mutual understanding of these matters.

In the early 1960's, I observed a group of people at Berkeley who had seen the motion picture *One Eyed Jacks* so many times that they knew every line by heart (e.g., "Git over here, you big tub of guts") and they "did" the entire picture from beginning to end around a table at a coffee house. This, of course, represents a kind of high of culturally based togetherness. Some groups were formed in this way over the teachings of Jesus. In a shining example of modern self-consciousness, the Beatles were reported to have remarked, "We're more popular than Jesus now."

It has long been a sociological truism that a human group that persists for any length of time will develop a "world view," a comprehensive scheme in which all familiar elements have a proper place. I am not certain that any group ever operated like this. Radical groups that meet periodically to try to hammer together an alternate viewpoint seem to drift aimlessly without dramatic ups and downs. This stands in marked contrast to the impact of their cultural productions, their mass protest demonstrations which shock the national consciousness. I am quite certain that if the idea that "a group develops a world view" holds a grain of truth, modernity reverses the relationship or inverts the structure. Modernized peoples, released from primary family and ethnic group responsibilities, organize themselves in groups around world views provided by cultural productions. The group does not produce the world view, the world view produces the group. A recent example is the Oriental guru phenomenon: visitors from afar promulgating a global vision in elaborately staged rallies surround themselves with devotees for the duration of their presence. Rock musicians' "groupies" and tour groups are other examples.

In industrial society, refinement of a "life-style" occurs through a process of emulating elites, or at least of keeping up with the Joneses. This requires designated leaders, so followers can know whom to obey, and regular meetings: church meetings, town meetings, board meetings, faculty meetings. The requisite of an internal group order, with its meetings of elites and followers, is disappearing with the coming of modernity. Life-styles are not expanded via emulation of socially important others until they have taken over an entire group. They are expanded by the reproduction of cultural models, a process that need not fit itself into existing group boundaries. The aborigines living near the missions in the Australian Outback have adopted a modified "Beachboy" look and play Hawaiian-style popular ballads on guitars.[18] The modern world is composed of movements and life-styles that exhibit neither "leadership" nor "organization" in the sense that these terms are now used by sociologists. World views and life-styles emerge from and dissolve into cultural productions.

From the standpoint of each cultural production (the screening of *Love Story*, for example, or a televised "Super Bowl" game), any population can be divided into three groups: (1) those who would not attend; (2) those who would attend: of those who would attend, there are (2a) those who would get caught up in the action and go along with it to its moral and aesthetic conclusion, and (2b) those who would reject the model, using their experience as a basis for criticising such "trash," "violence" or "fraud." In this last group are the American tourists who go to Russia in order to strengthen the credibility of their anti-Marxist, anti-Soviet proclamations.

It is noteworthy that recent trends in Western cultural production have been aimed at transforming the negative, critical audience into one that is "taken in" by the show. Recent fine art knows full well that it will be called "trash," and some of it does little to prevent the formation of this opinion: consider the display of ripe trash cans in art museums. Andy Warhol named one of his cinematic productions *Trash*. The effort here is basically democratic, to reach everyone with art, the detractors and the appreciators (who think of themselves as being "in" on the "put on") alike. Some of Frank Zappa's music could also serve as illustration.

Culture can continue, via its productions, to provide a basis for community even in our complex modern society. In fact, it is only culture—not empirical social relations—that can provide a basis for the modern community. Working through cultural productions, people can communicate emotions and complex meanings across class, group and generational lines. Music and games, for example, have always had deep roots in the human community because they permit anyone who knows the basic code to enjoy nuances and subtleties in the playing out of variations. Strangers who have the same cultural grounding can come together in a cultural production, each knowing what to expect next, and feel a closeness or solidarity, even where no empirical closeness exists. Their relationship begins before they meet. In modern society, not merely music and games but almost every aspect of life can be played at, danced, orchestrated, made into a model of itself and perpetuated without leadership and without requiring anyone's awareness or guidance.

As cultural productions provide a base for the modern community, they give rise to a modern form of alienation of individuals interested only in the model or the life-style, not in the life it represents. The academic provides some nice examples. Education in the modern world is increasingly represented as a form of recreation: suburban housewives vacillate between joining a reducing "spa" and taking a class at the university. Our collective image of the "college experience" emphasizes the swirling ambiance of the campus life-style, the intensity of the "rap sessions," the intimacy of even fleeting relationships between "college friends," "college pals" and "college buddies." The educational experience holds out the possibility of conversation, possibly sex, even friendship, with a "star" professor. The growth of the mind that is supposed to be the result of education can be exchanged for the attitudes that support the growth, an acceptance of change, an attachment to the temporary and a denial of comfort. A willingness, even a desire, to live in semifurnished quarters, moving often like a fugitive, holds the academic in its grip as an emblem at the level of an entire life-style of a restless spirit. There is an available esthetic of all aspects of the dark side of the college experience wherein, for example, the exhaustion of staying up all night, smoking, drinking coffee and studying for an examination with a friend is represented as a kind of "high" and, while painful at the moment, an alleged source of exquisite memories.

What I have described so far is the *model* of the educational experience found in cultural productions. No one need actually conform to it. The image of the tweedy, dry, humorless, conservative, absent-minded, pipe-sucking professor from the industrial age is being replaced by another image: that of a swinging, activist, long-haired, radical modern professor. But one finds in the *real* academic milieu some students and professors who embrace this life-style, who seem to have been attracted to their calling because they like the way it *appears* in our collective versions of it, and they want to make others see them as they see their ideal counterparts in the model.

In this academic group we find highly cultivated diversions, innocent copies of the serious aspects of scholarship. I have observed a party at which wine was served from numbered but otherwise unmarked bottles. The party was a little test. The celebrants carried cards and were supposed to indicate the house and vintage of each wine to win a prize for the most correct answers. On another occasion, a picnic, all the revelers got themselves up in full medieval drag, played on lutes and ate roast goat—theirs being a historical experience, one department of the college experience. For those who are in it for this kind of action, the university is less a house of knowledge than a fountain of youths.

Max Weber, consolidating his powerful comprehension of industrial society and looking ahead, perhaps to the present day, warned:

> No one knows yet who will inhabit this shell [of industrial capitalism] in the future: whether at the end of its prodigious development there will be new prophets or a vigorous renaissance of all thoughts and ideals or whether finally, if none of this occurs, mechanism will produce only petrification hidden under a kind of anxious importance. According to this hypothesis, the prediction will become a reality for the last men of this particular development of culture. Specialists without spirit, libertines without heart, this nothingness imagines itself to be elevated to a level of humanity never before attained.[19]

This mentality that Weber anticipated with great clarity and precision has become more or less "offical" in political and bureaucratic circles, among "the last men of this particular development of culture." While it continues to inhabit traditional fortresses of power, it is also clear that an alternate, postindustrial kind of mind is beginning to emerge in the interstices of modern culture.

Lewis Mumford discerned a dimension of this mind in the figure of Albert Schweitzer:

> In philosophy or theology, in medicine or in music, Schweitzer's talents were sufficient to guarantee him a career of distinction: as one of the eminent specialists of his time, in any of these departments, his success would have been prompt and profitable, just to the extent that he allowed himself to be absorbed in a single activity. But in order to remain a whole man, Schweitzer committed the typical act of sacrifice for the coming age: *he deliberately reduced the intensive cultivation of any one field, in order to expand the contents and significance of his life as a whole* . . . yet the result of that sacrifice was not the negation of his life but its fullest realization. . . .[20]

This emerging modern mind is bent on expanding its repertoire of experiences, and on an avoidance of any specialization that threatens to interrupt the search for alternatives and novelty. (This can be contrasted with the mind of industrial man, being in certain of its particulars a reaction against specialized and linear industrial processes.) *Tradition* remains embedded in modernity but in a position of servitude: tradition is there to be recalled to satisfy nostalgic whims or to provide coloration or perhaps a sense of profundity for a modern theme. There is an urgent cultivation of new people, new groups, new things, new ideas, and a hostility to repetition: a built-in principle of escalation in every collective work from war to music. There is a desire for greatly expanded horizons, a search for the frontiers of even such familiar matters as domestic relations. Finally, there is everywhere, including in our sociology, a repressive encircling urge, movement or idea that everyone ought to be coming together in a modern moral consensus.

## THE WORK EXPERIENCE

*Leisure* is constructed from cultural experiences. Leisure and culture continue to exist at a slight remove from the world of work and everyday life. They are concentrated in vacations, amusements, games, play, and religious observances. This ritual removal of culture from workaday activities has produced the central crisis of industrial society. In a fine early essay on "Culture, Genuine and Spurious" [1924], which, though available, has received too little attention in the human sciences, the linguist Edward Sapir wrote:

> The great cultural fallacy of industrialism, as developed up to the present time, is that in harnessing machines to our uses it has not known how to avoid the harnessing the majority of mankind to its machines. The telephone girl who lends her capacities, during the greater part of the living day, to the manipulation of a technical routine that has an eventually high efficiency value but that answers to no spiritual needs of her own is an appalling sacrifice to civilization. As a solution to the problem of culture she is a failure—the more dismal the greater her natural endowment.[21]

The mechanization Sapir stresses is only a part of the problem. Industrial society elevates work of all kinds to an unprecedented level of social importance, using as its techniques the rationalization and the deculturization of the workplace. As this new kind of rationalized work got almost everyone into its iron grip, culture did not enter the factories, offices and workshops. The workaday world is composed of naked and schematic social relations determined by raw power, a kind of adolescent concern for "status" and a furtive, slick sensualism all cloaked in moralistic rhetoric. Culture grew and differentiated as never before, escaping the elite groups that had previously monopolized it. It became popular, but it receded ever further from the workaday world.

Modern social movements push work and its organization to the negative margins of existence, and as our society follows these movements ever deeper into postindustrial modernity, the more widespread becomes the idea that not merely play and games but life itself is supposed to be fun. The world of work has not mounted a counteroffensive. It responds by shriveling up, offering workers ever increasing freedom from its constraints. I am suggesting that the old sociology cannot make much sense out of this if it stays behind studying work arrangements, class, status, power and related sociological antiquities.

Industrial society bound men to its jobs, but because of the extreme specialization and fragmentation of tasks in the industrial process, the job did not function to integrate its holder into a synthetic social perspective, a world view. As a solution to the problem of culture, industrial work is a failure. It repulses the individual, sending him away to search for his identity or soul in off-the-job activities: in music, sports, church, political scandal and other collective diversions. Among these diversions is found a cultural production of a curious and special kind marking the death of industrial society and the beginning of modernity: a museumization of work and work relations, a cultural production I call a *work display*.

Examples of work displays include guided tours of banks, the telephone company, industrial plants; the representation of cowboys and construction workers in cigarette advertisements; the chapters of *Moby Dick* on whaling, etc. Both machine and human work can be displaced into and displayed as a finished product: a work. Grand Coulee Dam on the Columbia River in Washington State is the greatest work display of all, both in the sense of the work it does while the tourist is looking on, and in its being a product of a mighty human labor. (Grand Coulee is also fittingly the tomb of some workers who fell in while pouring its concrete.) Labor transforms raw material into useful objects. Modernity is transforming labor into cultural productions attended by tourists and sightseers who are moved by the universality of work relations—*not* as this is represented through their own work (from which they are alienated), but as it is revealed to them at their leisure through the displayed work of others. Industrial elites were inarticulate when asked to explain the place and meaning of work, responding only with an abstraction: money. Today, the meaning of work of all types is being established in cultural productions.

Marx foresaw a clean division of capitalist society with workers on one side and owners on the other and an inevitable showdown with a classless aftermath. As industrial society developed, however, the work/no-work division did not eventually reside in neatly defined and socially important classes. In prerevolutionary societies such as our own, there are subproletarian "leisure" classes of idlers and the aged. And one by-product of the worker revolutions around the world is the creation of a sterile international class of displaced monarchs, barons, and ex-puppet dictators, numerically unimportant but a visible cultural element, nevertheless: they are called jet setters and Beautiful People.

The "class struggle," instead of operating at the level of history, is operating at the level of workaday life and its opposition to culture. In the place of the division Marx foresaw is an arrangement wherein workers are displayed, and other workers on the other side of the culture barrier watch them for their enjoyment. Modernity is breaking up the "leisure class," capturing its fragments and distributing them to everyone. Work in the modern world does not turn class against class so much as it turns man against himself, fundamentally dividing his existence. The modern individual, if he is to appear to be human, is forced to forge his own synthesis between his work and his culture.

# 2

## Sightseeing and Social Structure

### THE MORAL INTEGRATION OF MODERNITY

#### The Place of the Attraction in Modern Society

MODERN society constitutes itself as a labyrinthine structure of norms governing access to its workshops, offices, neighborhoods and semipublic places. As population density increases, this maze of norms manifests itself in physical divisions, walls, ceilings, fences, floors, hedges, barricades and signs marking the limits of a community, an establishment, or a person's space.[1] This social system contains interstitial corridors—halls, streets, elevators, bridges, water-ways, airways and subways. These corridors are filled with things anyone can see, whether he wants to or not. Erving Goffman has studied behavior in public places and relations in public for what they can reveal about our collective pride, shame and guilt.[2] I want to follow his lead and suggest that behavior is only one of the visible, public representations of social structure found in public places. We also find decay, refuse, human and industrial derelicts, monuments, museums, parks, decorated plazas and architectural shows of indus-trial virtue. Public behavior and these other visible public parts of society are tourist attractions.

#### Sightseeing and the Moral Order

The organization of behavior and objects in public places is func-tionally equivalent to the sacred text that still serves as the moral base

39

of traditional society. That is, public places contain the representations of good and evil that apply universally to modern man in general.

A touristic attitude of respectful admiration is called forth by the finer attractions, the monuments, and a no less important attitude of disgust attaches itself to the uncontrolled garbage heaps, muggings, abandoned and tumbledown buildings, polluted rivers and the like. Disgust over these items is the negative pole of respect for the monuments. Together, the two provide a moral stability to the modern touristic consciousness that extends beyond immediate social relationships to the structure and organization of the total society.

The tours of Appalachian communities and northern inner-city cores taken by politicians provide examples of negative sightseeing. This kind of tour is usually conducted by a local character who has connections outside of his community. The local points out and explains and complains about the rusting auto hulks, the corn that did not come up, winos and junkies on the nod, flood damage and other features of the area to the politician who expresses his concern. While politicians and other public figures like Eleanor Roosevelt and the Kennedys are certainly the leaders here, this type of sightseeing is increasingly available to members of the middle class at large. The *New York Times* reports that seventy people answered an advertisement inviting tourists to spend "21 days 'in the land of the Hatfields and McCoys' for $378.00, living in with some of the poorest people in the U.S. in Mingo County, West Virginia."[3] Similarly, in 1967, the Penny Sightseeing Company inaugurated extensive guided tours of Harlem.[4] Recent ecological awareness has given rise to some imaginative variations: bus tours of "The Ten Top Polluters in Action" were available in Philadelphia during "Earth Week" in April, 1970.

This touristic form of moral involvement with diverse public representations of race, poverty, urban structures, social ills, and, of course, the public "good," the monuments, is a modern alternative to systems of in-group morality built out of binary oppositions: insider vs. outsider, us vs. them. In traditional society, man could not survive unless he oriented his behavior in a "we are good—they are bad" framework. Although some of its remains are still to be found in modern politics, such traditional morality is not efficacious in the modern world. Social structural differentiation has broken up traditional loyalties. Now it is impossible to determine with any accuracy who "we" are and who "they" are. Man cannot therefore survive in the modern world if he tries to continue to orient his behavior in a traditional "we are good—they are bad" framework. As man enters the modern world, the entire field of social facts—poverty, race, class, work—is open to ongoing moral evaluation and interpretation. This craziness of mere distinctions forces the modern consciousness to explore beyond the frontiers of traditional prejudice and bigotry in its search for a moral identity. Only "middle Americans" (if such people actually exist) and primitives—peoples whose lives are "everyday" in the pejorative, grinding sense of the term—may feel fully a part of their own world. Modern man has been condemned to look elsewhere, everywhere, for his authenticity, to see if he can catch a glimpse of it reflected in the simplicity, poverty, chastity or purity of others.

## The Structure of the Attraction

I have defined a tourist attraction as an empirical relationship between a *tourist*, a *sight* and a *marker* (a piece of information about a sight). A simple model of the attraction can be presented in the following form:

[tourist / sight / marker]
attraction

Note that markers may take many different forms: guidebooks, informational tablets, slide shows, travelogues, souvenir matchbooks, etc. Note also that no *naturalistic* definition of the sight is possible. Well-marked sights that attract tourists include such items as mountain ranges, Napoleon's hat, moon rocks, Grant's tomb, even entire nation-states. The attractions are often indistinguishable from their less famous relatives. If they were not marked, it would be impossible for a layman to distinguish, on the basis of appearance alone, between moon rocks brought back by astronauts and pebbles picked up at Craters of the Moon National Monument in Idaho. But one is a sight and the other a souvenir, a kind of marker. Similarly, hippies are tourists and, at home in the Haight Ashbury, they are also sights that tourists come to see, or at least they used to be.

The distinguishing characteristic of those things that are collectively thought to be "true sights" is suggested by a second look at the moon rock example. *Souvenirs* are collected by *individuals*, by tourists, while *sights* are "collected" by entire societies. The entire U.S.A. is behind the gathering of moon rocks, or at least it is supposed to be, and hippies are a reflection of our collective affluence and decadence.

The origin of the attraction in the collective consciousness is not always so obvious as it is when a society dramatizes its values and capabilities by sending its representatives out into the solar system. Nevertheless, the collective determination of "true sights" is clear cut. The tourist has no difficulty deciding the sights he ought to see. His only problem is getting around to all of them. Even under conditions where there is no end of things to see, some mysterious institutional force operates on the totality in advance of the arrival of tourists, separating out the specific sights which are the attractions. In the Louvre, for example, the attraction is the Mona Lisa. The rest is undifferentiated art in the abstract. Moderns somehow know what the important attractions are, even in remote places. This miracle of consensus that transcends national boundaries rests on an elaborate set of institutional mechanisms, a twofold process of *sight sacralization* that is met with a corresponding *ritual attitude* on the part of tourists.

## Sightseeing as Modern Ritual

Erving Goffman has defined ritual as a "perfunctory, conventionalized act through which an individual portrays his respect and regard for some object of ultimate value to its stand-in."[5] This is translated into the individual consciousness as a sense of duty, albeit a duty that is often lovingly performed. Under conditions of high social integration, the ritual attitude may lose all appearance of coercive externality. It may, that is, permeate an individual's inmost being so he performs his ritual obligations zealously and without thought for himself or for social consequences.

Modern international sightseeing possesses its own moral structure, a collective sense that certain sights must be seen. Some tourists will resist, no doubt, the suggestion that they are motivated by an elementary impluse analogous to the one that animates the Australian's awe for his Churinga boards. The Australian would certainly resist such a suggestion. Nevertheless, modern guided tours, in Goffman's terms, are "extensive ceremonial agendas involving long strings of obligatory rites." If one goes to Europe, one "must see" Paris; if one goes to Paris, one "must see" Notre Dame, the Eiffel Tower, the Louvre; if one goes to the Louvre, one "must see" the Venus de Milo and, of course, the Mona Lisa. There are quite literally millions of tourists who have spent their savings to make the pilgrimage to see these sights. Some who have not been "there" have reported to me that they want to see these sights "with all their hearts."

It is noteworthy that no one escapes the system of attractions except by retreat into a stay-at-home, traditionalist stance: that is, no one is exempt from the obligation to go sightseeing except the local person. The Manhattanite who has never been to the Statue of Liberty is a mythic image in our society, as is the reverse image of the big-city people who come out into the country expressing fascination with things the local folk care little about. The ritual attitude of the tourist originates in the act of travel itself and culminates when he arrives in the presence of the sight.

Some tourists feel so strongly about the sight they are visiting that they want to be alone in its presence, and they become annoyed at other tourists for profaning the place by crowding around "like sheep." Some sights become so important that tourists avoid use of their proper names: in the Pacific Northwest, Mount Rainier is called "The Mountain," and all up and down the West Coast of the United States, San Francisco is called "The City."

Traditional religious institutions are everywhere accommodating the movements of tourists. In "The Holy Land," the tour has followed in the path of the religious pilgrimage and is replacing it. Throughout the world, churches, cathedrals, mosques, and temples are being converted from religious to touristic functions.

## The Stages of Sight Sacralization

In structural studies, it is not sufficient to build a model of an aspect of society entirely out of attitudes and behavior of individuals. It is also necessary to specify in detail the linkages between the attitudes and behavior and concrete institutional settings.

Perhaps there are, or have been, some sights which are so spectacular in themselves that no institutional support is required to mark them off as attractions. The original set of attractions is called, after the fashion of primitives, by the name of the sentiment they were supposed to have generated: "The Seven Wonders of the World." Modern sights, with but few exceptions, are not so evidently reflective of important social values as the Seven Wonders must have been. Attractions such as Cypress Gardens, the statue of the Little Mermaid in the harbor at Copenhagen, the Cape Hatteras Light and the like, risk losing their broader sociosymbolic meanings, becoming once more mere aspects of a limited social setting. Massive institutional support is often required for sight sacralization in the modern world.

The first stage of sight sacralization takes place when the sight is marked off from similar objects as worthy of preservation. This stage may be arrived at deductively from the model of the attraction

[tourist / sight / *marker*]
attraction

or it may be arrived at inductively by empirical observation. Sights have markers. Sometimes an act of Congress is necessary, as in the official designation of a national park or historical shrine. This first stage can be called the *naming phase* of sight sacralization. Often, before the naming phase, a great deal of work goes into the authentication of the candidate for sacralization. Objects are x-rayed, baked, photographed with special equipment and examined by experts. Reports are filed testifying to the object's aesthetic, historical, monetary, recreational and social values.

Second is the *framing and elevation* phase. Elevation is the putting on display of an object—placement in a case, on a pedestal or opened up for visitation. Framing is the placement of an official boundary around the object. On a practical level, two types of framing occur: protecting and enhancing. Protection seems to have been the motive behind the decision recently taken at the Louvre to place the Mona Lisa (but none of the other paintings) behind glass. When spotlights are placed on a building or a painting, it is enhanced. Most efforts to protect a sacred object, such as hanging a silk cord in front of it, or putting extra guards on duty around it, can also be read as a kind of enhancement, so the distinction between protection and enhancement eventually breaks down. Tourists before the Mona Lisa often remark: "Oh, it's the only one with glass," or "It must be the most valuable, it has glass in front." Advanced framing occurs when the rest of the world is forced back from the object and the space in between is landscaped. Versailles and the Washington Monument are "framed" in this way.

When the framing material that is used has itself entered the first stage of sacralization (marking), a third stage has been entered. This stage can be called *enshrinement*. The model here is Sainte Chapelle, the church built by Saint Louis as a container for the "true Crown of Thorns" which he had purchased from Baldwin of Constantinople. Sainte Chapelle is, of course, a tourist attraction in its own right. Similarly, in the Gutenberg Museum, in Gutenberg, Germany, the original Gutenberg Bible is displayed under special lights on a pedestal in a darkened enclosure in a larger room. The walls of the larger room are hung with precious documents, including a manuscript by Beethoven.

The next stage of sacralization is *mechanical reproduction* of the sacred object: the creation of prints, photographs, models or effigies of the object which are themselves valued and displayed. It is the mechanical reproduction phase of sacralization that is most responsible for setting the tourist in motion on his journey to find the true object. And he is not disappointed. Alongside of the copies of it, it has to be The Real Thing.

The final stage of sight sacralization is *social reproduction*, as occurs when groups, cities, and regions begin to name themselves after famous attractions.

Tourist attractions are not merely a collection of random material representations. When they appear in itineraries, they have a moral claim on the tourist and, at the same time, they tend toward universality, incorporating natural, social, historical and cultural domains in a single representation made possible by the tour. This morally enforced universality is the basis of a general system of classification of societal elements produced without conscious effort. No person or agency is officially responsible for the worldwide proliferation of tourist attractions. They have appeared naturally, each seeming to respond to localized causes.

Nevertheless, when they are considered as a totality, tourist attractions reveal themselves to be a taxonomy of structural elements. Interestingly, this natural taxonomic system contains the analytical classification of social structure currently in use by social scientists. A North American itinerary, for example, contains domestic, commercial and industrial establishments, occupations, public-service and transportation facilities, urban neighborhoods, communities and members of solidary (or, at least, identifiable) subgroups of American society. The specific attractions representing these structural categories would include the Empire State Building, an Edwardian house in Boston's Back Bay, a Royal Canadian mounted policeman, a Mississippi River bridge, Grand Coulee Dam, an Indian totem pole, San Francisco's Chinatown, a cable car, Tijuana, Indians, cowboys, an ante-bellum mansion, an Amish farm, Arlington National Cemetery, the Smithsonian Institution and Washington Cathedral.

Taken together, tourist attractions and the behavior surrounding them are, I think, one of the most complex and orderly of the several universal codes that constitute modern society, although not so complex and orderly as, for example, a language.

Claude Lévi-Strauss claims that there is no such system in modern society. I think it is worth exploring the possible base of this claim, which is by no means confined to Lévi-Strauss's offhand remarks. Erving Goffman has similarly suggested that:

> in contemporary society rituals performed to stand-ins for supernatural entities are everywhere in decay, as are extensive ceremonial agendas involving long strings of obligatory rites. What remains are brief rituals one individual performs for another, attesting to civility and good will on the performer's part and to the recipient's possession of a small patrimony of sacredness.[6]

I think that the failure of Goffman and Lévi-Strauss to note the existence of social integration on a macrostructural level in modern society can be traced to a methodological deficiency: neither of them has developed the use of systemic variables for his analysis of social structure. In my own studies, I was able to bypass Lévi-Strauss's critique by working up the very dimension of modernity that he named as its most salient feature: its chaotic fragmentation, its *differentiation*.

Interestingly, the approach I used was anticipated by Émile Durkheim, who invented the use of systemic variables for sociological analysis and who named tourist attractions ("works of art" and "historical monuments") in his basic listing of social facts. Durkheim wrote:

> Social facts, on the contrary [he has just been writing of psychological facts], qualify far more naturally and immediately as things. Law is embodied in codes . . . fashions are preserved in costumes; taste in works of art . . . [and] the currents of daily life are recorded in statistical figures and historical monuments. By their very nature they tend toward an independent existence outside the individual consciousness, which they dominate.[7]

Until now, no sociologist took up Durkheim's suggestion that "costumes," "art" and "monuments" are keys to modern social structure. The structure of the attraction was deciphered by accident by the culture critic Walter Benjamin while working on a different problem. But Benjamin, perhaps because of his commitment to an orthodox version of Marxist theory, inverted all the basic relations. He wrote:

> The uniqueness of a work of art is inseparable from its being imbedded in the fabric of tradition. This tradition itself is thoroughly alive and extremely changeable. An ancient statue of Venus, for example, stood in a different traditional context with the Greeks, who made it an object of veneration, than with the clerics of the Middle Ages, who viewed it as an ominous idol. Both of them, however, were equally confronted with its uniqueness, that is, its aura. Originally the contextual integration of art in tradition found its expression in the cult. We know that the earliest art works originated in the service of ritual—first the magical, then the religious kind. It is significant that the existence of the work of art with reference to its aura is never entirely separated from its ritual function. In other words, the unique value of the "authentic" work of art has its basis in ritual, the location of its original use value.[8]

Setting aside for the moment Marxist concerns for "use value," I want to suggest that society does not produce art: artists do. Society, for its part, can only produce the importance, "reality" or "originality" of a work of art by piling up representations of it alongside. Benjamin believed that the reproductions of the work of art are produced because the work has a socially based "aura" about it, the "aura" being a residue of its origins in a primordial ritual. He should have reversed his terms. The work becomes "authentic" only after the first copy of it is produced. The reproductions *are* the aura, and the ritual, far from being a point of origin, *derives* from the relationship between the original object and its socially constructed importance. I would argue that this is the structure of the attraction in modern society, including the artistic attractions, and the reason the Grand Canyon has a touristic "aura" about it even though it did not originate in ritual.

## ATTRACTIONS AND STRUCTURAL DIFFERENTIATION

In the tourists' consciousness, the attractions are not analyzed out as I present them type by type in the next sections and chapters. They appear sequentially, unfolding before the tourist so long as he continues his sightseeing. The touristic value of a modern community lies in the way it organizes social, historical, cultural and natural elements into a stream of impressions. Guidebooks contain references to all types of attractions, but the lively descriptions tend to be of the social materials. Modern society makes of itself its principal attraction in which the other attractions are embedded. Baedeker wrote of Paris:

> Paris is not only the political metropolis of France, but also the center of the artistic, scientific, commercial, and industrial life of the nation. Almost every branch of French industry is represented here, from the fine-art handicrafts to the construction of powerful machinery. . . .
>
> The central quarters of the city are remarkably bustling and animated, but owing to the ample breadth of the new streets and boulevards and the fact that many of them are paved with asphalt or wood, Paris is a far less noisy place than many other large cities. Its comparative tranquility, however, is often rudely interrupted by the discordant cries of the itinerant hawkers of wares of every kind, such as "old clothes" men, the vendors of various kinds of comestibles, the crockery-menders, the "fontaniers" (who clean and repair filters, etc.), the dog barbers, and newspaper-sellers. As a rule, however, they are clean and tidy in their dress, polite in manner, self-respecting, and devoid of the squalor and ruffianism which too often characterise their class.[9]

Georg Simmel began the analysis of this modern form of social consciousness which takes as its point of departure social structure itself. Simmel wrote:

> Man is a differentiating creature. His mind is stimulated by the differ-ences between a momentary impression and the one which preceded it. Lasting impressions, impressions which differ only slightly from one another, impressions which take a regular and habitual course and show regular and habitual contrasts—all these use up, so to speak, less consciousness than does the rapid crowding of changing images, the sharp discontinuity in the grasp of a single glance, and the unexpected-ness of onrushing impressions. These are the psychological conditions which the metropolis creates. With each crossing of the street, with the tempo and multiplicity of the economic, occupational and social life, the city sets up a deep contrast with the small town and rural life with reference to the sensory foundations of psychic life.[10]

Simmel claims to be working out an aspect of the *Gemeinschaft-Gesellschaft* distinction. It would be more accurate to say that he is de-scribing the difference between everyday life impressions, be they rural *or* urban, and the impressions of a strange place formed by a tourist on a visit, a vantage point Simmel knew well.[11]

Baedeker's and Simmel's stress on the work dimension of society is also found in touristic descriptions of New York City, which is always in the process of being rebuilt, and the waterfront areas of any city that has them. Similarly, Mideastern and North African peoples have traditionally made much use of their streets as places of work, and tourists from the Christian West seem to have inexhaustible fascina-tion for places such as Istanbul, Tangiers, Damascus and Casablanca, where they can see factories without walls.

Primitive social life is nearly totally exposed to outsiders who happen to be present. Perhaps some of our love for primitives is attached to this innocent openness.

Modern society, originally quite closed up, is rapidly restructur-ing or institutionalizing the rights of outsiders (that is, of individuals not functionally connected to the operation) to look into its diverse aspects. Institutions are fitted with arenas, platforms and chambers set aside for the exclusive use of tourists. The courtroom is the most important institution in a democratic society. It was among the first to open to the outside and, I think, it will be among the first to close as the workings of society are increasingly revealed through the opening

of other institutions to tourists. The New York Stock Exchange and
the Corning Glass factory have specially designated visitors' hours,
entrances and galleries. Mental hospitals, army bases and grade
schools stage periodic open houses where not mere work but Good
Work is displayed. The men who make pizza crusts by tossing the
dough in the air often work in windows where they can be watched
from the sidewalk. Construction companies cut peepholes into the
fences around their work, nicely arranging the holes for sightseers of
different heights. The becoming public of almost everything—a process that makes all men equal before the attraction—is a necessary part
of the integrity of the modern social world.

## TOURIST DISTRICTS

Distinctive local attractions contain (just behind, beside or embedded in the parts presented to the tourists) working offices, shops,
services and facilities: often an entire urban structure is operating
behind its touristic front. Some of these touristic urban areas are
composed of touristic *districts*. Paris is "made up" of the Latin Quarter, Pigalle, Montparnasse, Montmartre; San Francisco is made up of
the Haight Ashbury, the Barbary Coast and Chinatown; and London, of Soho, Piccadilly Circus, Blackfriars, Covent Gardens, the
Strand. Less touristically developed areas have only one tourist district and are, therefore, sometimes upstaged by it: the Casbah, Beverly Hills, Greenwich Village. An urban sociologist or an ethnographer might point out that cities are composed of much more than
their tourist areas, but this is obvious. Even tourists are aware of this.
More important is the way the tourist attractions appear on a regional
base as a model of social structure, beginning with "suggested" or
"recommended" *communities*, *regions* and *neighborhoods*, and extending
to matters of detail, setting the tourist up with a matrix he can fill in (if
he wishes) with his own discoveries of his own typical little *markets*,
*towns*, *restaurants* and *people*. This touristic matrix assures that the
social structure that is recomposed via the tour, while always partial,
is nevertheless not a skewed or warped representation of reality. Once
on tour, only the individual imagination can modify reality, and so

long as the faculty of imagination is at rest, society appears such as it is.

The taxonomy of structural elements provided by the attractions is universal, not because it *already* contains everything it might contain but rather, because the logic behind it is potentially inclusive. It sets up relationships between elements (as between neighborhoods and their cities) which cross the artificial boundaries between levels of social organization, society and culture, and culture and nature. Still, the resulting itineraries rarely penetrate lovingly into the precious details of a society as a Southern novelist might, peeling back layer after layer of local historical, cultural and social facts, although this is the ideal of a certain type of snobbish tourism. Such potential exists in the structure of the tour, but it goes for the most part untapped. Attractions are usually organized more on the model of the filing system of a disinterested observer, like a scientist who separates his passions from their object, reserving them entirely for matters of method; or like a carpetbagging politician who calculates his rhetoric while reading a printout of the demographic characteristics of the region he wants to represent. In short, the tourist world is complete in its way, but it is constructed after the fashion of all worlds that are filled with people who are just passing through and know it.

## THE DIFFERENTIATIONS OF THE TOURIST WORLD

Functioning *establishments* figure prominently as tourist attractions. Commercial, industrial and business establishments are also basic features of social regions, or they are first among the elements from which regions are composed. Some, such as the Empire State Building, the now-defunct Les Halles in Paris, and Fisherman's Wharf in San Francisco, overwhelm their districts. Others fit together in a neat structural arrangement of little establishments that contribute to their district's special local character: flower shops, meat and vegetable markets, shoe repair shops, neighborhood churches. Unlike the Empire State Building, with its elevators expressly for sightseers, these little establishments may not be prepared for the outside visitors they attract. A priest who made his parish famous had this problem, but apparently he is adjusting to the presence of tourists:

> For a time, in fact, St. Boniface became an attraction for tourists and white liberals from the suburbs. Father Groppi recalled that he had sometimes been critical of the whites who overflowed the Sunday masses at St. Boniface and then returned to their suburban homes.
>
> "But now I can understand their problems," he said. "They come from conservative parishes and were tired of their parish organizations, the Holy Name Society and that sort of nonsense."[12]

Under normal conditions of touristic development, no social establishment ultimately resists conversion into an attraction, not even *domestic establishments*. Selected homes in the "Society Hill" section of downtown Philadelphia are opened annually for touristic visitation. Visitors to Japan are routinely offered the chance to enter, observe and—to a limited degree—even participate in the households of middle-class families. Individual arrangements can be made with the French Ministry of Tourism to have coffee in a French home, and even to go for an afternoon drive in the country with a Frenchman of "approximately one's own social station."[13]

A version of sociology suggests that society is composed not of individuals but *groups*, and groups, too, figure as tourist attractions. Certain groups work up a show of their group characteristics (their ceremonies, settlement patterns, costumes, etc.) especially for the benefit of sightseers:

> At an open meeting yesterday of Indian businessmen, government officials and airline representatives, Dallas Chief Eagle, spokesman and director of the new United States Indian International Travel agency, said the cooperative hoped to be able to offer low-cost group tours to German tourists by June.[14]

Other groups, even other Indian groups, militantly resist such showmanship, even though their leaders are aware of their touristic potential, because this kind of behavior *for* tourists is widely felt to be degrading.[15] Given the multichanneled nature of human communication, these two versions of the group (the proud and the practical) need not be mutually exclusive. The following account suggests that a member of one of our recently emergent self-conscious minorities can do his own thing and do a thing for the tourists at the same time:

> New Jersey, Connecticut and even Pennsylvania license plates were conspicuous around Tompkins Square yesterday, indicating that the Lower East Side's new hippie haven is beginning to draw out-of-state tourists.
>
> "You go to where the action is," a blond girl in shorts said through a thick layer of white lipstick. The girl, who said her name was Lisa Stern, and that she was a Freshman at Rutgers University, added: "I used to spend weekends in Greenwich Village, but no longer." However, Lisa didn't find much action in Tompkins Square Park, the scene of a Memorial Day clash between about 200 hippies and the police. . . . Yesterday there was no question any more as to a hippie's right to sit on the grass or to stretch out on it.
>
> Some tourists from New Jersey were leaning over the guardrail enclosing a patch of lawn, much as if they were visiting a zoo, and stared at a man with tattooed arms and blue-painted face who gently waved at them while the bongo drums were throbbing.[16]

Other groups—the Pennsylvania "Dutch," The Amanas, Basques, and peasants everywhere—probably fall somewhere in between resistance and acquiescence to tourism, or they vacillate from self-conscious showiness to grudging acceptance of it.

Perhaps because they have a man inside, *occupations* are popular tourist attractions. In some areas, local handicrafts would have passed into extinction except for the intervention of mass tourism and the souvenir market:

> Palekh boxes are formed from papier-mâché and molded in the desired shape on a wood form. A single artist makes the box, coats it with layers of black lacquer, paints his miniature picture, adds final coats of clear lacquer and signs his name and the date. Each box represents two to three days' work. Some of Palekh's 150 artists work at home. . . . I watched Constantine Bilayev, an artist in his 50's, paint a fairytale scene he might have been doing for his grandchildren. It illustrated the story of a wicked old woman with a daughter she favored and a stepdaughter she hated. She sent the stepdaughter into the woods to gather firewood, hoping harm would befall the Girl. Instead, the stepdaughter triumphed over every adversity.[17]

In addition to this cute side of occupational sightseeing, there is a heavy, modern workaday aspect. In the same community with the box makers, there are *real* young ladies triumphing over adversity while serving as tourist attractions. The report continues:

> But the main attraction of this city of 400,000 people is the Ivanovo Textile Factory, an industrial enormity that produces some 25,000,000 yards of wool cloth a year. The factory represents an investment of $55 million. The factory's machinery makes an ear-shattering din. Ranks of machines take the raw wool and convert it into coarse thread, and successive ranks of devices extrude the thread into ever-finer filaments. The weaving machines clang in unison like a brigade on the march —Raz, Dva, Raz, Dva, Raz, Dva as an unseen Russian sergeant would count it out. The 7,500 workers are mostly young and mostly female. A bulletin board exhorts them to greater production in honor of the Lenin centenary.

Along with handicraft and specialized industrial work, there are other occupational attractions including glass blowers, Japanese pearl divers, cowboys, fishermen, Geisha girls, London chimney sweeps, gondoliers and sidewalk artists. Potentially, the entire division of labor in society can be transformed into a tourist attraction. In some districts of Manhattan, even the men in gray flannel suits have been marked off for touristic attention.

Connecting the urban areas of society are *transportation networks*, segments and intersections of which are tourist attractions. Examples are: the London Bridge, the Champs Elysées, Hollywood and Vine, Ponte Vecchio, the Golden Gate, Red Square, the canals of Venice and Amsterdam, Broadway, the Gate of Heavenly Peace, the rue de Rivoli, the Spanish Steps, Telegraph Avenue, the Atlantic City Boardwalk, the Mont Blanc tunnel, Union Square and New England's covered bridges. Along these lines is the following comment on an attraction that is not well known but for which some hopes have been raised:

> The city of Birmingham recently opened its first expressway. To do so it had to slice a gash through famed Red Mountain in order to complete construction and get people in and out of the city in a hurry. To the

> drivers of Birmingham the freeway means a new convenience, but to
> the thousands of visitors the giant cut at the crest of the mountain has
> become a fascinating stopping place . . . a new and exciting tourist
> attraction.[18]

In addition to roads, squares, intersections, and bridges, *vehicles*
that are restricted to one part of the worldwide transportation net-
work also figure as attractions: rickshaws, gondolas, San Francisco's
cable cars and animal-powered carts everywhere.

Finally, the system of attractions extends as far as society has
extended its *public works*, not avoiding things that might well have
been avoided:

> A London sightseeing company has added a tour of London's public
> lavatories to its schedule. The firm, See Britain, said the lavatories tour
> will begin Sunday and cost five shillings (60 cents). It will include
> lavatories in the City and the West End. A spokesman said visitors will
> see the best Victorian and Edwardian lavatories in the areas with a
> guide discussing the style of the interiors, architecture, hours of open-
> ing and history.[19]

*The* presentation of the inner workings of society's nether side is,
of course, the Paris sewer tour.

Although the tourist need not be consciously aware of this, the
thing he goes to see is society and its works. The societal aspect of
tourist attractions is hidden behind their fame, but this fame cannot
change their origin in social structure. Given the present sociohistorical epoch, it is not a surprise to find that tourists believe sightseeing is
a leisure activity, and fun, even when it requires more effort and
organization than many jobs. In a marked contrast to the grudging
acquiescence that may characterize the relation of the individual to his
industrial work, individuals happily embrace the attitudes and norms
that lead them into a relationship with society through the sightseeing
act. In being presented as a valued object through a so-called "leisure"
activity that is thought to be "fun," society is renewed in the heart of
the individual through warm, open, unquestioned relations, characterized by a near absence of alienation when compared with other
contemporary relationships. This is, of course, the kind of relation-

ship of individual and society that social scientists and politicians think is necessary for a strong society, and they are probably correct in their belief.

Tourist attractions in their natural, unanalyzed state may not appear to have any coherent infrastructure uniting them, and insofar as it is through the attraction that the tourist apprehends society, society may not appear to have coherent structure, either. It is not my intention here to overorganize the touristic consciousness. It exhibits the deep structure, which is social structure, that I am describing here, but this order need never be perceived as such in its totality. Consciousness and the integration of the individual into the modern world require only that one attraction be linked to one other: a district to a community, or an establishment to a district, or a role to an establishment. Even if only a single linkage is grasped in the immediate present, this solitary link is the starting point for an endless spherical system of connections which is society and the world, with the individual at one point on its surface.

# 3

# The Paris Case:
# Origins of Alienated Leisure

IN Paris, at the turn of the present century, sightseers were given tours of the sewers, the morgue, a slaughterhouse, a tobacco factory, the government printing office, a tapestry works, the mint, the stock exchange, and the supreme court in session. These establishments, and the activities they contain, are the concrete material representations of our most important institutions: law, economy, industry, the balance of man and nature and life and death. The twentieth century has made both a science (sociology) and a recreation (sightseeing) of the study of these institutions. The involvement of sightseers with touristic work displays qualifies as one of Lévi-Strauss's "sciences of the concrete."

The appearance of a mythology of work consigns it to a remote and formative period and marks the end of the industrial age. Work was once the locus of our most important social values and the exclusive anchor point connecting the individual and society. Now it is only one stop among many in tourists' itineraries.

I have termed visits to work displays of the sort listed above "alienated leisure" because such visits represent a perversion of the aim of leisure: they are a return to the work place. Some tourists never visit them, going in more for natural, historical and cultural attractions, or commercialized attractions of the "hyped-up" amusement park type. This makes the existence of visits to work displays and the infrastructure of displayed work that supports them all the more remarkable in that they run counter to common sense expectations for organized leisure activities. Work displays are not central to tourism itself but they are central to the more fundamental transformation of industrial society into modern society. Here, as elsewhere, sociohistorical forces deflect our attention away from the significant changes occurring around us. As work becomes a "mere" attribute of society, not its central attribute, the work display permits Industrial Man to reflect upon his own condition and to transcend it.

The shift from industrial to modern society is evidenced in changing family structure, new approaches to education, and modern social movements, as well as in the devaluation of work and in the rise of tourism and leisure. In this chapter, I examine the set of work displays for tourists in Paris at the turn of the century, the tobacco factory, the slaughterhouse, and the like. As nearly as I can tell from my research so far (described below), this is an exhaustive list. My hope is to expose the meanings embodied in these displays, and to discover in them, in simplified form, the inner core of our modern value system in the process of disentangling itself from industrial values.

In my analysis of Paris work displays, I have used (with some reservation) an expository method which seems to have been developed independently by Roland Barthes in his *Mythologies*[1] and H. Marshall McLuhan in his *Mechanical Bride*[2] in the mid-1950's. In these two "ur-texts" of modern structuralism, the authors present short, often crystalline analyses of aspects of popular culture: automobiles, magazines, comics, etc. In Barthes' book, relevant to the following, is a section on the Hachette *Guide Bleu* which Barthes criticises for its bias in favor of churches, monuments and hilly scenery. The problem with their epigrammatic method is its failure to trace the subterranean connections between its many subjects, or to arrive at the deep structure of modern culture. Lévi-Strauss corrected this to some degree in the manner in which he studied Native American myths, by setting them in relation to one another and searching for the inner logic of the totality.[3] I want to retain here some of the freedom of Barthes while modifying the method along the lines suggested by Lévi-Strauss's study of primitive social structure.

The data I use are descriptions of Parisian work displays from guidebooks written at the turn of the century. These descriptions are similar in style and format to the following familiar example from a recent Michelin guide to *New York City*:

GARMENT CENTER. Workshops, warehouses and factories line the streets jammed with trucks and frantic with delivery boys pushing racks of clothes on handtrucks at dizzy speeds between main factories and subcontractors, who often assemble the garments or add finishing touches. A typical sight is the rush at noon and after the factories close: solid waves of workers emerge, sweeping everything before them; a little later the Garment Center is a desert, where it is unwise to wander alone.[4]

I have gone back to the turn of the present century to examine these sights because this time represents the first moment when modern mass tourism and its support institutions were fully elaborated as we know them today. In a somewhat ironical passage, the historian of the American Express Company describes the situation on the eve of that other distinctively modern phenonenon—total global warfare:

Never was travel to Europe so pleasant as in the summer of 1914, never before and never again. The great modern ships had come in, the *Lusitania, Mauretania, France, Olympia, Aquitania,* and the German giants *Imperator* and *Vaterland.* Signor Marconi's invention had dispelled the dread mystery of the oceans, and Europe was only five days away. The new superliners were very elegant and far more comfortable than most people's homes. Travel on the Continent was easy and luxurious. The long years of peace had made conditions truly civilized and given a spurious air of permanence and progress to the European economy. No passports were needed in that enlightened summer. The hotels and luxury trains like the *Simplon-Orient* and the *Train Bleu* were in their heyday. . . . What wonder that the ships went out with tourists crowding them like swarming bees as 150,000 Americans started for a gay vacation abroad.[5]

Paris was selected for a case study of work displays because it was a focal point for tourism at the time. It had a fully elaborated touristic complex which was not yet repetitious or encrusted with commercialized attractions which only imprecisely reflect the elementary structures of tourism. There have been periods in the development of modern London, San Francisco, or Rome which would serve as well for such a case study, but none would serve better, and none is better documented.

From the standpoint of industrialization and modernization, Paris, 1900 is a far from arbitrary designation for a study of the origins of modern values. It is the capital of the nation that was, at that time, first among nations on most indicators of modernity. France had already had her revolutions. In so doing, she provided Marx with his model for the revolutions that would follow. Walter Benjamin suggested that nineteenth-century Paris was the origin of modernity itself: his working title of his *magnum opus*, unfinished at the time of his unfortunate death, was "Paris, the Capital of the Nineteenth Century."[6] In addition to attracting Marx, who was heading the other direction, Paris was an essential stop in the Grand Tours of British gentlemen, and was beginning to attract the new middle class of Britons and Americans in large numbers. The special reasons for travel (to visit a friend, fair, ceremony, or religious shrine, to do business or research, to shop for a special article) were giving way to the modern idea that no reason need be given to visit Paris except to see the city itself and its sights. The guidebooks of the time indicate that Paris was completely equipped with good temporary accomodations for tourists of limited means. A guidebook to the Paris International Exhibition of 1900 begins:

> Most of the visitors to Paris in 1900 will go, not only to see the exhibition, but to see Paris as well. For many the trip across the Channel will be the event of a lifetime. The publisher of the present guide has attempted to furnish those who wish to profit as much as possible by their visit, and enjoy it as fully as may be, the means of doing so easily and cheaply. The present Guide does not primarily appeal to the person who stays regardless of expense at the fashionable hotels, dines at the Grand Cafés, and shops at the Rue de la Paix, although every possible information concerning that life will also be found. . . . In "Exhibition Paris" will be found hints how to see Paris cheaply, how and where to live well and reasonably, how to save money.

For documentation I have selected two guides, the one just quoted from above, the *Anglo-American Practical Guide to Exhibition Paris: 1900* (London: William Heinemann), and Karl Baedeker's justly famous *Paris and Environs With Routes From London to Paris: Handbook for Travelers* (Leipsic, Karl Baedeker, Publisher, 1900).* Baedeker's

---

*References in this chapter to the *Anglo-American* guide will be in the text as "AAPG, p. 00," and the Baedeker guide as "*B*, p. 00."

guide contains a detailed description of every work display mentioned in the other guidebooks and traveler's accounts I have read.[7] The question of Baedeker's comprehensiveness, then, is academic. If a sight is not mentioned in any guides, it is unmarked, it is not an attraction from the standpoint of institutionalized tourism, and it is not likely to be visited much by tourists.

My use of the Baedeker guide did present another kind of difficulty, however. It retains, from its original use by the Grand Tourists, a distinctive upper-crustiness.[8] In the "Practical" guide, this is not the case: as already indicated in the quote above, it exhibits a penny-pinching middle-class stance as it immediately directs its readers away from the shops on the rue de la Paix. Baedeker, on the other hand, lists *only* the hotels and restaurants of "the highest class" and those of "almost equal rank" (*B*, p. 3), and for shopping Baedeker sends his reader straight to the rue de la Paix:

> SHOPS AND BAZAARS. With the exception of the houses in the aristocratic Faubourg St. Germain, there are few buildings in Paris which have not shops on the ground floor. The most attractive are those in the Grands Boulevards, the Rue de la Paix, Avenue de l'Opera, Rue Royale, Rue Vivienne, and Rue de Rivoli. (*B*, p. 39)

No matter how much they might have needed it, the users of the Baedeker guides would have been insulted by advice on how to cut corners, and Baedeker was careful not to give it.

The pronounced bias of Baedeker on the matter of selecting support facilities for tourists (hotels, restaurants, gift shops, etc.) did not influence his selection of *sights*. The "Practical" middle-class guide, which insists that "Paris is essentially a city of pleasure and amusements" (*AAPG*, p.v.), *is* biased in terms of selection of sights and omits mention of the slaughterhouse, for example. Baedeker calmly describes the sewers, the morgue, the slaughterhouse in their proper places in his suggested afternoon and morning walking tours (which cover almost the entire city) alongside his dry descriptions of fountains, paintings and monuments. He seems to be motivated only by a commitment, and sometimes a grudging one, to an ideal of responsible guide writing that requires descriptions of everything open to tourists. The result does not conform to the standards established by academic anthropology for ethnography, but it is still the best ethnography of modern cities so far available.

Baedeker's class bias did, it will soon be seen, influence the *way* he described work displays. I have used the "Practical" guide, with its less complete and less elevated viewpoint, to correct, wherever possible, Baedeker's disdain for everyday, especially workaday affairs.[9]

## The Work Displays

In industrial society, work is broken down into "occupations" and it provides livelihood and status on the individual level.[10] Modern society transforms this same work into a positive and negative aesthetic of production. The nature of work in an area (coal mining in Pennsylvania, musical instrument making in Northern Italy) is now understood to be an aspect of regional identity and an important component of the "quality of life" on the community level. The work displays about to be discussed, and work displays in general, unify economics and aesthetics and they begin to replace industrial concerns for social class and status with the modern concern for "lifestyle." They dramatize the enormous differentiation of the modern work force and, at the same time, reintegrate all classes of workers, from stock brokers to sewer cleaners, in a single system of representations. They obscure the distinction industrial society makes between human and machine labor by displaying the two as inextricably linked in unified designs as occurs, for example, in tours of assembly lines. The display of work creates the impression in the sightseer of having firsthand experience with society's serious side, even as the workers and the tourists are separated and the work is staged. On the other hand, the work display, unlike work itself, *does* open the most closed off areas of industrial society to almost everyone: men, women, and children of almost all ethnic origins and nationalities. Open display conveys the impression that work in all its forms is normal and routine, that no matter how dangerous or foul it may be, there is, nevertheless, "nothing to hide." The worker-as-tourist is permitted to "look down" on his comrades (even those holding a higher status position than his own in the industrial system), to offer remarks and suggestions expressive of great expertise and experience or moral superiority. There is a restructuring of the work place in response to its display; it is neutralized or modernized; practical joking stops; the "girlie" calendars come off the wall; traditional male solidarity is broken up. Politicians and other professionals spend almost all their time and resources building their "images" which are increasingly abstract and detached from the jobs they do. The worker was integrated *as worker* into industrial society. The worker is integrated into modern society as tourist and as tourist attraction (work display), as actor and spectator in the "universal drama of work."

*The Supreme Court:* Modernization is the opening up and dramatization of every important social institution, a process that creates "stars" and forecloses certain meanings and understandings that are based on rigid insider vs. outsider distinctions. "Democracy," whether based on the socialist conception of the "worker" or on the capitalist conception of the "electorate," is the ultimate political dramatization. Legal institutions, the courts, were the first to open up under pressures of modernization.

According to Baedeker (p. 220), the attraction of the supreme court in Paris, 1900 was the "opportunity of hearing some of the famous pleaders." Also, "the advocates in their black gowns are frequently seen pacing up and down the different galleries whilst the courts are sitting." The stress here is on the "star" lawyers whose work is represented as an anxious, thoughtful pacing. No mention is made of the complex principles which they have mastered, or of the legal research they have undertaken, preparatory to appearing bewigged and gowned before the court and the tourist.

The modern consciousness is perfectly divided between the thrill and mystery of stardom and a nostalgic longing to get back to the true inner principles of its complex institutions. Touristic understanding seems to be overpowering the other kind in the progress of modernity. Perhaps it was never possible to understand the complex inner workings of our institutions as such. In the Baedeker description, there is still the remote possibility that the tourists might decipher for themselves the institutional structures that are enacted in the legal process as they *hear* the famous lawyers. But this opening, provided by language, is beginning to disappear. Modern guides are written for a tourist class that knows only one language. (The same pressures are operating on our other institutions: in education, for example, one can cite the recent efforts to transform the American scholar into a "tourist intellectual" by removal of language studies from degree requirements.) As visual codes replace aural codes, modern social structure is represented as a dancing of the stars, something to see, an exciting drama. This exchange of an ear for an eye had already begun in 1900. The *Practical Guide* to the exhibition also contains an entry on the court, but its presentation is entirely transformed into the contemporary, visual mode: "The large hall, with the judges assembled in their robes, is well worth *seeing*" (*AAPG*, p.62; my emphasis).

Of course, Baedeker does not look down his nose at the supreme court and its respected workers, but he does draw a line, which seems strange from a modern vantage point, between the court and the stock exchange. Whereas today we tend to allocate our last reserves of disgust for work requiring physical contact with wet garbage and fecal matter, Baedeker was disgusted with the job of *the stockbroker*.

*The Stock Exchange:* As there were no restrictions as to who could enter the exchange for the purpose of doing business there, the main floor was open to anyone who wanted to come and speculate on the market. There was also one overhead gallery reserved for the use of sightseers. Baedeker describes the show below as follows:

> The tumultuous scene is best surveyed from the gallery. . . . The deafening noise, the vociferations, and the excited gestures of the speculators, produce a most unpleasant impression. Amidst the babel of tongues are heard the constantly recurring words, "*J'ai* . . . ; *qui est-ce qui a?* . . . ; *je prends; je vends*!" ["I have . . . who has? . . . I buy; I sell"; my translation]. (*B*, p.194.)

Again, the guide assumes that the reader knows French and perceives its job not as one of translating French into English, but of Noise into French. Also, implicit in the description is the reminder that high status once meant occupying a social position slightly above the need to make money. Baedeker looks down on men making money. The tone of the description of the stock exchange in the *Practical Guide* is quite different:

> It is a spectacle unique in Paris and perhaps the world. . . . Every type of speculator and financier may be seen there, from the millionaire, the banker, the jobber, the *coulissier*, the *rémissier* (tout who brings customers to the brokers), down to the poor ruined wretch

always hoping to recoup himself, or the retired *employé* who comes to
gamble there, as others gamble on the race course. (*AAPG*, p.133.)

Unlike Baedeker, this guide describes the scene at the exchange as
one into which a person of any status might fit, reserving the appellation "poor ruined wretch" only for those who fail at making money
there, not for everyone who is forced to make money, even those who
succeed at making considerable sums of it. The attitude of the *Practical Guide* reflects an essential victory of industrial capitalism over the
condescending survivors of an old life-style who were much in the
way at the time. The action of making money is transformed from
something that is "unpleasant" to an exciting spectacle.

*The Mint:* In moving from the stock exchange to the mint, the
tourist crosses another line dividing nonmanual from manual labor,
and enters the world of machinery. Baedeker evidently found the
sound of machines making money more tolerable than the sound of
men so engaged:

> The Ateliers, with their steam-engines, furnaces and machinery, are
> well worth visiting. . . . The machines invented by M. Thonnelier
> are highly ingenious, sixty pieces of money being struck by them each
> minute, while the whole of them in operation at once are capable of
> coining no fewer than two million francs per day. (*B*, p.248.)

It is probable that the Grand Tourists believed that this was the
proper way to make money, just as today some people think it proper
to delegate complex problem-solving to computers and dangerous
warfare to air force. Secreted within these desires is an effort to
bracket the presence of human workers, a pretense that The Job can
be done without human intervention. This is even now our "postindustrial" dream of an automatic society that runs without human
effort and allows mankind to enjoy perpetual childhood.

As I have suggested, the hope for a "postindustrial" society is, in
fact, only a touristic way of looking at work. It was apparently
especially difficult to routinize touristic visitation to work places
where manual labor was performed for several reasons, including the
embarrassment of appearing before "work people" whose life situation was less fortunate than that of the early tourists. The absence of

descriptions of workers at the mint is equivalent to the nice middle-class practice of averting the eyes from someone in a social predicament.

*The Government Printing Office:* A method of hiding the worker while displaying work is suggested in the following description of a print shop from the *Practical Guide:*

> Imprimerie Nationale, The: In the Court of honour is a statue of Gutenberg by David d'Angers; in the second court, a bas-relief by Le Lorrain, *Horses Drinking.* Eleven hundred work people of both sexes are employed by the Government in the Imprimerie Nationale. On the ground floor are the rooms in which are the presses (130 in number) the blocks, galvanos, and glazing apparatus. On the first floor: the director's office, containing four pictures by Pierre, and a clock by Boulle; the composition work rooms, the type rooms. The *Salon de Rohan* or *Salle des Poinçons* (dyes) has overdoors painted by Boucher. (*AAPG*, p.196.)

This mixture of mechanical and esthetic elements throws the work and the workers out of focus, and as the details blur, work becomes a mere part of an esthetic experience. The surface decorations provide something to look at should the work prove to appear "unpleasant." The tourist comes away from the shop able to construct for himself a belief that he has gained some inside knowledge of the industry, but so long as he never meets the gaze of the worker, he need not carry away an impression of the worker's actual situation. When the rules of etiquette intervene in this way between work and consciousness, as they do when workers are put on display for tourists, it is possible to omit the situation of the worker from the representation of the place of work in society. Here is the double character of work displays: they always appear as totalities and they convey vivid impressions, but they do not require that their viewer be responsible for seeing or remembering all their elements, or even their most essential elements, as he reconstructs them into his own firsthand version of society.[11] As anyone who tries to give (in absentia) clear directions over a route he drives daily can attest, when it comes to the exact relationships that hold between important details, experience is the worst teacher.

In his section on the print shop, in addition to noting the esthetic ornamentation, Baedeker is more precise about the work that takes place:

> The printing-office employs about 1200 work people of both sexes. The types are cast, the paper made, and the binding executed within the same building. Oriental characters are particularly well represented. The chief business consists in printing official documents of all kinds, books published at the expense of the government, geological maps, and certain playing cards (*viz.*, the "court cards" and the ace of clubs, the manufacture of which is a monopoly of the state). Visitors are admitted on Thurs. at 2 p.m. precisely. . . . (*B*, p.213)

Baedeker begins with the observation that an entire process is located under one roof, a fact which tenuously links the shop to its origins in handicraft. This linkage is not developed, however, and the main relationship presented is between a large force of workers and machinery and a finished product: books, maps, cards. The steps in the production process (type casting, paper making) are mentioned but the work itself is not described. Work is represented only up to the point where it would be necessary to begin commenting on human movements, skills and contact with machines.

This same strategy for describing work and workers is much used today. Instead of reproducing the sights, sounds and smells of the work place, the general characteristics of the aggregate of workers (number, composition by sex) are given along with their production figures. This approach, which obscures the concrete situation of the individual worker, is perhaps necessary when census-type information is used for economic and political projections. Its appearance in touristic descriptions (which often build images from the most precious details) is explicable only as a method of representing work while deflecting attention away from the worker. This "method" is not, of course, the product of conscious design. It has appeared as naturally as the work display itself appeared and developed with industrialization. The corresponding movement of the popular consciousness has been direct from the handicraft stage of production to the idea of a homogeneous industrial mass. The actual situation of the worker is elided and buried deep in the heart of modern society. Tourists are permitted to see the concrete situation of industrial workers but not to understand it in any meaningful sense.

"Experience" is the basic term in the rhetoric of modernity. That touristic experiences fall short of "understanding" (in the Weberian sense) is well-known. We do not, however, know the reasons why touristic experiences turn out to be so shallow. Common sense places the blame on the tourist mentality, but this is not technically correct. The tourist's inability to understand what he sees is the product of the structural arrangement that sets him into a touristic relationship with a social object, in this case, *work*. The tourist comports himself "as if" he has seen the things he has visited. It is through his sightseeing that he enters into a relationship to society. But this bond between the tourist and the social object is fragile and can be weakened if, even for a moment, the tourist perceives the distance that separates him from what he is seeing. Since the popular consciousness has a pronounced bias in favor of "experience" as the main route to understanding, it is through sightseeing that the tourist demonstrates better than by any other means that he is not alienated from society. If distance exists for the tourist, it is not between him and what he sees. As a tourist, he can only be alienated from the *meaning* of what he sees since this meaning is secreted in unnoticed details.

*The Gobelin Tapestry Weavers:* A concrete description of workers is found in Baedeker's section on the tapestry weavers:

> Only three looms are now engaged in producing Gobelin tapestry proper. At these the reverse side of the tapestry is turned toward the workmen, with the outline of the design drawn in black crayon on the stretched threads. At the workman's side are the picture to be copied and a basket with wool of every color and shade (about 14,000 tones in all). The weft threads are inserted by means of shuttles held in the hand. . . . Some families have been employed for generations in this industry. The work requires the utmost patience and the most prac-ticed eye. A skillful workman can complete 3 or even 4 square yds. in a year, but the average annual task is about 1½ yds. Many years are, therefore, sometimes requisite for the execution of the larger designs, which when complete are worth 2000 pounds and upwards. (*B*, pp.268-69.)

These workers seem almost museumized. Like the peasants under glass at the *Musée de l'Homme* at Trocadero, they appear to be outside of industrial time, working like spiders, weaving to perfection.

This appearance of being external to the industrial process— and therefore especially touristic from the common sense standpoint —is not, however, reflected in interior of the tapestry works nor in its historical origins. Gobelin remains a factory, a model factory, and factories are essential to industrialization. The industrial virtues of precision, fidelity to a boring task, and willingness to follow one's father into his line of work are what is on display. Gobelin seems to be a show of preindustrial handicrafts, but when it was first organized by Henri IV in the early seventeenth century and then reorganized under Louis XIV's finance minister, Colbert, the intent was to make it into the biggest, most modern and best-equipped factory in the world. It rated an entry in the famed French *Encyclopédie* (1765) and is characterized therein by the *philosophes* in terms less reminiscent of handicrafts than of modern heavy industry. Unlike Baedeker, who was so pleased by the quaint and patient master craftsmen he saw there, the *philosophe* was impressed, first of all, by its sheer output:

> The factory of the Gobelin is still the first of its kind in the world. The quantity of the works it has produced and the quantity of workers who were trained there is unbelievable. As a matter of fact France owes the progress of the arts and manufactures to this establishment.[12]

Industrialization has swirled past the Gobelin Tapestry Works but, in the beginning, it was at the cutting edge of the industrial movement. The tourist at the tapestry works may think he is watching old world craftsmen, but if they fascinate him in some indescribable way, it is because just beneath his consciousness he knows that he is really seeing a preserved fetus.

*The Tobacco Factory:* This place is not mentioned in the *Practical Guide* and apparently Baedeker was not especially interested in it:

> This extensive establishment, known as "du Gros-Caillou," is worthy of a visit, but the pungent smell of tobacco saturates the clothes and is not easily got rid of. About 2200 workpeople are employed here, and over 19 million lbs. of tobacco are annually manufactured. (*B*, p.281.)

In this brief description, there is no mention of a division of labor between the manual workers, of machines or of the different forms assumed by the product: cigars, pipe tobacco, snuff, quid. Manual labor has almost disappeared from this representation of work as if a man's tobacco is provided him, not by other men's labor, but directly from nature through a mysterious operation performed by work-in-the-abstract: i.e., "industry."

Interestingly, Baedeker does not mention esthetic details either. He is almost silent in the face of what must have seemed to him to be a kind of industrial nothingness. The guidebooks' descriptions of the paintings and sculptures at the mint and the print shops are reminders of early industry's struggle for integration in traditional cultural milieux. The tourists were supposed to be looking at the ornamentation and to be only indirectly interested in the work display. The structure is similar to that of the sewing machines offered for sale in early Sears and Roebuck catalogues, appealing for their iron-work morning-glory designs on their treadles and flywheels. The tobacco factory is a modern type of industrial attraction and it did not offer the same characteristic combination of mechanical and esthetic elements found on the sewing machine and at the mint and the press. As industrial society firmly established itself, its supplementary decorations were progressively erased from the surface of the industrial apparatus itself. Industrial design has become a subfield of economics, pushing the rhetoric of "form follows function" to the level of esthetic theory. At the same time, the ornaments of modern society have been displaced and concentrated in other attractions, monuments and museums, its official front. Whereas once the esthetics of industry were presented at the level of the factory, or even of individual machines, today the entire society is composed of parts of the Attraction. Its efficient, industrial side and its esthetic, ornamental aspect are mixed, measure for measure, in public representations at the macrostructural level.

Modern society divides its industrial and esthetic elements and reunites them on a higher social plane. Today, there is a general belief that esthetic objects ought to have utility and the work *process*, not merely its product, ought to look good or presentable. The tobacco factory is an early participant in this new dialectic of esthetics and utility. Emerging from this relationship are specialized supervisory personnel, arbiters of working class taste, comportment and standards, located at the center of the industrial process and at the top of their class. It is at the tobacco factory that Baedeker encounters this new type of worker:

> The *Ingénieurs aux Tabacs,* or higher officials, are educated at the Polytechnique School, and study two years at the "École d'application pour les Tabacs." (*B*, p.281.)

This is as close to an employed person as the Baedeker descriptions ever approach. Interestingly, the comment is not on the work done by the official, but on an aspect of his biography, his job qualifications, which he must obtain from other social establishments, special schools. The matrix of institutions at the base of modern society was already established while the older social order was in terminal decadence. The idea that anyone who is forced to earn his living should need qualifications, making some jobs a privilege and stigmatizing others, must have generated morbid fascination among persons of the smarter set (who were notorious for watching their own status relationships with great care). They could see a system, like a caricature of their own, only much larger, composing itself out of nothing but money and work and ranking persons who were, to them, uniformly socially inferior.

*The Morgue:* Baedeker's entry on the Morgue is polite and brief: "The painful scene attracts many spectators, chiefly of the lower orders" (*B*, p.227). It is necessary to turn to the *Practical Guide* for expanded commentary:

> The Morgue is a building in which the unknown dead picked up in the streets or in the river are publicly exhibited for identification. . . . The existing Morgue, a small sinister-looking building, dating 1864, consists of a central part, where the corpses are exposed in a room with refrigerating apparatus, and two wings. . . . In the left wing is the secretary's room, the dissecting room, the room in which judicial confrontations take place (*i.e.*, where persons suspected of a murder are examined in the presence of their supposed victims, a device that frequently leads to confession of the crime). . . . At the end of the [exhibition] room, in a dismal twilight, behind the glass panel of the refrigerator, the corpses are laid out on cast iron slabs. They are decently covered, and numbered, and being in a temperature of zero, it is possible to exhibit them for forty hours. . . . People go there to look at the corpses, as in other quarters they go to see the fashions and the

orange trees in flower. . . . The impression made by these rows of corpses is less moving and terrifying than it might be supposed, except in cases where a murder has been committed. Suicides and drowned persons look as if they had been embalmed, or were asleep. (*AAPG*, pp. 255-56.)

This final showing of working-class stiffs illustrates, as well as any other example, how the display of even a horrible object normalizes it. But such normalization works only up to a point. Although the show is alleged not to be terrifying, even as it tempts the tourist to try a look, it is gruesome enough to qualify as a kind of ultimate degradation ceremony.[13] The relationship of the tourist to the corpse is not merely that of life to death but of order to disorder as well. Ending up on the cold side of the glass in this establishment indicates a hasty and improper departure from the world and probably an unruly life-style which led to such an exit. The display of the corpses is ostensibly for the purpose of their identification, but what is represented is the importance of social order and of leaving society in an orderly way, preserving one's identity to the very end.

The display and degradation of the disorderly dead reflects some newly emergent status distinctions. In modern society, the workers are divided against themselves in three ways: First, there are those who must work but who are privileged to work in "careers" which can lead to what is called "success"—journalists, lawyers and other professionals, proprietors, high officials and other managers. Second are those who work, but only from day to day, week to week, and year to year, who must retire doing the same thing they did when they started, who can survive but not "succeed"—clerks, craftsmen and other regular hired hands of all sorts. Finally, there are those who do occasional work, the hard labor force kept at the ready by welfare and unemployment insurance—dishwashers, fruitpickers and holders of the other subproletarian "occupations." The Morgue brought representatives of these three types of workers into rare face-to-face contact. First, there are the middle-class tourists looking down on the members of the "lower orders" but not from a position so elevated that they cannot sneak their own peek at death. Then there is the main force of visitors who have been decent and orderly enough to stay alive and appear in public. Finally, there are the ones who died violently and/or anonymously.

It is at the Morgue that working-class people intrude onto tourist turf, showing up on the occasion of the death of their comrades as sightseers. When Mark Twain visited the Paris Morgue, he was horrified more by the living than by the dead:

> Men and women came, and some looked eagerly in and pressed their faces against the bars; others glanced carelessly at the body and turned away with a disappointed look—people, I thought, who live upon strong excitements and who attend the exhibitions of the Morgue regularly, just as other people go to see theatrical spectacles every night. Where one of these looked in and passed on, I could not help thinking: "Now this don't afford you any satisfaction—a party with his head shot off is what *you* need."[14]

Here, in fine, is the structure of touristic interpersonal solidarity: "they" ought to be respectful of each other; if "they" were more solidary with each other, I would be more solidary with them. The tendencies here, when radicalized, result in each individual's aloneness before death.

*The Slaughterhouse:* An original form of work is the killing and preparation of food animals. It is possible to read out of this kind of work the major oppositions of Western consciousness: life *vs.* death and man *vs.* nature. Part of the horror that attaches itself to slaughter seems to derive from the return to nature represented by the kill. In killing, man imitates the beasts, and not in one of their nice social acts either, like the dance of the bees or the conversation of the dolphins. Rather, he recreates one of their most animal relationships: predator and prey. Except for Christianity, the major (and most of the minor) religions dictate what animals may be killed and eaten, the exact manner of the slaughter and the office of the man who performs the act. Jews may not eat camel, hare and swine nor the blood of any animal. Moslems may not eat swine or the blood of any animal except that of locusts and fish. Hindus may not eat meat.[15] Among some peoples, the act of slaughter has no *work* connotations at all since it is entirely circumscribed by ritual. This ritual attention to the killing of food animals secures the act a place among tourist attractions in the modern world:

> Visitors are also usually permitted to visit the adjoining Abattoirs de la Villette, or slaughter-houses, beyond the canal. The chief entrance to

them is in the Rue de Flandres, on the N.W. side, beside which are two sculptured groups of animals, by A. Lefeuvre and Lefèvre-Deslong-champs. The busiest time here is also in the morning, but the scene is not one which will attract many visitors, though the premises are kept scrupulously clean. The buildings include about 20 courts, with 250 scalding-pans. About 1200 bullocks, 500 calves, and 800 sheep are slaughtered here daily: sometimes even more. (*B*, p.203.)

What is represented here is a victory of modern methods over traditional religious values, or the end of religious privilege to designate the type of animal and the manner of killing it proper to society. In the modern slaughterhouse, animals are killed according to the same rational method regardless of their species. A visit to the slaughterhouse locates the tourist in a postreligious relationship to meat production. Features of the earlier ceremonies (like cleanliness) are preserved, but only in the interests of efficiency—which is not a god in the true sense.

I have suggested that for many attractions, the fact of their being open for tourists is more significant than the collective experience produced by actual visits. This is especially the case with the slaughterhouse. Baedeker notes that the Abattoirs are not popular sights. They are not even mentioned in the more middle-class guidebooks.[16] By opening the slaughterhouse to visitors, the establishment communicates that it has nothing to hide, even to those who do not visit the place. Avoidance where there is openness of this sort is technically the sole responsibility of the individual tourist: his queasiness keeps him from the attraction. The structure is not one in which his sensibilities are being protected from the attraction's grisliness by some paternalistic authority. This frank and open attitude toward meat production extends to the neighborhood butcher of today. There is some suppression of bloody hands, aprons and of the sound of knives being sharpened, but not so much suppression that everyone has not had some opportunity to see a butcher at work. In fact, the modern butcher provides one of the few examples where a worker routinely demands (and gets) his onlooker to join him in a work display: while the housewife is watching, he sharpens his knife and, resting the sharpened edge against the surface of the meat he is cutting for her, he turns and looks into her face and she gives a little nod of assent as the signal for him to press down.

*The Sewers:* The sewers of Paris, into which the main characters of French novels and the motion picture actors who follow them are sometimes introduced, indicate the power behind the movement to open basic areas of complex society for touristic visitation. The very dread that attaches itself to this forbidden nether world seems to have been converted into an important factor in touristic motivation. A modern day tourist writes:

> The sewers of Paris! The words alone carry an aura of romance and adventure that London, with all its modern sewage treatment works, can never equal. The sewers of Paris evoke memories of Lon Chaney lurking deep in the ground below the opera house in "The Phantom of the Opera." The sewers of Paris mean Jean Valjean, the long-suffering protagonist of Victor Hugo's *Les Misérables*, escaping death at the barricades by fleeing into the sewers, with the police at his heels and treacherous quicksand just ahead.[17]

The realization that all the social establishments of the city, be they domestic, commercial, industrial, or cultural, no matter how unrelated they are on the surface, are interconnected underground, excites powerful touristic passions. Baedeker, who was a bit put off by the smell of the tobacco factory, does not try to hide his enthusiasm for the sewers:

> In the Place du Châtelet is one of the usual entrances to the vast network of *sewers* (Egouts) by which Paris is undermined. They are generally shown to the public on the second and fourth Wednesday of each month in the summer. . . . The visit, in which ladies need have no hesitation in taking part, lasts about 1 hr., and ends at the Place de la Madeleine. Visitors are conveyed partly on comfortable electric cars, partly in boats, so that no fatigue is involved. (*B*, p.64.)

The guidewriter's solicitous concern that everyone have an opportunity to be introduced to this murky underlife, regardless of age or sex, is augmented today by an ability of the sewer workers to represent their activities as an object of touristic interest. The writer of the *New York Times* article conducted an interview:

> No, there were no criminals or corpses or valuables to be seen in the sewers. No, they had never heard of quicksand in the sewers which, in

fact, were lined with cement. Even worse, they had never heard of Valjean. The only possible danger, they said, is being drowned by a sudden rise in water. Sewermen no longer fall prey to the "malignant fevers" listed by Hugo because "They're always giving us injections." As for objects of value, they never saw any. Seeing my disappointment, one of the men, a weather-beaten, cheerful fellow with scarcely a half dozen teeth left, reminded his colleagues, "Of course, there was the time you found that sword wrapped in paper. It was a nice one." (*NYT*, p.6.)

These shy and pallid gentlemen who work in the bowels of the city are developing, it seems, a skill once monopolized by writers and motion picture makers. They exhibit a professional responsibility to contribute to the universal drama of work. As they select out (or fabricate) details of their jobs which they feel will be of interest to tourists (the danger, the injections) or have intrinsic appeal (the sword), they create one more bridge between men and make their small contribution to the solidarity of the modern world thereby.

In 1900, as today, there existed a widespread notion of a class of objects known as "articles de luxe," or sometimes as "articles de Paris" which Baedeker lists as "real and imitation jewelry, artificial flowers, toys, articles in leather and carved wood, etc." (*B*, p.xxvii). These items set Paris off from other cities. Along with the naughty stage reviews, they are elements of the essential Paris in the modern tourists' consciousness. ("Paris is essentially a city of fun and amusements.") The overall image they present is opposite to that which appears through the medium of the work display. Paris made her *articles de luxe* famous as souvenirs. The presentation of Paris' everyday life is hidden behind these more pleasant memories. They are its mystification. The work displays, which might have been seen even if they are eventually suppressed from memory and buried in the tourists' unconscious, did not involve the making of *articles de luxe*, nor of any other distinctively Parisian object. What was shown was work that is requisite for the operation of any modern society. The tourist, lured by the West's most seductive city, is permitted to peek beneath her fancy skirts where he can catch a fleeting glimpse of her basic functions—varieties of work in the first place, and not mere work: but fundamentally important work.

# 4

## The Other Attractions

WE like to think of nature and other societies as being outside of historical time and beyond the boundaries of our own cultural experience. In this way, we can draw upon them as endless resources for social change and development. But this exteriority of nature and otherness is mainly fictional as modernity expands and draws every group, class, nation and nature itself into a single framework of relations.

Modern culture stands in sharp contrast to that of the seventeenth and eighteenth centuries. In the preindustrial era, *Society* was defined as an exclusive subgroup of the collectivity, much as we try to define "high society" today. The lives of members of this *Society* were apparently quite coordinated: culture in the form of concerts, operas, portrait sittings, poetry readings, music lessons and the like fit in not so much as optional extras but as standard equipment. At the very heart of the human community were the opera halls, cathedrals, cafés and salons which accommodated this *Society* and its very high culture. The relics of this system survive today as tourist attractions embedded in a greatly expanded system of attractions including factory tours, inner city tours, museums of all types, historical and industrial monuments, parks and pageants. The attractions in this expanded system are still concentrated in the heart of the human community, but they are also dispersed throughout society and nature. They are much more accessible: they stand in the open air or, in the case of museums, are open to the general public throughout the day.

# THE FUNCTION OF THE MUSEUM
# IN MODERN CULTURE

Although museums are often seen by their curators as important tools of modernization, as forces of resocialization of traditional peoples, and as reinforcers of modern values, I am not prepared to go so far here and accord them causal status.[1] They are only a part of the modern cultural complex. They are emblematic of modern solidarity, however, and some of the necessary experiments toward the modernization of the human mentality have been conducted in museums as these were being converted from collections for scholarly research to the public places they are today. A recent report of the United Nations defines a museum as:

> a building to house collections of objects for inspection, study and enjoyment. The objects may have been brought from the ends of the earth—coral from the Great Barrier Reef of Australia, a brick from the Great Wall of China, an ostrich egg from Africa or a piece of magnetic ore from Greenland; they may be things of today or things of the distant past—a model of a jet-propelled aeroplane or a fossil from the Coal Measures; they may be of natural origin or man-made—a cluster of quartz crystals or a woven mat from India.[2]

Museums and departments of museums are consecrated to *social*, *historical*, *cultural* and *natural* objects. It is by means of their specificity that they can set the totality of the modern world in motion in the tourist's imagination.

The function of museums is not entirely determined by what is shown; the way in which the objects are shown is also important. There are two main types of museum display: *collections* and *re-presentations*. A re-presentation is an arrangement of objects in a reconstruction of a total situation. Re-presentation always requires an arbitrary cutoff from what would have surrounded it in its original context, a frame, and usually a certain amount of filling in on the part of the museum: painted background, façades of native huts, department store mannequins for the period costumes. Re-presentations of *habitats* are popular features of natural history museums: some nicely preserved specimens of birds and small rodents in realistic postures may be shown occupying their ecological niches among the sands and grasses of the display case. Re-presentation aims to provide the viewer with an authentic copy of a total situation that is supposed to be meaningful from the standpoint of the things inside of the display; from the standpoint of the neolithic man shown crouching in his cave, or the lion cub stalking through the tall grass behind its mother. Re-presentations are occasions for *identification*.

The idea behind a *collection* is to bring together and catalogue diverse examples of a type of object: Eskimo snowshoes, oil paintings, African masks. There is no effort to rebuild a natural, cultural or historical totality. Order is superimposed by an arbitrary scheme like the Dewey decimal system. Whereas re-presentations demand identification, collections require an esthetic. They often generate a juxtaposition of objects that would be meaningless at other than the level of individual taste. A theoretician of museum display writes:

> The skill of collection is a true skill, binding separate objects into a new unity.

> The courage and skill of museum officials within the last fifteen years have brought the exhibition of objects to a fine art. To some extent they have borrowed the technique of early religious instruction; their material has been dramatized, creating a pageantry of objects that affects the mind directly through the eye.[3]

Another asks rhetorically:

> Where is the museum where visual chamber concerts would be offered, with a few works of art stemming from different cultures being orchestrated with a beautiful crystal, a rare map, a photograph of excellence, or an exquisite flower arrangement?[4]

Although the taste is different, this same idea, perhaps not so consciously articulated, seems to have animated the collection in a museum in Paris at the beginning of the century where, Baedeker noted, one could see Marat's snuff box, Voltaire's armchair, Napoleon's writing desk, the door of Balzac's bedroom, a copy of the constitution bound in human skin among other interesting items. (*B*, pp.215-16)

The esthetics of collection are, in part, economically determined, especially when it comes to the collection of rare objects such as art masterpieces. The justifications in terms of "harmony" or "subject matter" for historically meaningless arrangements of paintings in American art museums would not be necessary if the museums had enough paintings. At well-stocked museums such as the Louvre or the Prado, there is usually a group of masterpieces representing every "period" with a logical place, therefore, in the totality for each individual masterpiece.

Re-presentations tend to be associated with natural history museums and collections with art museums, but there is much crossing and recrossing of this line. Some natural history museums are filled with stuffed animals classified not by habitat but according to kingdom, phylum, subphylum, class, order, and species so the dogs are not found among the men, but with the wolves next to the bears. And in the basement of the *Musée de l'Art Moderne* in Paris is Brancusi's workshop, allegedly exactly as it was when he died, every tool in place.

## PARKS

Modernity is transforming *nature* from a cruel alternative to community life into a place of play. Leisure-time uses of nature are of two main types, recreational and esthetic. The recreational uses of nature include sport hunting and fishing, rock and mountain climbing, crosscountry jeep, snowmobile and motorcycle racing, skiing, rockhounding, sailing, skydiving. Esthetic uses of nature include sightseeing of two types. One involves looking at *scenery* in the sense of a landscape taken in as a totality or appreciated for qualities spread evenly throughout—mountain ranges, plains, foothills, forests, coastlines. The other involves *landmarks* or outstanding features of the landscape —high-rise mountain peaks, grotesque rock formations, caves, very old trees, a large waterfall. Recreational interests in nature can be reconciled with a love for scenery and vice versa, as in fishing, but they may also be separated. Sometimes there is an antagonism between recreational and esthetic uses of nature. Rockhounds must remove a mountain in order to enjoy it.

Powerful human passions evoked by nature were once available in a wide variety of situations: in the hunt, in the forest on the edge of camp, at sea beyond the horizon. The human group could, and did, draw heavily on the unknown forest and sea for inspiration in the creation of social solidarity out of opposition of man and nature. The naturalistic standpoint in the human sciences and the control of nature provided by modern life-sciences have done much to undercut this important resource for the construction of solidarities. However, at the same time, modern tourism is reorganizing nature and the touristic experience of it so it may continue to serve as a basis for unity in the family of man. The modern touristic version of nature treats it not as a force opposing man, something we must join together to fight against, but as a common source of thrills, something we must try to preserve. Tours of natural wonders organize the thrills nature provides into discrete experiences, guaranteeing results for those who would take in the approved sights. The following somewhat vulgar account of a trip to Niagara Falls indicates that this touristic normalization of the "thrill of nature" is at least 100 years old:

> Oh Aunt! what can I say that shall give you the least inkling of that wonderful sight! We were silenced, awed by the scene. Alfred, poor fellow! squeezed my hand . . . I returned the pressure; such scenes are so overpowering . . . As for Alfred's friend Plenderleath, he would do nothing but suck on the end of his cane, and ejaculate "By Gad!" at intervals.[5]

The writer wants us to believe that her relationship with Alfred has been strengthened by Mother Nature. This link of social solidarity with nature is integral with modern consciousness and modern social structure. After the nationalization of Yellowstone in 1872, the people of the U.S.A. developed and put into practice the idea that society has the capacity to preserve nature or to institutionalize scenery and landmarks. One of William Catton Jr.'s respondents in a study of the attractiveness of the national parks explained his refusal to answer the questionnaire:

> To rate one more attractive than the others is like asking a person which is more valuable, your eyesight or hearing. Collectively, the national parks help to form a composite representation of the "crown jewels" of our nation. Each in its own way contributes to the whole.[6]

Paralleling the opening up of visitors' galleries at social establishments such as the stock exchange and factories has been a corresponding process of installing social arrangements for sightseers into our newly institutionalized natural settings. At national parks, the rangers delineate and number campsites, pipe and pump in a water supply, provide communal garbage and toilet facilities, grade and blaze roads and paths. At some of the more developed natural areas, there are central campfire rings for group singing and nature talks, public showers, coin-operated laundromats, ironing rooms, and, in each campsight, food storage lockers and stoves. For their part, the visitors bring food, tents, beds, chairs, lamps, and trucks and trailers outfitted like little homes. The incorporation of "nature" as an aspect of modernity, with a particular role to play in the modern world is not complete, but it is quite advanced.

## TRADITION

Every society necessarily has another society inside itself and beside itself: its past epochs and eras and its less developed and more developed neighbors. Modern society, only partly disengaged from industrial structures, is especially vulnerable to overthrow from within through nostalgia, sentimentality and other tendencies to regress to a previous state, a "Golden Age," which retrospectively always apppears to have been more orderly or normal. In a recent, helpful study, César Graña has written:

> The destruction of local traditions and the assault upon "the past" perpetuated by industrialization and world-wide modernization seem to make large numbers of people susceptible to an appetite for relics of pre-industrial life. This appetite is so intense that it accounts in part for one of the major and nost characteristically modern industries: tourism. The most ambitious monuments of earlier life-styles, such as the stately homes of England, and even whole nations, like the prototypically picturesque Spain, have now been reduced to the conditions of *objets d'art*. "In the family" events, like the bullfight or royal pageantry, whose mystique was once accessible only to natives, are now marketed to foreign visitors by the well-organized bureaucracies of popularized cultural romance, both private and governmental—that is to say, travel agencies, tourist bureaus, and even tourist ministries.[7]

Graña understands the psychology of slightly snobbish and sentimental tourism, but he has not located the sights and spectacles that service these sentiments alongside the other attractions or analyzed the contribution of the total system of attractions to the solidarity of modernity. Restored remnants of dead traditions are essential components of the modern community and consciousness. They are reminders of our break with the past and with tradition, even our own tradition. But they are not the only basis for tourism and sightseeing. Tour companies in Paris offer both "Paris Historique" and "Paris Moderne."

Graña might have noted that the tourists' quest is not limited to a search for traditional elements restored and embedded in the modern world; they also search for natural and contemporary social attractions in the same matrix. When tradition, nature and other societies, even "primitive" societies, are transformed into tourist attractions, they join with the modern social attractions in a new unity, or a new universal solidarity, that includes the tourist. Traditional life-styles and modern tourists are brought into face-to-face contact by ethnological exhibits in museums. Care is taken in the setting up of such exhibits not to break up the fragile solidarity of modernity. For example, a student of museum display advises:

> "It seems wise to introduce cultural behavior and values that diverge considerably from those of the monocultural learner, not in terms that stress traditional differences, but rather in terms of common problems." This principle is most directly realized when the re-interpretation attempts to link the foreign reality [in the exhibit] with the visitors' own occupational or hobby interests. The approach may succeed in creating a feeling of appreciation of and admiration for the ways in which some primitive peoples have solved difficult environmental and technical problems with minimal means.[8]

The solidarity of modernity, even as it incorporates fragments of primitive social life, the past and nature, elevates modernity over the past and nature. There is nothing willful in this; it is automatic; it is a structure *sui generis*. Every nicely motivated effort to preserve nature, primitives and the past, and to represent them authentically contributes to an opposite tendency—the present is made more unified against its past, more in control of nature, less a product of history. The future of museums has been linked directly to modernization by a United Nations document which foresees a day in which museums serve social (industrial) purposes on a regional level and the regions of the world are linked up through their museums:

> And what of the future? One thing is clear—that in many countries, museums which had no active teaching programme now take a very keen interest in this kind of work. What other impulses are actuating museums today? There is, for example, the development of the specialized regional museum. In France, one museum traces the history of the "wine civilization" in Burgundy from Roman times to the present, and displays, for purposes of comparison, material assembled from lands near and far. In this field of museum work, we may well see the start of rational planning (in the past the specialized museum was often a matter of chance), whereby each region will have a museum to record the historical background of its basic local industry, its effect on folklore and the traditional culture of the region and its links with regions of similar character.[9]

This ideal of the museum is one that contributes to the unification of the modern world, to control over tradition and over nature.

Modern museums and parks are anti-historical and un-natural. They are not, of course, anti-historical and unnatural in the sense of their destroying the past or nature because, to the contrary, they preserve them, but as they preserve, they automatically separate modernity from its past and from nature and elevate it above them. Nature and the past are made a part of the present, not in the form of are unreflected inner spirit, a mysterious *soul*, but rather as revealed objects, as tourist attractions.

The museums, monuments, parks and restorations of modern society indicate that the staging of otherness and the organization of disparate elements in collections and representations into a single design of modern making, with the modern world flowing past its designated attractions, renders history, nature and traditional societies only aspects of the structural differentiation of the modern world, and not privileged aspects either, or at least no more privileged than the other attractions.

## HISTORY

There are two major scientific approaches to history being subsumed by the development of modern society and culture. *Positivism* holds that societies everywhere are composed of the same set of elements which combine in varying quantities to form each particular society. History, from the standpoint of this positivist perspective, is a matter of increase or decrease in the amount of a societal element or elements. The causes of development or historical change are usually claimed to be external forces: geography, climate, an infusion of money or ideology or the good or evil genius of a "great" man. Evolutionism is the most sophisticated theory of historical change within the positivist perspective. The second approach, *materialist dialectics*, holds that societies and historical periods are qualitatively different from one another, and that they undergo total change as a result of internal contradictions. The cause of change is claimed to be internal force, traditionally applied by the industrial proletariat. Revolutionary praxis is the most logical approach to social change within the dialectical materialist perspective.

Dialecticians such as Marx and Mao are committed to the priority of the material substratum over theory and ideas. For them, positivism and dialectical materialism are only two opposing world views, that is, merely two different ways of thinking about the world. But the modern world has the capacity to organize itself around ideas, especially the ideas of bourgeois idealists. The entire touristic complex is, in a sense, a dematerialization of basic social relations as, for example, between a man and his work.

One would expect, then, to find enormous opposition to tourism and sightseeing in the socialist world. But this is far from the case. In the Soviet Union, tourism comes close to being the official state "religion", as is evidenced, for example, by the Industrial Park on the outskirts of Moscow, the Hermitage, Lenin's Tomb, the practice of displaying artistic masterpieces in the subway, the recent unrestricted issuance of internal passports to all Soviet citizens over the age of eighteeen years and subsidies for recreational travel.

As our modern kinds of societies (both socialist and capitalist) develop, they eventually arrive at a point where they can develop no further, and they turn in on themselves, elaborating ever more refined internal reflections on their own structure. It is at this moment, when all the miracles they can perform and all their horrors are fully exposed, that they can change. I think we are living in this moment at the present time, and we may be trapped in it for some time to come. Even the lines drawn for the ultimate purpose of warfare, excepting the standpoint of a handful of politicians, are arbitrary, as between "North" and "South" Vietnam. Real wars are without ideological significance and resemble the war games between the Red and the Blue armies.

Modernity is arriving at its impasse. The West cannot be moved by the East nor the East by the West. The capitalists cannot move the socialists nor the socialists the capitalists. The Third World is holding its own. Bourgeois idealists freely press their plans into reality everywhere, but in so doing, they have sterilized their old motive forces for change. Nature, history, culture and great men are being transformed from agents of change into mere sources for inspiration, into attractions. Socialists press their plans into reality everywhere and in so doing sterilize their old motive force for change: nowhere is the industrial proletariat so nicely domesticated as in the Soviet Socialist bloc. The socialist dream of being the negation of capitalism appears now as a rather limited vision. As the modern world completes itself, socialism is only a part of the equation, not its solution. Modernity is staggering right now, not so much as a result of its "internal contradictions" as of plenitude and stagnation. A civilization in this condition, dizzy with its own fullness, is vulnerable to revolutionary forces within and without.

It is not now possible to describe the end of this particular development of culture. If our consciousness fails to transcend this, it will resolve itself in paroxysm of differentiation and collapse. A more hopeful ending, perhaps, would be the emergence of a reflexive self-consciousness on a community level which would organize history, nature and tradition in distinctive and logical arrangements, and systematically develop their implications. The revolution according to this hypothesis, would be replaced by the cultural revolution— the Chamber of Commerce by the Chamber of Culture—a process already visible in the appointment of Commisars of Tourism and boards and bureaus of tourism.

The eventual results of this development are still hidden in the heart of the worldwide process we call "modernization", which contains many alternative experimental models for cultural re-vision. Cuba alone, for example, provides several imaginative variations on the structure of modernization: with its population dispersed beyond its merely political boundaries, growing colonies in the developed world, in the U.S.A.; with its dramatic juxtaposition of revolution and socialism on the island with capitalism and counterrevolution on the continent; with its traditional charismatic leadership and its modern paranoic, underground involvements with counterintelligence agencies, the CIA; with its appeal to middle-class North American youth who, as tourist-revolutionaries, depart each year from Canada for a vacation in Cuba where they help cut the cane. Of course, not all modernizing nations have quite so complex a collective self-consciousness as has Cuba: most stick closer to tried and true formulas, "Westernization" vs. revision and reorganization of existing tradition.

Even in the developed world, the war between history and modernization is far from over. But here, as the last fragments of the past are incorporated into modernity, the process is beginning to have both comic and tragic overtones. Our history is increasingly an occasion for a kind of mopping-up operation.

> In public works projects in the Italian capital scholars hover near the laborers most of the time. This is the reason—though not the only one—why the Roman subway is taking so long to build. . . . Pasquale Cutitta, an immigrant from Naples who has for the last six years been ripping open Rome's surface in various construction jobs, says with a grin: "If I see any old stones, I cut right through with the jackhammer. Isn't the Colosseum enough of a ruin for Rome?"[10]

In this crude and final confrontation of past and present, the historical totality is broken into bits and pieces which are admitted into the modern present selectively and one at a time. The safest fragment of the past to admit (from the standpoint of any possible threat to the integrity of modernity) is one of its lone remaining representatives. The most striking example of this mode of accommodation occurred in San Francisco in 1911 when the anthropologists Kroeber and Waterman brought the last surviving member of a California Indian tribe to live out the short remainder of his life in the University of California museum. His story was told much later by Kroeber's wife:

> The museum was overrun with mountebanks and plain and simple exploiters with their offers. There were the impresarios . . . one of whom had the imagination to offer to "take over" both Kroeber and Ishi [the Indian], to promote them as a two man act under a billing of

"educational" and "edifying". . . . Would-be exploiters and show-men soon dropped off, but a problem remained. Ishi was an attraction, something Waterman and Kroeber had somehow not taken into account until the reality threatened to disrupt all normal activities of the museum. How to cope with the friendly crowd? It could not be put off as could the exploiters. It meant no harm to Ishi, and asked nothing for itself but to be allowed to see, and if possible to shake hands with, to touch, to "know" the last wild man in America. . . .

The museum staff felt a duty to a public it hoped to make its own, as well as to Ishi. The problem was how to do right by both. Waterman remarked gloomily to Kroeber that the only solution he saw was to put Ishi in an exhibition case during visiting hours, where people could see him but would at least be prevented from touching him.[11]

The negative attitude so prevalent in modern society toward anything that is old, *dépassé* or alien dissolves into sentimentality and respect whenever the object in question is the last of its kind.

This turnabout was evident in the case of the "last wild man" in America. It also occurs in the contact of modern society and wild animals such as wolves, which were once feared and hated by men but whose rights to existence are now protected by special laws. Similarly, bits and pieces of outdated material culture are preserved:

The 46-year-old paddleboat Delta Queen—wooden superstructure and all—will again ply the water of the Mississippi—under a bill passed by Congress. . . . Owned by the Greene Line Steamers Inc., of Cincinnati, the Delta Queen stopped operations several weeks ago under a safety law requiring boats with 50 or more overnight passengers to have metal superstructures. . . . Congress wanted to "assist in saving the last symbol of a bygone era".[12]

In modern society, "symbols" of the past are collected in museums when they are small enough, and when they are too large, they are left outside in parks and called "monuments."[13] Some, as in the case of the paddleboat, San Francisco's cable cars and large old homes, are restored and kept functioning as "living reminders" of the past.

It is by means of these museums, monuments and living reminders that the present frames up its history. Sometimes a little license is exercised, especially by the living reminders. At a Columbus Day parade in Philadelphia, a reporter gathered the following:

(A) man dressed like Columbus said he was Filindo Masino, a lawyer. "Columbus was a man of the world," Masino said. "He was not Italian, Irish or Jewish. That's the way I feel about it." . . .

"This is one of those days that you have an obligation to take the kids down to see what the past is like," said Frank Gormley . . . who had his nine-year-old daughter with him. "Knowing the past is the best way to understand the present."

Stalking through the crowd was a tall gentleman made up to look like Abraham Lincoln. He identified himself as Albert L. Johnson, of San Jose, Calif., who said he is retired and now travels the country to "recreate the spirit of Lincoln".[14]

Even when modern society gets its historical facts and relationships right (if this is technically feasible), the appearance of the past through the vehicle of the tourist attraction may be loaded in favor of the present which is not shown as an extension of the past but as a replacement for it. An advertisement for the Bureau of Travel Development of Pennsylvania reads: "GO WHERE THE ACTION WAS. . . . Come tour history in Pennsylvania."[15]

# 5

## Staged Authenticity

THE modernization of work relations, history and nature detaches these from their traditional roots and transforms them into cultural productions and experiences. The same process is operating on "everyday life" in modern society, making a "production" and a fetish of urban public street life, rural village life and traditional domestic relations. Modernity is quite literally turning industrial structure inside out as these workaday, "real life," "authentic" details are woven into the fabric of our modern solidarity alongside the other attractions. Industrial Man could retreat into his own niche at his work place, into his own neighborhood bar or into his own domestic relations. Modern Man is losing his attachments to the work bench, the neighborhood, the town, the family, which he once called "his own" but, at the same time, he is developing an interest in the "real life" of others.

The modern disruption of real life and the simultaneous emergence of a fascination for the "real life" of others are the outward signs of an important social redefinition of the categories "truth" and "reality" now taking place. In premodern types of society, *truth* and *nontruth* are socially encoded distinctions protected by norms. The maintenance of this distinction is essential to the functioning of a society that is based on inter*personal* relationships. The stability of interpersonal relations requires a separation of truth from lies, and the stability of social structure requires stable interpersonal relations. This pattern is most pronounced in the primitive case where family structure *is* social structure. In modern settings, society is established through cultural representations of reality at a level above that of interpersonal relations. Real life relations are being liberated from their traditional constraints as the integrity of society is no longer dependent on such constraints. No one has described the impact of this social structural change so well or so closely as Erving Goffman. He has found that it is no longer sufficient simply to *be* a man in order to be perceived as one. Now it is often necessary to *act out* reality and truth.

I began my analysis of the problem of authenticity by starting across the bridge between structure and consciousness built by Goffman. I found it necessary to extend his conception a little to make it to the other side.

## FRONT, BACK AND REALITY

Paralleling a common sense division, Goffman analyzed a structural division of social establishments into what he terms *front* and *back regions*. The front is the meeting place of hosts and guests or customers and service persons, and the back is the place where members of the home team retire between performances to relax and to prepare. Examples of back regions are kitchens, boiler rooms, executive washrooms, and examples of front regions are reception offices and parlors. Although architectural arrangements are mobilized to support this division, it is primarily a *social* one, based on the type of social performance that is staged in a place, and on the social roles found there. In Goffman's own words:

> Given a particular performance as the point of reference, we have distinguished three crucial roles on the basis of function: those who perform; those performed to; and outsiders who neither perform in the show nor observe it. . . . (T)he three crucial roles mentioned could be described on the basis of the regions to which the role-player has access: performers appear in the front and back regions; the audience appears only in the front region; and the outsiders are excluded from both regions.[1]

The apparent, taken-for-granted reality of a social performance, according to Goffman's theory, is not an unproblematical part of human behavior. Rather, it depends on structural arrangements like this division between front and back. A back region, closed to audiences and outsiders, allows concealment of props and activities that might discredit the performance out front. In other words, sustaining a firm sense of social reality requires some *mystification*.

The problem here is clearly one of the emergent aspects of life in *modern* society. Primitives who live their lives totally exposed to their "relevant others" do not suffer from anxiety about the authenticity of their lives, unless, perhaps, a frightening aspect of life suddenly becomes *too* real for them. The opposite problem, a weakened sense of reality, appears with the differentiation of society into front and back. Once this division is established, there can be no return to a state of nature. Authenticity itself moves to inhabit mystification.

A recent example of a mystification designed to generate a sense of reality is the disclosure that chemical nitrates are injected into hams for cosmetic purposes to make them more pink, appetizing and desirable, that is, more hamlike.[2] Similarly, go-go girls in San Francisco's North Beach have their breasts injected with silicones in order to conform their size, shape and firmness to the characteristics of an ideal breast. Novels about novelists and television shows about fictional television stars exemplify this on a cultural plane. In each of these cases, a kind of strained truthfulness is similar in most of its particulars to a little lie. In other cases, social structure itself is involved in the construction of the type of mystification that supports social reality.

In fact, social structural arrangements can generate mystifications without the conscious manipulation on the part of *individuals* that occurred in the ham and breast examples. The possibility that a stranger might penetrate a back region is one major source of social concern in everyday life, as much a concern to the strangers who might do the violating as to the violated. Everyone is waiting for this kind of intrusion not to happen, which is a paradox in that the absence of social relationships between strangers makes back region secrets unimportant to outsiders or casual and accidental intruders. Just having a back region generates the belief that there is something more than meets the eye; even where no secrets are actually kept, back regions are still the places where it is popularly believed the secrets are. Folklorists discover tales of the horror concealed in attics and cellars, attesting to this belief.

## BACK REGIONS AND SOCIAL SOLIDARITY

As yet unexplored is the function of back regions—their mere existence intimating their possible violation—in sustaining the common-sense polarity of social life: the putative "intimate and real" as against "show." This division into front and back supports the popular beliefs regarding the relationship of truth to intimacy. In our society, intimacy and closeness are accorded much importance: they are seen as the core of social solidarity and they are also thought by some to be morally superior to rationality and distance in social relationships, and more "real." Being "one of them," or at one with "them," means, in part, being permitted to share back regions with "them." This is a sharing which allows one to see behind the others' mere performances, to perceive and accept the others for what they really are.

Touristic experience is circumscribed by the structural tendencies described here. Sightseers are motivated by a desire to see life as it is really lived, even to get in with the natives, and at the same time, they are deprecated for always failing to achieve these goals. The term "tourist" is increasingly used as a derisive label for someone who seems content with his obviously inauthentic experiences.

The variety of understanding held out before tourists as an ideal is an *authentic* and *demystified* experience of an aspect of some society or other person. An anonymous writer in an underground periodical breathlessly describes her feelings at a women's liberation, all-female dance where she was able, she thought, to drop the front she usually maintains in the presence of men:

> Finally the men moved beyond the doorway. And We Danced—All of us with all of us. In circles and lines and holding hands and arm in arm, clapping and jumping—a group of whole people. I remember so many other dances, couples, men and women, sitting watching, not even talking. How could I have consented to that hateful, possessive, jealous pairing? So much energy and life, and sensuality, we women have so rarely and ineffectively expressed. But we did, on Saturday. The women in the band were above performing and beyond competition, playing and singing together and with we [sic] who were dancing. And We Danced—expressing for and with each other.[3]

An earlier, one-sided version of this connection between truth, intimacy and sharing the life behind the scenes is found in descriptions of the ethnographic method of data collection. Margaret Mead has written:

> The anthropologist not only records the consumption of sago in the native diet, but eats at least enough to know how heavily it lies upon the stomach; not only records verbally and by photographs the tight clasp of the baby's hands around the neck, but also carries the baby and experiences the constriction of the windpipe; hurries or lags on the way to a ceremony; kneels half-blinded by incense while the spirits of the ancestors speak, or the gods refuse to appear. The anthropologist enters the setting and he observes. . . .

These writers base their comments on an implicit distinction between false fronts and intimate reality, a distinction which is not, for them, problematical: once a person, or an observer, moves off-stage, or into the "setting," the real truth begins to reveal itself more or less automatically.

Closer examination of these matters suggests that it might not be so easy to penetrate the true inner workings of other individuals or societies. What is taken to be real might, in fact, be a show that is based on the structure of reality. For example, Goffman warns that under certain conditions it is difficult to separate front from back, and that these are sometimes transformed one into the other:

> (W)e can observe the up-grading of domestic establishments, wherein the kitchen, which once possessed its own back regions, is now coming to be the least presentable region of the house while at the same time becoming more and more presentable. We can also trace that peculiar social movement which led some factories, ships, restaurants, and households to clean up their backstages to such an extent that, like monks, Communists, or German aldermen, their guards are always up and there is no place where their front is down, while at the same time members of the audience become sufficiently entranced with the society's id to explore the places that had been cleaned up for them. Paid attendance at symphony orchestra rehearsals is only one of the latest examples.[5]

Under the conditions Goffman documents here, the back-front division no longer allows one to make facile distinctions between mere acts and authentic expressions of true characteristics. In places where tourists gather, the issues are even more complex.

## AUTHENTICITY IN TOURIST SETTINGS

Not all travelers are concerned about seeing behind the scenes in the places they visit. On occasion, and for some visitors, back regions are obtrusive. Arthur Young, when he visited France in 1887 to make observations for his comparative study of agriculture, also observed the following:

> Mops, brooms, and scrubbing brushes are not in the catalogue of the necessaries of a French inn. Bells there are none; the *fille* must always be bawled for; and when she appears, is neither neat, well dressed, nor handsome. The kitchen is black with smoke; the master commonly the cook, and the less you see of the cooking the more likely you are to have a stomach to your dinner. The mistress rarely classes civility or attention to her guests among the requisites of her trade. We are so unaccustomed in England to live in our bedchambers that it is at first awkward in France to find that people live nowhere else. Here I find that everybody, let his rank be what it may, lives in his bed-chamber.[6]

Among some, especially some American, tourists and sightseers of today, Young's attitude would be considered insensitive and cynical even if there was agreement that his treatment of the facts was accurate, as apparently it was. One finds in the place of Young's attitude much interest in exactly the details Young wanted not to notice.

A touristic desire to share in the real life of the places visited, or at least to see that life as it is really lived, is reflected in the conclusion of a tourist's report from a little Spanish town:

> Finally, Frigliana has no single, spectacular attraction, such as Granada's Alhambra or the cave at Nerja. Frigliana's appeal lies in its atmosphere. It is quaint without being cloying or artificial. It is a living village and not a "restoration of an authentic Spanish town." Here one can better see and understand the Andalusian style of life.[7]

There are vulgar ways of expressing this liberal sentiment, the desire

"to get off the beaten path" and "in with the natives." An advertisement for an airline reads:

> Take "De tour." Swissair's free-wheeling fifteen day Take-a-break
> Holiday that lets you detour to the off-beat, over-looked and unex-
> pected corners of Switzerland for as little as $315. . . . Including car.
> Take de tour. But watch out for de sheep, de goats and de chickens.[8]

Some tourists do in fact make incursions into the life of the society
they visit, or are at least allowed actually to peek into one of its
back regions. In 1963, the manager of the Student Center at the
University of California at Berkeley would occasionally invite visitors
to the building to join him on his periodic inspection tours. For the
visitor, this was a chance to see its kitchens, the place behind the
pin-setting machines in the bowling alley, the giant fans on the roof,
and so forth, but he was probably not a typical building manager.
This kind of hospitality is the rule rather than the exception in the
areas of the world that have been civilized the longest, a factor in the
popularity of these areas with Anglo-Americans. A respondent of
mine told me she was invited by a cloth merchant in the Damascus
bazaar to visit his silk factory. She answered "yes," whereupon he
threw open a door behind his counter exposing a little dark room
where two men in their underwear sat on the floor on either side of a
hand loom passing a shuttle back and forth between them. "It takes a
year to weave a bolt of silk like that," the owner explained as he closed
the door. This kind of happening, an *experience* in the everyday sense
of that term, often occurs by accident. A lady who is a relative of
mine, and another lady friend of hers, walked too far into the Canadian Rockies near Banff and found themselves with too much traveling back to town to do in the daytime that was left to do it in. They
were rescued by the crew of a freight train and what they remember
most from their experience was being allowed to ride with the engineer in the cab of his locomotive. A young American couple told me
of being unable to find a hotel room in Zagreb, Yugoslavia. While
they were discussing their plight on the sidewalk, an old woman
approached them and led them by a circuitous route to a small
apartment where they rented a blackmarket room, displacing the
family of workers who slept on a couch behind a blanket hung as a
curtain in the living room.

Certain individuals are prone to the kind of accident that leads to these experiences because they seek out situations in which this type of thing is most likely to occur. A report from the Caribbean suggests that a taste for action of this type can be cultivated:

> "But tourists never take the mail boats," said the hotel manager. That clinched the matter. The next afternoon, I jumped from the dock at Potter's Cay in downtown Nassau to the rusted deck of the Deborah K., swinging idly at her spring lines. . . . [The writer describes island hopping on the mail boat and ends his account with this observation.] The next day, while aloft in a Bahamas Airways plane, I spotted the Deborah K. chugging along in the sound toward Green Turtle Cay. She is no craft for the queasy of stomach and has a minimum of the amenities that most people find indispensable, but she and her sister mail boats offer a wonderfully inexpensive way to see life in the Bahamas—life as the natives live it, not the tourists.[9]

Given the felt value of these experiences, it is not surprising to find social structural arrangements that produce them.

## STAGED AUTHENTICITY IN TOURIST SETTINGS

Tourists commonly take guided tours of social establishments because they provide easy access to areas of the establishment ordinarily closed to outsiders. School children's tours of firehouses, banks, newspapers and dairies are called "educational" because the inner operations of these important places are shown and explained in the course of the tour. This kind of tour, and the experiences generated by it, provide an interesting set of analytical problems. The tour is characterized by social organization designed to reveal inner workings of the place; on tour, outsiders are allowed further *in* than regular patrons; children are permitted to enter bank vaults to see a million dollars, allowed to touch cows' udders, etc. At the same time, there is a staged quality to the proceedings that lends to them an aura of superficiality, albeit a superficiality not always perceived as such by the tourist, who is usually forgiving about these matters.

An account from Cape Kennedy provides illustration:

> No sightseers at the Manned Spacecraft Center ever had a more dramatic visit than those who, by design or accident of time, found them-

selves touring the facility last month during the unforgettable mission of Apollo 13. . . . In a garden-like courtyard outside the News Bureau in Building 1, a group of tourists visiting the Manned Space-craft Center here stared at the working correspondents through the huge plate-glass windows. The visitors, too, could hear the voice of Mission Control. A tall young man, his arm around his mini-skirted blonde girl friend, summed up the feelings of the sightseers when he said, half aloud, "Being here's like being part of it." "Dear God," his girl whispered earnestly, "please let them come home safe."[10]

The young man in this account is expressing his belief that he is having an almost authentic experience. This type of experience is produced through the use of a new kind of social space that is opening up everywhere in our society. It is a space for outsiders who are permitted to view details of the inner operation of a commercial, domestic, industrial or public institution. Apparently, entry into this space allows adults to recapture virginal sensations of discovery, or childlike feelings of being half-in and half-out of society, their faces pressed up against the glass. Some political radicals and conservatives consider "swinging," "massage therapy" and "wide-screen cunnilin-gus" to be indices of a general relaxation of society's moral standards. These are, however, only special cases of reality displays, public orgasm worked up in the interest of social solidarity.

Other basic (that is, biological process) examples of staged inti-macy are provided by the tendency to make restaurants into some-thing more than places to eat:

The newest eating place in Copenhagen is La Cuisine, strategically located on the Stroeget, the main strolling street of the city. Everyone is flat-nosing it against the windows these days watching the four cooks. In order to get to the cozy, wood-paneled restaurant in the back of the house, the guest must pass the kitchen. If he is in a hurry he may eat in the kitchen, hamburger joint-style.

"The kitchen" bit is a come-hither, actually, admits Canadian-born, Swiss-educated Patrick McCurdy, table captain and associate manager. "A casual passer-by is fascinated by cooks at work, preparing a steak or a chicken or a salad."[11]

What is being shown to tourists is not the institutional *back stage*, as Goffman defined this term. Rather, it is a staged back region, a kind of living museum for which we have no analytical terms.

## THE STRUCTURE OF TOURIST SETTINGS

A student of mine has told me that a new apartment building in New York City exhibits its heating and air conditioning equipment, brightly painted in basic colors, behind a brass rail in its lobby. From the standpoint of the social institutions that are exposed in this way, the structure of their reception rooms reflects a new concern for *truth* and *morality* at the institutional level. Industry, for example, is discovering that the commercial advantages of appearing to be honest and aboveboard can outweigh the disadvantages of having to organize little shows of honesty. There is an interesting parallel here with some of the young people of the industrial West who have pressed for simplicity and naturalness in their attire and have found it necessary assiduously to select clothing, jewelry and hair styles that are especially designed to *look* natural. In exposing their steel hearts for all to see and in staging their true inner life, important commercial establishments of the industrial West "went hippie" a decade before hippies went hippie. Approached from this standpoint, the hippie movement is not technically a movement but a basic expression of the present stage of the evolution of our society.

The current structural development of society is marked by the appearance everywhere of touristic space. This space can be called a *stage set*, a *tourist setting*, or simply, a *set* depending on how purposefully worked up for tourists the display is. The New York Stock Exchange viewed from the balcony set up for sightseers is a tourist setting, since there is no evidence that the show below is *for* the sightseers. The exhibitions of the back regions of the world at Disneyland in Anaheim, California are constructed only for sight-seers, however, and can be called "stage sets." Characteristics of sets are: the only reason that need be given for visiting them is to see them—in this regard they are unique among social places; they are physically proximal to serious social activity, or serious activity is imitated in them; they contain objects, tools and machines that have specialized use in specific, often esoteric, social, occupational and industrial routines; they are open, at least during specified times, to visitation from outsiders.

Touristic consciousness is motivated by its desire for authentic experiences, and the tourist may believe that he is moving in this direction, but often it is very difficult to know for sure if the experience is in fact authentic. It is always possible that what is taken to be entry into a back region is really entry into a front region that has been totally set up in advance for touristic visitation. In tourist settings, especially in industrial society, it may be necessary to discount the importance, and even the existence, of front and back regions except as ideal poles of touristic experience.

Returning to Goffman's original front-back dichotomy, tourist settings can be arranged in a continuum starting from the front and ending at the back, reproducing the natural trajectory of an individual's initial entry into a social situation. While distinct empirical indicators of each stage may be somewhat difficult to discover, it is *theoretically* possible to distinguish six stages of this continuum. Here, the exercise of a little theoretical license might prove worthwhile.

*Stage one:* Goffman's front region; the kind of social space tourists attempt to overcome or to get behind.

*Stage two:* a touristic front region that has been decorated to appear, in some of its particulars, like a back region: a seafood restaurant with a fishnet hanging on the wall; a meat counter in a supermarket with three-dimensional plastic replicas of cheeses and bolognas hanging against the wall. *Functionally*, this stage (two) is entirely a front region, and it always has been, but it is cosmetically decorated with reminders of back region activities: mementos, not taken seriously, called "atmosphere."

*Stage three:* a front region that is totally organized to look like a back region; simulations of moonwalks for television audiences; the live shows above sex shops in Berlin where the customer can pay to watch interracial couples copulating according to his own specific instructions. This is a problematical stage: the better the simulation, the more difficult to distinguish from stage four.

*Stage four:* a back region that is open to outsiders; magazine exposés of the private doings of famous personages; official revelations of the details of secret diplomatic negotiations. It is the open characteristic that distinguishes these especially touristic settings (stages three and four) from other back regions; access to most nontouristic back regions is somewhat restricted.

*Stage five:* a back region that may be cleaned up or altered a bit because tourists are permitted an occasional glimpse in: Erving Goffman's kitchen; factory, ship, and orchestra rehearsal cases; news leaks.

*Stage six:* Goffman's back region; the kind of social space that motivates touristic consciousness.

That is theory enough. The *empirical* action in tourist settings is mainly confined to movement between areas decorated to look like back regions, and back regions into which tourists are allowed to peek. *Insight*, in the everyday, and in some ethnological senses of the term, is what is obtained from one of these peeks into a back region.

## TOURISTS AND INTELLECTUALS

There is no serious or functional role in the production awaiting the tourists in the places they visit. Tourists are not made personally responsible for anything that happens in the establishments they visit, and the quality of the insight gained by touristic experience has been criticized as less than profound. David Riesman's "other-directed" and Herbert Marcuse's "one-dimensional" men are products of a traditional intellectual concern for the superficiality of knowledge in our modern society, but the tourist setting *per se* is just beginning to prompt intellectual commentary. Settings are often not merely copies or replicas of real-life situations but copies that are presented as disclosing more about the real thing than the real thing itself discloses. Of course, this cannot be the case, at least not from technical stand-points, as in ethnography, for example. The Greyline guided tours of the Haight Ashbury when the hippies lived there cannot be substi-tuted for the studies based on participant observation undertaken at the same time. The intellectual attitude is firm in this belief. The touristic experience that comes out of the tourist setting is based on inauthenticity and as such it is superficial when compared with careful study. It is morally inferior to mere experience. A mere experience may be mystified, but a touristic experience is always mystified. The lie contained in the touristic experience, moreover, presents itself as a truthful revelation, as the vehicle that carries the onlooker behind false fronts into reality. The idea here is that a false back is more insidious and dangerous than a false front, or an inauthentic demystification of social life is not merely a lie but a superlie, the kind that drips with sincerity.

Along these lines, Daniel Boorstin's[12] comments on sightseeing and tourism suggest that critical writing on the subject of modern mass mentality is gaining analytical precision and is moving from the individual-centered concepts of the 1950's to a structural orientation. His concept of "pseudo-event" is a recent addition to a line of specific criticism of tourists that can be traced back to Veblen's "conspicuous leisure"[13] or back still further to Mark Twain's ironic commentary in *The Innocents Abroad*.[14] In his use of the term "pseudo-event", Boorstin wants his reader to understand that there is something about the tourist setting itself that is not intellectually satisfying. In his own words:

> These [tourist]"attractions" offer an elaborately contrived indirect experience, an artificial product to be consumed in the very places where the real thing is as free as air. They are ways for the traveler to remain out of contact with foreign peoples in the very act of "sight-seeing" them. They keep the natives in quarantine while the tourist in air-conditioned comfort views them through a picture window. They are the cultural mirages now found at tourist oases everywhere.[15]

This kind of commentary reminds us that tourist settings, like other areas of institutional life, are often insufficiently policed by liberal concerns for truth and beauty. They are tacky. We might also suggest that some touristic places overexpress their underlying structure and thereby upset certain of their sensitive visitors: restaurants are decorated like ranch kitchens; bellboys assume and use false, foreign first names; hotel rooms are made to appear like peasant cottages; primitive religious ceremonies are staged as public pageants. This kind of naked tourist setting is probably not as important in the overall picture of mass tourism as Boorstin makes it out to be in his polemic, but it is an ideal type of sorts, and many examples of it exist.

Boorstin is insightful as to the nature of touristic arrangements but he undercuts what might have developed into a structural analysis of sightseeing and touristic consciousness by falling back onto individual-level interpretations before analyzing fully his "pseudo-event" conception. He claims that touists themselves *cause* "pseudo-events." Commenting on the restaurants along superhighways, Boorstin writes:

> There people can eat without having to look out on an individualized, localized landscape. The disposable paper mat on which they are served shows no local scenes, but a map of numbered super highways with the location of other "oases." *They feel most at home above the highway itself, soothed by the auto stream to which they belong.*[16]

None of the accounts in my collection support Boorstin's contention that tourists want superficial, contrived experiences. Rather, tourists demand authenticity just as Boorstin does. Nevertheless, Boorstin persists in positing an absolute separation of touristic and intellectual attitudes. On the distinction between work ("traveling") and sightseeing, he writes:

> The traveler, then, was working at something; the tourist was a pleasure-seeker. The traveler was active; he went strenuously in search of people, of adventure, of experience. The tourist is passive; he expects interesting things to happen to him. He goes "sight-seeing". . . . He expects everything to be done to him and for him.[17]

As I have already suggested, the attitude Boorstin expresses is a commonplace among tourists and travel writers. It is so prevalent, in fact, that it is a part of the problem of mass tourism, not an analytical reflection on it.

In other words, we still lack adequate technical perspectives for the study of "pseudo-events." The construction of such perspectives necessarily begins with the tourists themselves and a close examination of the facts of sightseeing. The writers of the accounts cited earlier in this chapter express Boorstin's disappointment that their experiences are sometimes fleeting and insulated. They desire to get in with the natives, but, more important here, they are willing to accept disappointment when they feel they are stopped from penetrating into the real life of the place they are visiting. In fact, some tourists are able to laugh off Boorstin's disappointment. The account of a trip to Tangier from which the following is excerpted was given by a writer who clearly expected the false backwardness she found there and is relaxed about relating it.

> A young Arab pulled a chair up to our table. He had rugs to sell, but we insisted we were not interested. He unrolled his entire collection and spread them out on the ground. He wouldn't leave. I could see beneath his robes that he was wearing well-tailored navy blue slacks and a baby blue cashmere sweater.[18]

Similarly, the visitor to La Vegas who wrote the following has seen through the structure of tourist settings and is laughing about it:

> Along with winter vacationists by the thousands, I will return to lively Las Vegas, if only to learn whether Howard Hughes, like the Mint Casino, has begun issuing free coupons entitling the visitor to a back-stage tour of his moneymaking establishment.[19]

For these tourists, exposure of a back region is casual part of their touristic experience. What they see in the back is only another show. It does not trick, shock or anger them, and they do not express any feelings of having been made less pure by their discoveries.

## CONCLUSION

Daniel Boorstin calls places like American superhighways and the Istanbul Hilton "pseudo," a hopeful appellation that suggests that they are insubstantial or transitory, which they are not. It also suggests that somewhere in tourist settings there *are* real events accessible to intellectual elites, and perhaps there are. I have argued that a more helpful way of approaching the same facts is in terms of a modification of Erving Goffman's model of everyday life activities. Specifically, I have suggested that for the study of tourist settings *front* and *back* be treated as ideal poles of a continuum, poles linked by a series of front regions decorated to appear as back regions, and back regions set up to accommodate outsiders. I have suggested the term *stage setting* for these intermediary types of social space, but there is no need to be rigid about the matter of the name of this place, so long as its structural features and their influences on ideas are understood.

I have claimed that the structure of this social space is intimately linked to touristic attitudes and I want to pursue this. The touristic way of getting in with the natives is to enter into a quest for authentic experiences, perceptions and insights. The quest for authenticity is marked off in stages in the passage from front to back. Movement from stage to stage corresponds to growing touristic understanding. This continuum is sufficiently developed in some areas of the world that it appears as an infinite regression of stage sets. Once in this manifold, the tourist is trapped. His road does not end abruptly in some conversion process that transforms him into Boorstin's "traveler," "working at something" as he breaks the bounds of all that is pseudo and penetrates, finally, into a real back region. Tourists make brave sorties out from their hotels, hoping, perhaps, for an authentic experience, but their paths can be traced in advance over small increments of what is for them increasingly *apparent* authenticity proffered by tourist settings. Adventuresome tourists progress from stage to stage, always in the public eye, and greeted everywhere by their obliging hosts.

In highly developed tourist settings such as San Francisco and Switzerland, every detail of touristic experience can take on a showy, back-region aspect, at least for fleeting moments. Tourists enter tourist areas precisely because their experiences there will not, for them, be routine. The local people in the places they visit, by contrast, have long discounted the presence of tourists and go about their business as usual, even their tourist business, as best they can, treating tourists as a part of the regional scenery. Tourists often *do* see routine aspects of life as it is really lived in the places they visit, although few tourists express much interest in this. In the give-and-take of urban street life in tourist areas, the question of who is watching whom and who is responding to whom can be as complex as it is in the give-and-take between ethnographers and their respondents. It is only when a person makes an effort to penetrate into the real life of the areas he visits that he ends up in places especially designed to generate feelings of intimacy and experiences that can be talked about as "participation." No one can "participate" in his own life; he can only participate in the lives of others. And once tourists have entered touristic space, there is no way out for them so long as they press their search for authenticity. Near each tourist setting there are others like the last. Each one may be visited, and each one promises real and convincing shows of local life and culture. Even the infamously clean Istanbul Hilton has not excluded all aspects of Turkish culture (the cocktail waitresses wear harem pants, or did in 1968). For some Europeans I know, an American superhighway is an attraction of the first rank, the more barren the better because it is thereby more American.

Daniel Boorstin was the first to study these matters. His approach elevates to the level of analysis a nostalgia for an earlier time with more clear-cut divisions between the classes and simpler social values based on a programmatic, back *vs.* front view of the true and the false. This classic position is morally superior to the one presented here but it cannot lead to the scientific study of society. Specifically, Boorstin's and other intellectual approaches do not help us to analyze the expansion of the tourist class under modernization, or the development on an international scale of activities and social structural arrangements made *for* tourists, social changes Boorstin himself documents. Rather than confront the issues he raises, Boorstin only expresses a long-standing touristic attitude, a pronounced dislike, bordering on hatred, for other tourists, an attitude that turns man against man in a *they are the tourists, I am not* equation.[20]

The touristic attitude and the structure that produces it contribute to the destruction of the interpersonal solidarity that is such a notable feature of the life of the educated masses in modern society. This attitude has nowhere been so eloquently expressed as it was by Claude Lévi-Strauss:

> Travel and travellers are two things I loathe—and yet here I am, all set to tell the story of my expeditions. But at least I've taken a long while to make up my mind to it; fifteen years have passed since I left Brazil for the last time and often, during those years, I've planned to write this book, but I've always been held back by a sort of shame and disgust. So much would have to be said that has no possible interest: insipid details, incidents of no significance. . . . That the object of our studies should be attainable only by continual struggle and vain expenditures does not mean that we should set any store by what we should rather consider as the negative aspect of our profession. The truths that we travel so far to seek are of value only when we have scraped them clean of all this fungus. It may well be that we shall have spent six months of travel, privation, and sickening physical weariness merely in order to record—in a few days, it may be, or even a few hours—an unpublished myth, a new marriage-rule, or a complete list of names of clans. But that does not justify my taking up my pen in order to rake over memory's trash-cans: "At 5:30 a.m. we dropped anchor off Recife while the seagulls skirled around us and a flotilla of small boats put out from the shore with exotic fruits for sale. . . ."
> And yet that sort of book enjoys a great and, to me, inexplicable popularity.[21]

# 6

## A Semiotic of Attraction

A relationship between cultural systems and systems of belief is implicit in most sociology and anthropology extending back to Durkheim, but only recently have some students elected to make this relationship explicit. Most notably, Noam Chomsky and Claude Lévi-Strauss, in their theoretically quite similar studies of language and culture, have independently concluded that there is a universal mind underlying all linguistic and culture behavior.

It is now possible, I think, by applying recently developed techniques in the field of semiotics, to move beyond Lévi-Strauss's and Chomsky's hypothesis to actual studies of the relationship of mind and society.

Semiotics is the science of signs. Its most distinctive theoretical characteristic is its negation of the division of subject from object which is the keystone of traditional Western science. Semiotics locates the *sign*, which it treats as an original unification of subject and object, in the place of the old subject-object split at the center of scientific investigation. In Charles Sanders Peirce's original formulation, *a sign represents something to someone.*

I have suggested that tourist attractions are signs. It was my goal, in my formulation of the attraction as a relationship between a sight, marker and tourist, that it conform precisely to the empirical characteristics of actual tourist attractions *and*, if possible, to the theoretical definition of the sign established by Peirce. The esthetics of the eventual symmetry I was able to achieve between the two, between

109

the theory and its application to tourism, was a source of great
personal pleasure:

> [represents / something / to someone]   sign
>
> [marker / sight / tourist]   attraction

Given the homology between the two, it is possible to remove the
development of understanding of signs and modern culture from the
realm of theoretical speculation and locate it in empirical studies. In
this chapter and the two that follow, we will undertake an explication
of touristic consciousness, trying to discover aspects of the relationship between modern society and the mind of modern man.


## MARKERS

Usually, the first contact a sightseer has with a sight is not the
sight itself but with some representation thereof. The proliferation of
touristic representations was apparently quite widespread even before the recent information explosion. Charles Dickens, in what
appears to be hyperbole, makes what is, in truth, a factual observation: "There is, probably, not a famous picture or statue in all Italy,
but could easily be buried under a mountain of printed paper devoted
to dissertations on it."[1] Modifying everyday usage somewhat, I have
adapted the term *marker* to mean information about a specific sight.
The information given by a sight marker often amounts to no more
than the name of the sight, or its picture, or a plan or map of it.

The conventional meaning of "marker" in touristic contexts tends
to be restricted to information that is attached to, or posted alongside
of, the sight. A plaque reading "George Washington, the First President of the United States, Slept Here," is an example. My use of the
term extends it to cover any information about a sight, including that
found in travel books, museum guides, stories told by persons who
have visited it, art history texts and lectures, "dissertations" and so
forth. This extension is forced, in part, by the easy portability of
information. Tourists carry descriptive brochures to and from the
sights they visit. Some steal plaques and carry them off as trophies.

The official National Monument sign, "George Washington Slept Here," then, will be termed a marker whether it is located over a bed in a room at Mt. Vernon or in a boy's room at an Ivy League college fraternity house. Where it is necessary to distinguish between information found at its sight and information that is separated from its sight, I will use the terms *on-sight marker* and *off-sight marker*.

While extending the conventional meaning "marker" in this way, to include both on- and off-sight markers, I want to limit its use in another way. In common use, "marker" often refers to both *information* and the *vehicle* for the information (to the stone as well as to the inscription on it, in the case of grave "markers"), but here it refers only to the information or the inscription. The distinction I want to preserve here is a common one at the time when a stone or plaque is selected, or when a new one is set in place. But it seems to erode with time. So, for example, the nice separation between plaque and inscription, made by the reporter who filed the following item, is not always so evident as he makes it:

> London, August 12 (AP)—Karl Marx, the father of communism, was commemorated Saturday in this city of capitalism. A round blue plaque was unveiled at 28 Dean Street in the Soho district, one of five places where Marx lived in the 34 years he spent in London. The plaque reads: "Karl Marx 1818-1883 lived here 1851-1856."[2]

It is necessary to preserve this kind of distinction between inscriptions and the vehicles which carry the inscription. Some of these vehicles are themselves tourist attractions requiring separate consideration: totem poles, the Rosetta Stone and the obelisks called "Cleopatra's Needle" in New York, London and Paris.

## SIGHT INVOLVEMENT AND MARKER INVOLVEMENT

Sightseers do not, in any empirical sense, *see* San Francisco. They see Fisherman's Wharf, a cable car, the Golden Gate Bridge, Union Square, Coit Tower, the Presidio, City Lights Bookstore, Chinatown, and, perhaps, the Haight Ashbury or a nude go-go dancer in a North Beach-Barbary Coast club. As elements in a set called "San Francisco", each of these items is a symbolic marker. Individually, each item is a sight requiring a marker of its own. There are, then, two frameworks which give meaning to these attractions. The sightseer may visit the Golden Gate Bridge, seeing it as a piece of information about San Francisco which he must possess if he is to make his being in San Francisco real, substantial or complete; or, the sightseer visits a large suspension bridge, an object which might be considered worthy of attention in its own right. The act of sightseeing can set in motion a little dialectic wherein these frames are successively exchanged, one for the other, to the benefit of both: that is, both San Francisco and the Golden Gate Bridge are felt to have gained a little weight in the act of looking at the bridge—or they are held to have been, at least to some extent, *meaningfully experienced*.

There is a second possibility. The sightseer perceives the bridge only as a piece of San Francisco and unworthy in itself of his attention. A better way of describing this second possibility would be to say that the bridge has lost its markers and is incomplete as an attraction. This is expressed in the complaint: "So what's there to see? The Verrazzano Narrows is a lot bigger than that."

I will term the sightseeing situation in which a sight has no markers, whether this occurs because they have been taken over by another sight as in the last example, or because the sightseer simply lacks relevant information, *sight involvement*. Mark Twain exhibits little interest in the information made available to him on the occasion of his visit to see a much admired painting, and, consequently, he expresses a high level of sight involvement:

> "The Last Supper" is painted on the dilapidated wall of what was a little chapel attached to the main church in ancient times, I suppose. It is battered and scarred in every direction, and stained and discolored by time, and Napoleon's horses kicked the legs off most the disciples when they (the horses, not the disciples) were stabled there more than half a century ago.
>
> This picture is about thirty feet long and ten or twelve high, I should think, and the figures are at least life-size. It is one of the largest paintings in Europe. The colors are dimmed with age; the countenances are scaled and marred, and nearly all expression is gone from them; the hair is a dead blur upon the wall, and there is no life in the eyes. Only the attitudes are certain.[3]

One result of sight involvement is *disappointment*. Mark Twain also expresses some marker involvement, with quite a different result:

> I recognized the old picture in a moment—the Saviour with bowed head seated at the center of a long, rough table with scattering fruits and dishes upon it, and six disciples on either side in their long robes, talking to each other—the picture from which all engravings and all copies have been made for three centuries. Perhaps no living man has ever known an attempt to paint the Lord's Supper differently. . . . There were a dozen easels in the room, and as many artists transferring the great picture to their canvases. Fifty proofs of steel engravings and lithographs were scattered around, too. And as usual, I could not help noticing how superior the copies were to the original, that is, to my inexperienced eye. Whenever you find a Raphael, a Rubens, a Michelangelo, a Carracci, or a da Vinci . . . you find artists copying them, and the copies are always the handsomest.[4]

Mark Twain means to be ironic, but ironic humor does not succeed unless it exposes some truth. The truth is that marker involvement can prevent a tourist's realizing that the sight he sees may not be worth his seeing it. Mark Twain is trying to combat a tendency on the part of some sightseers to transfer the "beauty" of the calendar version of *The Last Supper* to the original, but his is a losing battle.

Children, more than adults, have a capacity for being at once sight-involved and marker-involved. Some are quick to point out that a specific sight is hardly worth seeing but the information associated with it makes a visit worthwhile anyway:

> New York (AP)—Less than an ounce of moon rock went on display at the American Museum of National History, and 42,195 people, the largest one-day crowd in the museum's history, turned out to see it. "It looks like a piece of something you could pick up in Central Park," one 13 year-old boy said. "But it's cool that it's from the moon."[5]

The examples begin to make clear that the important element in (pleasant?) sightseeing need not be the sight. More important than the sight, at least, is some marker involvement.

Thus, we find that the State of Iowa, which may be as free of sights as any state in the United States, is nevertheless not without its attractions. A brochure reads, in part:

*Free Guide:* An invitation to the beautiful 5 by 80 area. . . . 5 cooperating towns along Interstate 80. See the historical places in the picture window of Iowa. [The word "Iowa" appears inside an outline map of the state.] Bring your camera. Wonderful picture-taking opportunities at all these attractions.[6]

Descriptions of the attractions are provided by the guide. Following are several examples:

Kunkle cabin site. In 1848 Benjamin Kunkle and his family became the first permanent settlers of Guthrie County. Mr. Kunkle raised the first hogs in the county. The marker is attached to a large elm tree in the Myron Godwin farmyard.

Casey's Tall Greeter. One of Iowa's tallest living Christmas Trees. In 1921, this tree was planted in memory of Jesse Kite—a World War I casualty. It overlooks a small park and when decorated at Christmas time it is the landmark of the town.

Dale City. . . . about 4 miles west of Dale City on the north side of the road is Glacier Ridge. The Wisconsin Glacier ended here, leaving rich gravel deposits for road building.

More interesting, from a technical (and a touristic) standpoint, is the star attraction of this area. As a sight, it amounts to no more than a patch of wild grass, but it was recently provided with an elaborate off-sight marker by the motion picture industry. The fortuitous acquisition of this new marker apparently caught the promoters of the area by surprise as the following information in the brochure is overstamped in red ink: VISIT THE BONNIE AND CLYDE SHOOTOUT AREA. Also overprinted in red ink is a square box surrounding a sight description that appeared in the original printing of the brochure.

Quaker Ridge. The hills on the south side of the South Raccoon River. In 1933 the notorious Barrow Gang camped here near Dexfield Park. Two were captured—the other three, including Bonnie Parker, escaped—to be killed later in Louisiana.

Visitors to the "Bonnie And Clyde Shootout Area" cannot be disappointed as Mark Twain was when he visited *The Last Supper*. They do not arrive expecting to see anything and are content to be involved with the marker. An unusual degree of contentment with sight markers was exhibited by a young couple I observed at the Washington, D.C. zoo in midwinter when many of the birds had been removed from their outdoor cages for protection from the low temperatures. The couple proceeded methodically from empty cage to empty cage, reading and discussing the illustrative markers on each. Even where there *is* something to see; a tourist may elect to get his thrills from the marker instead of the sight. After completing his sociological survey of park visitors, William Catton Jr. visited a museum in Yellowstone and described his response as follows:

> Realizing I was seeing the very spot where mercenery [sic] thoughts were submerged under a noble vision at that 1870 campfire, I felt my spine tingle. A few moments later, in a plain glass case in this little museum, I saw a facsimile copy of The Yellowstone Act. I read these quietly momentous words: "Be it enacted by the Senate and House of Representatives of the United States of America in Congress assembled, That the tract of land in the Territories of Montana and Wyoming. . . ." I swallowed, and squared my shoulders.[7]

It is necessary to qualify these examples of marker involvement. The behavior of the couple at the zoo is unusual, Iowa is no capital of tourism, and Catton is not an ordinary tourist. There is a practical limit on how far a marker can go in covering over an absence of sights. A raised tablet beside the highway near the Wind River Indian Reservation in Wyoming proclaims the spot where early settlers stopped and broke open the sod under which they found natural deposits of ice which they used in mixing their drinks. This is an interesting piece of information, but not many sightseers are attracted to the place now that better ice supplies are available.

Another sight of the work display type that fails to attract, even though it seems more qualified for this purpose than a prairie, is a car smasher. The reporter followed a lead provided by an advertisement she read in a Wilmington, Delaware newspaper:

> It offered to pay a "reward" for automobiles "dead or alive," with the added inducement: "Come See Your Car Crushed Before Your Eyes." Arthur Ploener, who bought and paid for the advertisement, thought he might have to put up bleachers to accommodate people watching the

death throes of their automobiles. Not so. The day I was there no one
wanted to watch except me. . . . Watching a car-crusher at work is an
exciting interlude for tourists, and especially rewarding for those who
would enjoy seeing a few vehicles eliminated from blighted roadsides.

Three compact cars make a wafer about as thick as a standard model.
The noise of crunching metal is not as loud as the motor of the fork-lift
truck. The crusher operator enjoys a fringe benefit: When he sweeps
out the crusher bed after each operation, he usually finds some of the
small change people are always losing behind the seats. The profit
averages about $1 a day.[8]

Famous rocks, it was noted, are attractive to Manhattanites, but
manifestly equally famous dust failed to attract the citizens of a
nearby city which has some infamous dust of its own:

Pittsburgh, October 9 (Special to the *New York Times*)—Area residents
are not excited by the opportunity to see samples of moon dust brought
back to earth by Apollo 11 astronauts. University of Pittsburgh officials say that their moon dust display is attracting about as much
attention as a sack of coal dust. "We never get more than a dozen people
at the display," a spokesman said. "We thought they'd be breaking
down the doors to get in."[9]

Georg Simmel, who was apparently not much concerned about lit-
terbuggery and other forms of man's rape of nature, once suggested
that the interest value of archaeological ruins can be traced to the way
they reveal a contest between nature and culture, and a proof that the
cultural object (the ruin) can resist the ravages of nature. To this I
would add that the ruin is emblematic of all tourist attractions which
are subject to physical and informational deterioration.

Its markers notwithstanding, moon dust can fail to attract as moon
rock attracts, and even though "watching a car crusher can be an
exciting interlude for a tourist," an advertisement in a Wilmington
newspaper apparently provides insufficient information, or information of the wrong kind, so only a journalist follows its lead. Nevertheless, it must be noted that all the attractions figuring in this section,
the Wyoming ice deposits, the *Last Supper*, the "Bonnie and Clyde
Shootout Area," etc., have markers, generate some marker involvement, and attract at least a few sightseers—as do even the empty

birdcages at the Washington, D.C. zoo. The boy's comment on the moon rock ("it's cool") reminds us that there are some all-purpose markers available for the sightseers to add to existing ones, or to supply in the case of an unexpected attraction, when other markers are lacking.

## THE RELATIONSHIP OF MARKERS (SIGNIFIER) TO SIGHTS (SIGNIFIED)

The most important discovery of the first semiotic, that of Charles Peirce and Ferdinand de Saussure, was the principle of the arbitrariness of the relationship between the signifier and the signified. The example most often cited as illustration of this principle is the absence of natural connections between the sound of a word such as "tree" and the object it signifies. This is especially evident when words from different languages that mean the same thing (tree, *arbre*, *Baum*) are compared. In the "Introduction" to a forthcoming book, Peter K. Manning provides some interesting nonlinguistic illustrations of the arbitrariness of the sign:

> The association between the wide-brimmed hat and cultural values of land-owning haciendados in Andalusia . . . ; between orchids and casting of spells to rid persons of evil or of bodily afflictions . . . ; between types of grain and connotations of wealth, purity or spatial locale . . . ; or between crow's meat and incest . . . are *symbolic* and can be understood only by unraveling the *system of signs* in which these associations become unquestioned.

The world of tourism is crowded with similar relationships: the connection between liberty and the Statue of Liberty is a monumental example.

Even as it elucidates the principle of the arbitrariness of the relationship of signifier and signified, the first semiotic can retain traces of the old subject-object duality so long as the signifier is always understood to be a psychological fact, a mental image or idea, while the signified is always understood to be an objective fact "out there." This unnecessarily restricted version of semiotics fits itself neatly into established scientific frameworks by equating signifier with *concept* and signified with *observation* preserving, thereby, the separation of theory from reality or subject from object.

One implication of the analysis of the tourist attraction in the following sections is that the "principle" of the arbitrariness of the relationship of signifier to the signified is only a corollary of a more fundamental principle: namely, that of the *interchangeability* of the signifier and the signified. For example, the word asterisk signifies one of these: ****. The presence of an asterisk in a text signfies additional information.* The asterisk is both signified and signifier. The referent of a sign is another sign. On a more complex level, the field of the sociology of knowledge has begun to discover that scientific theories, in addition to being reflections of empirical reality, themselves reflect the structure of the groups and classes in which they originate. Men have ideas about things, and these ideas are readily transformed into the object of critical study. If a group elevates things over ideas, or ideas over things, this is only a matter of social values and has nothing to do with the essential structure of meaning which is much more plastic than values (for example, scientific values, or common sense values) make it out to be.

In the actual operation of social life everything appears firmly attached to its meaning. Science is locked in combat with common sense because the way the world ordinarily works is intuitively obvious to anyone who occupies a fairly stable position in his society. It makes no difference if the meaning he attaches to an observation is not correct from the standpoint of science or of someone in another social class or from another culture. Ordinary reality remains intuitively obvious in the way it is structured. The social world is simply saturated with meaning in such a way that does not call attention to itself as it is in the process of becoming meaningful. This is its most mysterious and its most social quality. The immediate meaningfulness of social reality depends on a system of transformations of things into ideas (as is accomplished, for example, by modern science), and ideas into things such as gestures, books, monuments and other cultural objects. Additional analysis of the structure of the attraction provides specific illustrations.

*Located at the bottom of the page.

In the world of the tourist, common sense easily and rigidly segregates information about an object from the object itself (marker from sight) so easily, in fact, that special terms seem unnecessary. Closer examination reveals, to the contrary, that where a distinction is made between a marker and a sight, it is secured through the intervention of modern civilization. The designation of an object as a sight, a factory process, a bit of moon dust, is most often accomplished without any esthetic assistance from the object. Its elevation to sight status is the work of *society*. Markers are sometimes made out of the same stuff a sight is made out of—they might even be a chip off the sight—but once they are in the hands of an individual, they can only be souvenirs, memories of the thing itself.

Any difference between signifiers and signifieds is the result of the superimposition of a system of social values. Nature does not present itself as a collection of signifiers on the one hand and a collection of signifieds on the other. We assign it esthetic and utilitarian values according to our own social structure and social organization. Interestingly, even the language we use in everyday discourse does not automatically distinguish between signifiers and signifieds (between markers and sights). Following is an excerpt from an advertisement for a book, which in this case is a kind of marker for the archeological sights of Egypt. The writer of the advertisement has made clever use of the failure of the language to distinguish sight from marker:

> I would like to examine ANCIENT EGYPT. Please send it to me for ten days' free examination and enter a trial subscription to the GREAT AGES OF MAN series. If I decide to keep ANCIENT EGYPT I will pay $4.95 (plus shipping and handling).[10]

At that price, no one is likely to confuse ancient Egypt with *Ancient Egypt*. Apparently P. T. Barnum was able to bank on the confusion of some visitors to his "Greatest Show on Earth" who, expecting to see a wonderful sight, followed the signs reading "This Way to the Egress" and had to pay a second admission to get back in again.

In the absence of a universal system of values such as those provided by a religion, the capitalist mode of production or modern tourism, we are thrust by our language into a dazzling dialectic of meaning. For example, the relationship between man and his work is potentially far more complex than the way it is presented within Protestantism, capitalism or tourism. Tourism makes an attraction of the relationship of man and his work and in so doing is often arbitrary and capricious about which aspects of the relationship it elevates to the status of attraction. Consider, for example, a recent case, carefully watched over by specialists in these matters, of a classical kind of work display, a self-portrait of an artist at work. This case involves a painting hanging in a museum in Vienna called *The Painter in His Studio* which bears the mark of the Dutch Master, Pieter de Hoogh. The sight the visitor comes to see is the painting. The marker is the piece of information: this is a picture of Pieter de Hoogh at work. In this case, as is possible in every case, this information is apparently misinformation. *The Painter in His Studio* is now believed to have been painted by Vermeer, de Hoogh's mark having been fraudulently added by an unscrupulous seller before Vermeer's work became more valuable than de Hoogh's in the masterpiece marketplace.[11] The information that the canvas was painted by de Hoogh, information once held to be so important that someone took the trouble to fake it, has now become a curious part of Vermeer's painting, an aspect of the sight with a marker of its own.

The transformation of marker into sight turns the painting into a display of an even more important painter's work. Suddenly, the entire surface of the painting is alive with new information: so that is what Vermeer looked like, so that is the way his studio looked! As the marker is turned into the sight, the sight turns into a marker, and the esthetics of production are transformed into the esthetics of consumption and attraction. The writer of the following account apparently believes that all Dutch paintings function in this way as Time Machines and as fancy travel posters:

> The backgrounds of the paintings of the Flemish masters of the 15th and 16th centuries seem to be identifiable in Brussels and, more especially, in Bruges and Ghent. The people of today's Belgium appear to step out of the paintings of David Teniers, the people of Holland still laugh the way they did in Franz Hals' work and Rembrandt's subjects swarm through Amsterdam. A visit to the area can become a low-key excursion into an earlier age.[12]

A serious art critic might protest that to turn paintings into pictures is to deform them, but such protests are directed at real acts of real viewers (called "naive") and it is with these latter that the human scientist is necessarily concerned.

## CONTACT AND RECOGNITION

Sight → marker → sight transformations are not merely something that may occur in the act of sightseeing. They are an essential element of the act. Tourists have been criticized for failing, somehow, to *see* the sights they visit, exchanging *perception* for mere *recognition*.[13] The polemic is not worth entering, but the point that sightseers have the capacity effortlessly to recognize a sight on first contact with it is correct, interesting and worthy of careful description. First, it is necessary to note that not all sightseers recognize what they see as sights. A woman passing a painting by Michelangelo in the National Gallery in London does not stop, but says to her friend, "I just *love* pictures in a round frame!" This lady hangs a marker on the painting in passing, but her marker, nicely intended as it is, does not combine with the sight to make of it an attraction. It is a near miss, though: she *almost* stops to admire the painting just because it has a round frame. The incident reveals that the elementary material of first contact recognition is (1) an off-sight marker that is carried to the sight by the sightseer (in his hand or in his head) and (2) a clear view of a substantial sight.

Mark Twain describes the recognition process on the occasion of his arrival in Paris:

> In a little while we were speeding through the streets of Paris and delightfully recognizing certain names and places with which books had long ago made us familiar. It was like meeting an old friend when we read "Rue de Rivoli" on the street corner; we knew the genuine vast palace of the Louvre as well as we knew its picture; when we passed the Column of July we needed no one to tell us what it was or to remind us that on its site once stood the grim Bastille.[14]

Recognition, as Mark Twain describes it, is a marker → sight replacement. Information about the object gives way to the object itself. This happens quickly, in less than a second perhaps, but the speed of the process should not be allowed to cover the details of its structure. It is possible to examine more carefully this instant which is accepted so naturally, and which is a part of the delight of the sightseer. The analyst is fortunate—"natural" means for slowing down the recognition process are available. Towers for sightseers are constructed, like the "Space Needle" at the Seattle World's Fair, which complicate, minaturize and shift the usual perspective from which the famous objects below are viewed. A guidebook describes for the visitor to the 1900 Paris Exposition what he can expect in the way of experience if he uses the Eiffel Tower:

> The Exhibition with its marvellous palaces and pavilions, its gardens and terraces, is seen to the greatest advantage, and produces an effect of confused architectural magnificence never to be forgotten, recalling in many ways one of those fantastical panoramas conjured up by the vivid imagination of Martin in his extraordinary pictures of ancient Babylon, Rome and Jerusalem. Far away beyond the Champ Elysée [sic] can be seen standing out against the horizon the domes and towers of buildings whose fame is world-wide. Notre Dame, the Louvre, the Tower of St. Germain des Prés, and St. Sulphice [sic], the dome of the Panthéon and the towers of a hundred other landmarks celebrated in history and romance. The night panorama from the Eiffel Tower is even more wonderful than that to be seen by daylight.[15]

What is interesting about this claim is its emphasis on the wonderful quality of seeing actual objects *as if they are pictures, maps or panoramas of themselves.* Apparently the instant just before the sightseer completes his recognition of a famed sight is regarded highly enough by some that they will employ mechanical aids to prolong and savor it. From the Eiffel Tower it is possible both to recognize the Palace of the Louvre and to have an inkling of it.

When the Louvre first comes into view, then, it may not be recognized at all. Partially recognized, it has the momentary status of information about a famous building which the viewer "should know." It appears as an incomplete plan, model or image of itself. Its label or name is not attached to the sight; it is said to be, rather, on the "tip of the sightseer's tongue." The uncertain tourist, less knowledgeable than Mark Twain, may check the image provided by the actual Louvre against its other markers—a picture in his guide, for example—before he completes first contact recognition. The process can be diagrammed as follows:

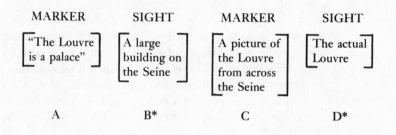

| MARKER | SIGHT | MARKER | SIGHT |
|---|---|---|---|
| "The Louvre is a palace" | A large building on the Seine | A picture of the Louvre from across the Seine | The actual Louvre |
| A | B* | C | D* |

Mark Twain described a sudden replacement of Marker A by sight D omitting the embedded sight marker transformation → (B → C) wherein the sight itself serves as the last piece of information the sightseer obtains before definitive first contact recognition. When this happens very rapidly, as Mark Twain claims it did to him, the embedded stage (B → C) may go unnoticed. When it happens a little more slowly the sightseer may do what is called a "double take," turning his head toward the sight, and then away, and then suddenly turning back again. The asterisks in the diagram indicate the points in the process at which the sightseer's head turns toward the sight in a double take.

## THE DOMINATION OF A SIGHT BY ITS MARKERS

*Constructed recognition: Sightseers* have the capacity to recognize sights by transforming them into one of their markers. *Society* has the capacity to "recognize" places, men and deeds by building a marker up to the status of a sight. Compare, for example, *The Painter in His Studio* with the Tomb of the Unknown Soldier in Washington, D.C. The tomb was constructed as a tableau of information, or a carrier of official inscriptions that serves at the same time as a sight for visitors. It is a monumental analogue of de Hoogh's forged signature, standing in for the anonymous but worthy dead man, selected almost at random, who was actually behind or beneath the visible object. Both exhibit the structure of formal recognition. It is characteristic of formal recognition that the sightseer is not permitted to attach the last marker to the sight according to his own method of recognition. The marker and sight are fused in a single representation, guaranteeing a certain on-the-spot appreciation or marker involvement.

*Identification:* A second type of marker → sight displacement occurs when an individual seeks to identify himself with a sight by sacralizing one of its markers. This is best represented by a common use of travel posters. Some of these have been made to abandon their original function and have been elevated to become decorative objects. This may not be the case for those found on the walls of the office of a travel agent, which retain some meaning as off-sight markers. It is where they are used to "brighten up" a student's room, or a "French" restaurant in London's Chelsea, that they tend to become just sights, or rather, off-sight markers that are transformed into sights. Under conditions where this achieved with an economy of means, that is, where it is not necessary, as in the case of tombs, to erect a marble edifice on which to hang the marker, we may speak of a simple marker → sight displacement or identification. Many, not all, souvenirs are displaced replicas or effigies of the sight they mark, serving simultaneously as one of its markers and as a little sight in its own right. These are called "charms" and women wear them on charm bracelets. It is also possible to purchase charms that are not effigies of a sight but effigies of a sight marker. For example, in Paris one can buy a little blue and white enamel copy of the street sight that reads "Rue de Rivoli." (Little plastic copies are also available, as are little gold ones.) This street sign charm is a double identification:

|         | MARKERS | SIGHTS |
|---------|---------|--------|
| SIGHTS  | [Actual street sign] | [Actual street] |
| MARKERS | $\begin{bmatrix} \text{Inscription on the} \\ \text{charm} \end{bmatrix}$ | [Actual charm] |

First, the real street sign displaces the street as the object of touristic recognition, then the charm displaces the street sign as a sight. Only the inscription on the charm, the words "Rue de Rivoli," and the actual street have singular status in this set of relationships, the former as marker, the latter as sight. The street sign and the charm are at once both markers and sights. And this is what makes a charm charming (or a totem totemic).

*Obliterations:* In the early 1950's, a large (perhaps 100′ x 200′) animated neon sign mounted on the top of a building in Tacoma, Washington occasioned a public outcry because it blocked the view of Mount Rainier for some city residents. The sign was an advertisement for an oil company, not a marker for the mountain. In fact, something like the reverse was the case, as each glance toward "The Mountain" from certain districts of the town became a glance at the oil company's trademark. Advertising is an inexact science, as its practitioners are quick to admit, and only rarely does it accomplish its goals with the precision and economy manifest in this example. One might go so far as to say that advertising does not know its exact methods. If these are ever organized and classified, they would include a kind of marker → sight transformation that might be reformulated as being a trademark → commodity obliteration. What this means, in theory, is a supplanting of a commodity by the *name* of one brand of that commodity. This goal has been reached on several occasions: by "vacuum cleaners," which was an early brand of a class of commodities then called "suction sweepers," by jeep, kleenex, zipper and napalm. "Xerox" and "Coke" make a legal point of their being specific copyrighted trade names and not generic terms. Usually, however, when advertisements obliterate an object, it is not their competitor's product but something else, and when the audience for the advertising is the sightseer, it may obliterate a sight. At the intersection of advertising and tourism, a conflict can and does occur between markers and the sight the visitor comes to see:

> Montpelier, Vermont—Beginning tomorrow, travelers to a heavily visited section of Vermont will find themselves part of an experimental project that substitutes color-and-picture coded directional signs for billboards and other off-premise roadside signs.
>
> This is the latest step in Vermont's effort to preserve one of its major attractions—its natural scenic beauty—by ending billboard blight.

The state-owned-and-operated sign system has already been installed. Signs are grouped in clusters never more frequent than five or six miles along the road, nor closer than five miles to a built-up area.

Vermont's struggle to pass anti-billboard legislation, and the subsequent delays in its implementation, are suggestive of the problems inherent in this type of "esthetic pollution" program. While the bill was approved in just one session of the Legislature, it was not without strong opposition from billboard companies and some legislators. Typical was a prediction from the Senate floor that "in the name of esthetics, we're on the merry road to socialism." However, the billboard lobby's traditional friends—the hotel, motel, and restaurant associations—were lined up this time in favor of the bill. They came to the conclusion that their proliferating signs were polluting the very scenery their patrons came to see.[16]

This pragmatic move on the part of the people of Vermont may solve some economic problems but it is not a solution to the problem of marker → sight obliteration as it is claimed to be. If they achieve the goal of making the state more attractive to tourists who come to partake of the newly unobstructed view, the increased numbers of tourists will reobstruct the view. In August, the first sign that one is approaching Old Faithful Geyser in Yellowstone National Park is a traffic jam extending down the road for several miles on either approach to the sight. This is also a marker → sight obliteration. It is noteworthy that the capacity of an aggregate of tourists and their accommodations to block views seems greater than any set of signs yet devised. An example from London, which has reached a more advanced stage of touristic development than Vermont, illustrates:

It is only in recent years that London has permitted the construction of high-rise buildings. The first was the Hilton Hotel, built in the early '60's in the face of bitter public opposition. Permission was only granted after a cabinet decision ruled that it was in the interest of the British economy to encourage American tourists, and it was felt that the Hilton would serve this end. That set the precedent for many other tower blocks in and around the city center. The biggest threat to the Georgian areas of London is not offices, but hotels, being rapidly built to cater for the 10 million tourists who will visit Britain every year in the '70's. "The irony is," says Mr. Jenkins, "that they are destroying the very character and scale of the city their customers are coming to see."[17]

The same thing occurs on a smaller scale. The Paris International Automobile Salon, held annually in the Fall, allows visitors— as the New York Show does not—to touch and enter the automobiles on display and to look under their hoods at the engines. In midafternoon on a weekday at the 1970 Salon, persistent search from a dais ten feet above the floor on which over 400 automobiles were on view revealed not a visible trace of a car, or even a small part of a car, except for one experimental model that was suspended by its exhibitors in the air above the spectators. One could only see the backsides of viewers stooped over the cars.

*The last transformations:* The section on obliteration suggests that sightseeing is a self-destroying structure, but such a conclusion is too hasty. An aggregate of sightseers is one indicator that there is a sight nearby, or a marker, and like all markers it can be transformed into a sight. Mark Twain provides an example from another Paris exposition:

> Of course, we visited the renowned International Exposition. All the world did that. We went there on our third day in Paris—and we stayed there *nearly two hours*. That was our first and last visit. To tell the truth we saw at a glance that one would have to spend weeks—yea, even months—in that monstrous establishment to get an intelligible idea of it. It was a wonderful show, but the moving masses of people of all nations we saw there were a still more wonderful show. I discovered that if I were to stay there a month, I should still find myself looking at the people instead of the inanimate objects on display.[18]

The conservation-conscious epoch in which we live tends to define all marker → sight obliterations as a kind of blight, while in fact this is not the case once the marker is reconverted into a sight. The nongambling visitor to Las Vegas and the shy stroller in the section of Baltimore known as "The Block" may engage in a little interesting sightseeing. If they do, the sights they see are mainly the fanciful signs that are used to advertise gambling casinos (in Las Vegas) and burlesque houses (in Baltimore).

It is noteworthy that *marker involvement* is an original form of a sight → marker obliteration. This is especially evident when a sight is dominated by some *action* that occurred in the past. This was the case for the "Bonnie and Clyde Shootout Area," where it was hoped that marker involvement would obscure the fact that here was nothing to see. Mark Twain, exhibiting more enthusiasm for a certain tree than he did for the *Last Supper*, provides a similar example:

> I will not describe the Bois de Boulogne. I cannot do it. It is simply a beautiful, cultivated, endless, wonderful wildnerness. It is an enchanting place. It is in Paris now, one may say, but a crumbling old cross in one portion of it reminds one that it was not always so. The cross marks the spot where a celebrated troubadour was waylaid and murdered in the fourteenth century. It was in this park that that fellow with an unpronounceable name made the attempt upon the Russian czar's life last spring with a pistol. The bullet struck a tree. Ferguson [Twain's hired guide] showed us the place. Now in America that interesting tree would be chopped down or forgotten within the next five years, but it will be treasured here. The guides will point it out to visitors for the next eight hundred years, and when it decays and falls down they will put up another there and go on with the same old story just the same.[19]

Without its marker, this tree that he admired so much would be just a tree. It is the *information* about the tree (its marker) that is the object of touristic interest and the tree is the mere carrier of that information.

The withering away of the sight makes possible a common kind of misrepresentation where correct information is given but attached to the wrong object. Twain mentions that someday another tree may be substituted for the "interesting tree" that he saw. He does not reflect on the possibility that this switch may have been made before he saw the tree, or that the bullet missed the tree as well as the Czar and is buried in the ground. The use of the Bois de Boulogne as the duelling grounds for Paris no doubt qualified many of its trees as candidates to be the tree in the story. Any obliteration of a sight by its marker allows a little fraud when it comes to presenting the actual sight, but more interestingly, it forces on the honest keepers of certain sights a special set of problems involving reverse fraud: How does one make a convincing display of honest honesty? Is it possible to construct a true-seeming marker on the veritable spot where the beloved leader fell?

Great historical events of the outdoor variety (wars) often occur in little-distinguished surroundings, and the surviving parties to these events tend to be fastidious in the way they clean up the mess they made. The winning dead are often sent home for honorable burial. The losing dead from the local team may be stripped down to the fillings in their teeth, counted, put in plastic bags and burnt. This leads future keepers of the hallowed grounds precious little to work with in the way of sights, and can lead to some tedious marking procedures. At Verdun, this is not the case: the forest has not grown back; the French have not landscaped the trenches; the remains of the over half million men who were killed there in 1916 have not been much disturbed. At other battlefields, more marking is required. Recorded martial music is broadcast at Waterloo. Watts, the district of Los Angeles burned by dissidents in 1965, marks its event with a spectacle, an annual festival held in the first week of August. At Gettysburg, there are automated reconstructions of battles with military units indicated by flashing colored lights.

Battlefields provide excellent examples of marker → sight obliterations. The sight yields to a standard set of markers, including The Cemetery, The Museum (with its displays of rusted arms), The Monument to a General or Regiment, The Polished Cannon with its welded balls, The Battle Map and the (optional) Reconstructed Fortification. Standardization, here, leads back to the very anonymity it is designed to combat, an anonymity that is only partly relieved by the special markers cited above: the recorded music, festivals and automated maps. Normandy Beach is giving up as an ex-battlefield and is taking on a new identity as a suburban resort community. The identity problem for battlefields is compounded in the case of the famous encampment where cannon, battle plans and fortifications are relatively meaningless bits of marking paraphernalia. Inadequately marked, the preserved encampment, even more than the preserved battlefield, is in danger of being mistaken for a golf course. Tourists arriving at Valley Forge are directed to an "Information Center" where they are politely but firmly requested to watch a free, narrated slide show of Valley Forge before (or even instead of) visiting the actual "sights." (At Waterloo, movies are shown.) The sight of Valley Forge is especially problematical to its keepers. Unlike Normandy and Mark Twain's tree, Valley Forge is in no danger of blending into its surroundings. Rather, it stands out, but the qualities which make it appear so different from its current surroundings (as a barrier, in fact, to the westward movement of suburban Philadelphia)—its acres of clipped grass and carefully maintained roads, trees, picnicking, and parking facilities—are not much related to expectations for a winter camp of a large revolutionary army. If the tourist does not avail himself of the free slide show, Valley Forge has nothing of the revolutionary encampment about it. It has become a big, clean, grassy backyard for the city of Philadelphia, and on the Fourth of July that is just what it is used for by center-city residents (who do not stop at the "Information Center" to have it transformed for them back into an encampment).

*People watching:* Just as the great lighted signs at Las Vegas can be converted into sights, it is possible to transform the tourists themselves into attractions. This is not, as yet, a widespread phenomenon. Occurrences of people-watching are clustered at specific locations: the Boardwalk at Atlantic City where the municipality has constructed public alcoves filled with benches facing the walk; Telegraph Avenue in Berkeley; the Spanish Steps in Rome; the late Haight Ashbury and North Beach in San Francisco; the "Boul' Mich' " in the Latin Quarter in Paris; Dam Rak in Amsterdam and Trafalgar Square in London. These areas are not usually filled with local residents but with students, visitors and travelers, a fact which renders the attraction of people watching, in these little capitals of people watching, not that of people in general but of fellow aliens. Mark Twain provided an old example from the Paris Expo of 1868 (cited above), which is a case of sightseeing where the sight seen is a sightseer. The sight, its marker and its seer are the same, or, if they are not exactly the same, two tourists can take turns being all three. This is the most economical kind of sightseeing from the standpoint of sight presentation and the cash and energy outlay of the viewer. It is to be expected, therefore, that its adherents are mainly recruited from economically dependent classes: the aged and infirm and students. It does not necessarily follow, however, that the *behavior* of the students who gather at Dam Square in Amsterdam in the summer is little distinguishable from that exhibited by an outdoors gathering of old folks.[20] Nevertheless, this appears to be the case. The routines are few: dozing in the sun; quiet conversation interrupted by long silent periods; a following with the head and sometimes upper body of almost anything that is moving—a scrap of paper blown by the wind perhaps; a slow-motion greeting of an acquaintance without conversational follow-up. The students, who need not fear that the gesture can be read as "symptomatic," rest their heads on their arms more; the old folks seem to smile more. Excepting these differences, the summer population occupying the bricks around the monument in Dam Square is interchangeable with that occupying the green benches along Central Avenue in the retirement community of St. Petersburg, Florida, as far as its public behavior is concerned. Unlike the middle-aged tourist, who tends to define the urban outdoors as a tangle of corridors between monuments and museums, the old and young at times define it as a kind of big TV room wherein they are spectator and image alike.

## THE MARKER AS SYMBOL

There are two superficially different ways in which a locality can be represented symbolically to a tourist. San Francisco, for example, may be symbolized by food to the tourist who, eating cracked crab and garlic bread at Fisherman's Wharf, believes he is capturing the flavor of the city. The other kind of symbolic representation is that found on some travel posters. In 1968, the United States Travel Service, campaigning to attract European visitors, distributed a poster depicting two cowboys riding across a desert while over their heads, in the sky, appears a large sign: "U.S.A." The idea is that cowboys are symbolic of the U.S.A. We have, it seems to me, given too much attention to the differences between these two types of symbolism, going so far as to include only the travel poster type in discussions of symbols. There are similarities between the two. Both examples suggest that touristic symbolism does not involve a simple cutting off of a part to represent the whole. Care is exercised in the matter of what part of the whole is selected, the choice being limited to sights that are well-marked in their own right: Fisherman's Wharf, San Francisco, American cowboys.

One result of the analysis of sights and markers clarifies the structure of touristic *symbolism*. A touristic symbol is a conventionalized sight → marker → sight transformation. Thus, the Empire State Building is a sight which serves as a symbolic marker for the sightseer's Manhattan. Or, the Statue of Liberty is a sight which serves as a symbolic marker for the United States. Under conditions where the symbolization occurs at the sight, as for example, in Paris at the Eiffel Tower, where the tourist partakes of something of the city by taking in the Tower, the transformation can be diagrammed as follows:

MENTAL IMAGE

$$\text{Sight} \quad \rightarrow \quad [\text{Marker} \quad \rightarrow \quad \text{Sight}]$$

or

$$\begin{matrix}\text{Actual} \\ \text{Eiffel} \\ \text{Tower}\end{matrix} \quad \rightarrow \quad [\text{Symbolizes} \quad \rightarrow \quad \text{Paris}]$$

When the Eiffel Tower is used as a symbol of Paris on a travel poster or the cover of a Paris guidebook, the transformation is diagrammed:

PICTORIAL IMAGE

$$[\text{Sight} \quad \rightarrow \quad \text{Marker}] \quad \rightarrow \quad \text{Sight}$$

or

$$\begin{bmatrix}\text{Actual} & \rightarrow & \text{Symbol of} \\ \text{Tower} & & \text{Tower}\end{bmatrix} \quad \rightarrow \quad \text{Paris}$$

In the first transformation the symbolic marker is a mental image (someone might call it an "idea" or "feeling" of Paris) while in the second it is a physical image or picture of the Eiffel Tower representing Paris. Again, it is necessary to note that in the structural analysis of touristic information, some common sense distinctions between "subjective" and "objective" are neither "natural" nor helpful.

After all the marker → sight transformations, the point is that tourist attractions are plastic forms: the eventual shape and stability they have is, like signs, socially determined. It is social determination that makes the attractions, the structural differentiations of society, appear as *things* to consciousness. And society, not the individual, divides reality into what is to be taken as a *sight* and what is to be taken as *information* about a sight. Through the institutionalization of attractions, material that is capable of being either subjective or objective is made to appear as only one or the other.

*Negations:* A simple illustration of the social base of the relationship of sights and markers is provided by a class of markers designed to discredit their sights. The American tourists' commonplace that the canals of Venice smell of sewage is a negative marker which could presumably be analyzed by way of a series of references to the Anglo-American "olfactory code" which organizes our collective concerns about armpits and canals. A rare, complete presentation of a negative marker and its socially encoded link with its sights is provided by an advertisement which read, in part: "THE EIFFEL TOWER HAS RUSTY BOLTS." The link between the famous tower and this particular piece of information about it is alive with implications. The tower is presented as old and rundown and, perhaps, dangerous.

$$\text{SIGHT} \quad [\text{Eiffel Tower}] \quad \text{MARKER} \quad \begin{bmatrix} \text{Has rusty} \\ \text{bolts} \end{bmatrix}$$

This advertisement was made for a 1968 United States Government campaign to keep tourists home. The rest of the advertisement read: "SEE AMERICA FIRST."

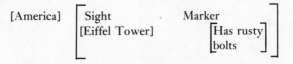

$$\text{SIGHT} \qquad\qquad \text{MARKER}$$
$$[\text{America}] \begin{bmatrix} \text{Sight} & \text{Marker} \\ [\text{Eiffel Tower}] & \begin{bmatrix} \text{Has rusty} \\ \text{bolts} \end{bmatrix} \end{bmatrix}$$

The original sight-marker relationship marks "America" by negating her touristic rival. The method is not very efficient because it depends on the patriotic residues that may be left in American society: [See] *America First.*

# 7

# The Ethnomethodology
# of Sightseers

Information that has a limited audience is bound by formal considerations. Scientific information appears in scholarly monographs; political information in speeches, pamphlets, editorials and wall posters; commercial information in advertisements and catalogues; news in reports. Each special informational format presupposes a set of methods and has its own version of reliability, validity and completeness. Becoming a scientist or a politician means, in part, learning and adhering to, even "believing in," the standards and techniques of one's profession. The process of becoming a tourist is similar except that the methods followed by tourists have not been made partially explicit to the point where they can be taught in college courses as is the case for professions properly so called.

Touristic information is found in guidebooks and travel writings, but it is more thoroughly diffused throughout the modern world than is the case for some other types of information, and the taken-for-granted reality which it presupposes and supports is also much more general. An ethnomethodology of sightseers would explore the touristic consciousness of otherness, and the ways tourists negotiate the labyrinth of modernity. In this chapter I want to present some observations I have made of an interesting but limited aspect of the ethnomethodology of sightseeing: on the authentication of experience or the accomplishment of touristic certainty.

In order to keep the following observations in perspective, it is necessary to recall that they fit into the structure discussed in the previous chapter. The ideas we have about the things we see are already organized before we see them in terms of the sight-marker relationship. The structure of modernity is composed of a system of linkages attaching specific bits of information to concrete representations of society and social relations. Each individual act of sightseeing must replicate one of these linkages more or less exactly, or modernity will eventually decompose. A close examination of the act of sightseeing does reveal the individual making his own sight-marker linkages and constructing (or reconstructing) his own part of the modern world. As is always the case when it comes to social behavior, the energy that is devoted to the task, and the accuracy of the results, varies from individual to individual—structure is a collective accomplishment.

## "WHEN I ACTUALLY SAW IT FOR THE FIRST TIME"

Sightseeing is most usually done in a small group of intimates such as family members. This small group is often embedded in a larger group of tour mates not previously acquainted. The sightseeing task may be made routine and unproblematical by on-sight markers and a good guide, but even when it is highly streamlined, tour intimates are expected to say something to one another when they arrive in the presence of the attraction. Minimally, they might say "Gee, that's really something." In other words, the act of sightseeing culminates in the tourist linking to the sight a marker of his very own. In so doing, he is supposed to indicate whether or not the sight has lived up to his expectations. If the tourist is also a guide, as when someone takes out-of-town relatives around to show them the sights, the marker he provides at these moments is supposed to make the sight interesting so the others have a memorable experience.

In the last moments of the sightseeing act, there is a little flurry of activity during which markers are passed back and forth, added and subtracted, and eventually organized in a final composition relating several markers, the tourist and the sight. There are some standardized arrangements for these compositions. For example, the individual may represent his perception of the actual sight as a marker superior to the others and say to himself or a friend "It's more beautiful than I had imagined." This formula can also be inverted, of course.

Interestingly, just seeing a sight is not a touristic experience. I know a lady who lived at the foot of a famous mountain in Northern California, who saw it every day for three years, and who was perfectly aware of the name of the mountain and its fame, but who did not know that "her" mountain was "that" mountain. An authentic touristic experience involves not merely connecting a marker to a sight, but a participation in a collective ritual, in connecting one's own marker to a sight already marked by others.

## "TRUTH" MARKERS

The movement from marker to marker that ends with the tourist's being in the presence of the sight is not a simple adding up of information. Any new piece of information may contradict the others while claiming for itself the status of the truth. This also happens on an interpersonal level in areas of social life policed by gossip, innuendo and slander. But the social organization of the truth is not exactly the same on this interpersonal level as it is in the realm of tourism. When the method detaches itself from interpersonal relations, it becomes far more difficult to check out competing claims for the truth, and far less important to do so as the difference between truth and nontruth becomes inconsequential. The following item from a Paris guide may serve as illustration:

> In olden days the site now occupied by the Louvre was covered by a forest swarming with wolves. In order to lessen the number of these savage beasts a hunting-lodge was built in the forest, and was called the Louverie, hence the name Louvre. This is the romantic derivation of the word, but the more probable though prosaic derivation is from the Saxon *leowar* or *lower*, meaning fortified camp.[1]

In this passage, which is by no means unique and is, in fact, characteristic of the rhetoric of tourism, *leowar* and *lower* are serving as truth markers.

Truth markers function to cement the bond of tourist and attraction by elevating the information possessed by the tourist to privileged status. A human guide at Independence Hall in Philadelphia explains:

> It is commonly believed that the Liberty Bell cracked because it was rung too hard celebrating American Independence.
>
> Actually [this is the truth marker] the Bell was not manufactured properly at the factory where it was made in England.

Truth markers are not markers of a distinctive type. Any type of marker can serve as a truth marker: those provided by the guide, those provided by the tourist, on-sight markers, off-sight markers. Truth markers are produced in touristic discourse out of simple opposition to other markers. On-sight markers usually have more authority than off-sight markers but this is not always the case. In the following transcript of part of a taped conversation between two university professors discussing a sightseeing trip they had taken together a few months earlier, the second professor opposes an off-sight marker to an on-sight marker (a picture that was taken to the pointer on the telescope at the sight) in order to arrive at the truth:

> *First Professor:* (handing over a photograph) Here is the picture I took of Alcatraz from that tower while you were trying to park the car.
> *Second Professor:* That's not Alcatraz. It's Treasure Island or something.
> *First Professor:* Huh. (pause) I checked the pointer on the telescope.
> *Second Professor:* Well it's not Alcatraz. It's another island. Alcatraz is little. This is too big.
> *First Professor:* Really?

A mechanical engineer provides a similar example from a trip he took to Grand Coulee Dam in the early 1950's.[2]

> A guide pointed at these big pipes going over the mountain and said that the electricity generated by the dam was conducted through these pipes.
>
> I just couldn't believe that. That's not a known means of conducting electricity.

On a train in France an American girl asks her American tour guide (a "know-it-all" type) how, when she arrives in Paris, she can find the Sorbonne. The guide replies:

> Don't bother. Everyone thinks it's the University but the Sorbonne itself is just a dormitory. There is no real university in Paris. It's scattered all over.

It is clear from the examples that a touristic truth marker need not have any truth value from a scientific or a historical perspective. Truth emerges from a system of binary oppositions to information that is designated as nontruth. In the original illustration *leowar* (meaning a fortified camp) was opposed to Louverie (wolf lodge) as the true derivation of the name Louvre. Consider the possibilities. A truth marker can be made by opposing good information to bad (*leowar* is correct and Louverie is incorrect just as the guide says); by opposing bad information to bad information (*leowar* and Louverie are *both* incorrect); and by opposing bad information to good information (Louverie was correct all along and it is *leowar* that is incorrect).

Some of these oppositions can be resolved to the satisfaction of the tourists in the act of sightseeing itself, in their own final organization of information and experience. Gross misrepresentation is subject to ongoing collective correction. The results of this activity are not to be denied. I have already indicated that I believe the consensus about the structure of the modern world achieved through tourism and mass leisure is the strongest and broadest consensus known to history. Nevertheless, it is also worthwhile to examine the workings of this consensus. Its strength seems to be based on the same principle as its weakness: by refusing to distinguish between truth and nontruth, the modern consciousness can expand freely, unfettered by formal considerations. At the same time, it is necessarily undermined by an agonizing doubt.

Even the most careful efforts to arrive at the truth within the context of touristic experience can have quite the opposite results. In the following example, all the scientific virtues of logic, empirical observation, contrast and comparison are applied, each operation carrying the tourists further from the truth while increasing their certainty that they are getting closer to it. Two English-speaking young ladies in an art gallery in Zürich examine a painting by an Italian artist named Pio Piso. They have several pieces of information about the painting, but nothing written in a language they understand perfectly.

> *First Young Lady:* This is an interesting painting for an "op" artist.
> *Second Young Lady:* I wonder what his name is. We should write it down.
> *First Young Lady:* At the top of the gallery guide it says "Pio Piso."
> *Second Young Lady:* That can't be his name. It means "first floor" in Italian. That's just a part of this gallery's address because it's located on the first floor.

The artist's name was Pio Piso, but the Second Young Lady has used some linguistic sophistication to transform it into the gallery's address:

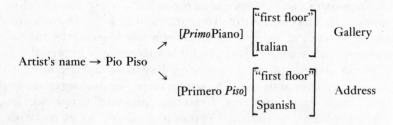

Having eliminated the artist's name as a possible candidate to be the artist's name, the young ladies press their search, examining new information. The conversation continues:

> *First Young Lady:* It says "Öl auf Leinwand" on the plaque here.
> *Second Young Lady:* That must be his name. It's by Öl auf Leinwand. It sounds Scandinavian. And here's another by him only in a different style.

The young ladies went on to find many other paintings "by" Öl auf Leinwand (which means "oil on cloth" in German), so many others, in fact, that they began to doubt their original procedures.[3]

The version of the "truth" contained in these examples, the basis of touristic certainty, is adapted to a type of society in which social relationships are arbitrary, fleeting and weightless, in which growth and development takes the form of an interplay of differentiations.

Within this manifold, the individual is liberated to assemble and destroy realities by manipulating sociocultural elements according to the free play of his imagination. This is the worst feature of modernity and, at the same time, the grounds of our greatest hope: perhaps we can individually or collectively put together the "right combination" of elements and make it through to a better world or a higher stage of civilization.

## THE CONSTRUCTION OF SOCIAL REALITY

Today, everywhere on the face of the earth, there are patches of social reality growing out of the collective experiences of tourists. The original macrodifferentiations of the tourist world were labeled by outsiders—The Wild West, The Dark Continent, The Mysterious East—but with the growth of modern mass tourism, the imagery has become more complex and comprehensive, and there is a systematic effort to bring the consciousness of the insider into alignment with that of the outsider:

> Ottawa, Nov. 4—An official report complained today that Canada's swinging modern character was being obscured at home and abroad because too many people still think of her as the land of the Mounties and "Rose Marie." . . . "For a great many years," [the authors of] the report said, "Canadian Government information officers in other countries have been working to correct the cliché image of Canada that is both irritating to Canadians and hardy as a weed. This is the Canada of Rose Marie and Maria Chapdelaine, the land of ice and snow, Mounties, Eskimos and not much else.
>
> "Somehow, however, the International Service of the C.B.C., a public corporation, failed to get the message. It put on a special winter centennial schedule of programs and distributed it to countries around the world. The program included illustrations of the Parliament buildings in midwinter; prairie wheat fields; a hockey game; the Fathers of the Confederation; a winter landscape; the musical ride of the Royal Canadian Mounted Police and a Canadian Indian in ceremonial dress. So much for the swinging new Canada. Nelson Eddy lives, and be sure to bring your skis."[4]

The Canadian officials may not be able to get rid of Rose Marie, but they can probably banish her to a small town in Manitoba as they build up a more "swinging" image. It is here in the organization and reorganization of touristic experience that modern culture and consciousness are being assembled and their direction established.

The kind of mentality manifest in the Canadian case contrasts sharply with the mind of industrial man. Our industrial forebears seemed to struggle endlessly with the problem of their identity. They elaborated theories to account for their own motives as being hidden deep in mysterious religious and sexual impulses. The modern consciousness builds images and remodels them to suit its changing moods, creating new religions, making a recreation out of sex and rewriting history to make it accord with new reality. It is also making a routine out of the controversy and conflict accompanying the process:

> The Pilgrims who embarked for the New World . . . would be startled to see what a monumental beanfest the anniversary of their sailing is going to be. Not that Plymouth hasn't always made the Pilgrims and the Mayflower the subjects of a busy local industry, as the windows of every olde gift shoppe and the souvenir ashtrays testify. So do the signboards—like Mayflower Hair Stylists, Mayflower Sandwich Bar and Restaurant, Mayflower Insurance Brokers, even Mayflower TV Rentals. . . . The plans for the anniversary hit some early squalls. Other English places with stakes in the Pilgrim Fathers industry accused Plymouth of cashing in, hogging the limelight and even of twisting historical facts a little in the interest of publicity. The Mayor of Southhampton, Mrs. Kathie Johnson, indignantly accused the Lord Mayor of Plymouth of "filching our history."[5]

Just as the individual tourist is free to make his own final arrangements of sights and markers, the modernizing areas of the world are also free to assemble their own images in advance of the arrival of the tourists. The most extreme case of arbitrary touristic imagery I have found, a controversial travel poster advertising an English resort, was reported in the *International Herald Tribune*. Under a picture of a pretty girl, gesturing as if to protect her eyes from blinding sun, is this explanation:

> Where did you say?—This poster of a sun-tanned girl (American), standing on the Beach (Tunisian), shot by a photographer (German) and bought from an agency (Italian) is designed to attract tourists to the seaside resort of Exmouth, on the Devonshire coast (English).[6]

The underlying structure of touristic imagery is absolutely plastic, so its eventual form is a perfect representation of the collective conscience, including those aspects of the collective conscience which strive for clarity, precision and accuracy. The people of the area advertised by the poster have the opposite kind of problem from that of the mayor of Southhampton: they were awarded some history that was not theirs and which they apparently did not want. Perceiving that a great deal had been made from misinformation, these people became concerned. Sixteen months after the *Herald Tribune* report, the following item appeared in the *New York Times* under the headline "Girl and Sea in Poster Called Alien to Resort."

> Deal, England (Reuters)—Billboards advertising in this Southeast England coastal resort show a lovely gray-eyed blonde against a beautiful blue ocean backdrop. Local residents are campaigning to get the poster changed on the ground that it is inaccurate. They say that the girl on the poster never set foot in Deal, and the picture of the blue ocean was taken in Greece.[7]

The local people at the resort have begun to set the record straight. The same process by which touristic reality is constructed can be used to dismantle reality. Now all that remains to be discovered is whether the picture was taken in Greece or Tunisia, whether the resort it advertises is Exmouth or Deal, and/or whether the two news items are even related to the same incident.

In stressing the plasticity of the touristic image and the freedom which we enjoy in the construction of touristic reality, I do not want to suggest that this freedom is always used. Modernization, even before it begins, runs up against traditional concerns and constraints. When justifiable national pride intervenes, for example, there may be much concern that the eventual form of the touristic representation be *accurate*. And accuracy *is* one of the many possible forms that touristic imagery can take. It is nicely manifest in national museums and in historical reconstructions. My point in examining extreme deviations from accurate representation was only to explore the possibilities inherent in the form: not to malign or undermine concerns for accuracy, only to show what they are up against, and to explicate the pure potentiality of modern cultural expression as we seem to be trying to turn ourselves into an enormous work of art.

# 8

# Structure, Genuine
# and Spurious

THE model of modern culture presented in the last several chapters was designed to explicate its most salient and mysterious qualities: the ability to change and transform itself endlessly found in a seemingly paradoxical combination with its great strength, power and presence. I have found the solidarity of modernity to be grounded in objective relations, in history and in social facts. But unique to the modern world is its capacity to transform material relations into symbolic expressions and back again, while continuing to differentiate or multiply structures. The expansion of alternative realities makes the *dialectics of authenticity* the key to the development of the modern world. The question of authenticity transcends and subsumes the old divisions of man vs. society, normal vs. deviant, worker vs. owner. The field of criminology and the sociology of deviance are now in the process of radical reformulation as they attempt to adapt themselves to modern reality. Predictably, they are confused as to what constitutes a "real" deviant as modern society races ahead of existing theories, decriminalizing social differences, turning the differences between the normal and the deviant into mere differentiations, into dramatic as opposed to legal categories. The field of social psychology which once made something of an absolute out of the division between the individual and the group is abandoning this for the more complex realm of the ethnography of everyday life, discourse analysis and the sociology of face-to-face interaction. Here also the question of authenticity, in this case the question of the authenticity of the self, has subsumed the old differentiation of man from society. Social class

145

distinctions are blurred by the universal quest for authentic experience. In sightseeing, all men are equal before the sight. The Emperor of Japan visited the statue of the Little Mermaid in the harbor at Copenhagen, Henry Kissinger visited the Great Wall, Pope Paul visited the Wailing Wall, Jackie Kennedy Onassis visited just about everything.

Interestingly, the subfield of sociology which is reputed to be the most radical—culture criticism—has adapted the least to the evolution of modernity. With the possible exception of the work of Theodor W. Adorno, culture criticism remains traditionally social-psychological. That is, current culture criticism of both Freudian and Marxist types, the work of Marcuse, Habermas, Slater, Brown, Laing and others, is based on a man vs. society division. The formula for work of this sort is that society, civilization or culture have an adverse effect on the individual: his labor is exploited or his sexuality repressed.

The findings of culture criticism include: modern society is too complicated, competitive, rat racy, dog-eat-dog, racist, exploitative, slick, superficial and corrupt. Accomplishment reduces to status-seeking or ego-tripping. Individuals who aspire to, and reach, responsible positions are power mad and probably impotent. Behind the calm and seemingly concerned face of the political leader lurks anxious and brutal indifference. Official images are unbelievable. Non-ordinary reality, hallucination, is to be preferred over unmodified experience which has itself become artificial, pseudo, illusory. The individual is powerless and his life is meaningless. Creativity is sublimated to sheer production, and insecurity and other-directedness are necessary for success. The sciences pretend to be objective in their research for truth but they are, at best, amoral and often a vicious political program is hiding beneath their cool pronouncements. Right, Left and Center rapidly degenerate into mere ideological justifications for attacking, often killing, "extremists." Interpersonal relationships are temporary, authoritarian and restrictive. And the individual seems to enjoy all this, to revel in his own alienation.

In this chapter, I want to suggest that this social-psychological version of modernity and its discontents is now in the process of being absorbed into the dialectics of authenticity. Current intellectual criticism of modernity is based on the assumption of the ultimate perfectibility of society, after an as yet unattained authentic ideal. This ideal is not the invention of culture critics and other intellectuals. It is the inevitable product of modernization or differentiation. Culture critics have only given it expression in the outmoded social psychological language of the industrial age. The intellectual critique of society assumes the inauthenticity of everyday life in the modern world. It is based on a concern about the structure of social reality which goes beyond the openly stated concerns for alienation and sublimation. In the next section I begin the exploration of the structural grounds of the inauthentic in modern society, which is also, I think, an exploration of the implicit assumptions of some current culture criticism.

## SPURIOUS STRUCTURE

The spurious side of the social structure of modernity is composed out of the information, memories, images and other representations which become detached from genuine cultural elements, from the "true" sights, and are circulated and accumulated in everyday life. This is no longer a simple matter of an occasional souvenir ashtray or the little bars of soap from The Motel that are stored away with the pressed and dried wildflower. It is now possible to build an entire life out of these and other spurious elements. Amateur photography permits the tourist to create his own touristic imagery with himself and his family at the center, or just off to the side of the great sight or moment.

Bits of touristic information such as subway tokens saved from the Senior Trip to the Big City are sometimes cherished as souvenirs alongside other tokens of heightened moments: a snapshot of the first girl who "went all the way," a trophy for placing in a swimming race, ticket stubs from a rock concert, the shift lever handle from a first automobile, wine bottles, baby booties. Touristic souvenirs are found in every corner of daily life and embedded in every system of information. For example, a steamer trunk or an urbane monologue in a conversation well-plastered with names of famous places is also operative in the system of *status signs* that so interests sociologists. *Marks of group affiliation* such as political campaign buttons and the facial scars of German university students are sometimes taken over as souvenirs.

An anthropologist friend of mine brought me some Red Guard lapel buttons from the Great Proletarian Cultural Revolution. *Identity badges* such as those used at the conventions of professional groups also appear in touristic contexts and are later saved as souvenirs. American students hitchhiking in Europe during their country's unpopular involvement in Vietnam sometimes carried a large sign written in several languages reading "CANADIAN STUDENT." Apt to become most intermixed with touristic information are *mementos of rites of passage* such as wedding and birth announcements, which are often stored in the same box or pinned on the same bulletin board with steamship ticket receipts and matchbooks picked up at famous sights. Heightened moments of an individual's life and social reality are combined in this way in a single representation resembling a collage. Middle-class Anglo-Americans tend to think of trips made by girl scout troups and college study abroad programs as rites of passage. It is a common practice of young ladies who avail themselves of their college's Junior Year Abroad program to refer irreverently to the experience as their "Junior Affair Abroad."

Everywhere in the minutiae of our material culture, we encounter reminders of the availability of authentic experiences at other times and in other places. Pictures of important sights, moments and men appear on ashtrays depicting the Leaning Tower of Pisa, the Capitol, the face of Richard Nixon. Names and labels appear on pencils stamped "Disneyland," "Property of the State Department" and the like. Picture postcards circulate throughout the world tying tourists together in networks and linking the tourist to the attraction and to his friends at home. Pictures and descriptions of sights are also found on the covers of matchbooks distributed by commercialized attractions such as Coney Island, and by commercial establishments operating under the nimbus of noncommercial sights: the Mount Rushmore Cafe, for example, or the Plymouth Rock Restaurant. In addition to matchbooks, postcards, pencils and ashtrays that carry the name and/or the picture of a sight, there are the less common items such as touristic dish towels and dust cloths overprinted with drawings of Betsy Ross' House or Abraham Lincoln's Birthplace. These are not intended to serve their original purposes, but are fixed instead so they can be hung on kitchen walls. There is also a special type of square pillow covered with a white silklike cloth, fringed in gold braid, that is made to serve as the canvas for little paintings of sights like Niagara Falls. These latter items are spurious elements that have come out of the closet, occupying visible places in the domestic environment. Similarly, school lunch pails, pencil boxes and notebooks sometimes carry in addition to such items as Western cattle brands, images of steamer-trunk stickers bearing the strange sounding names of far-away places. Popular songs are also a source of touristic imagery but they will not be discussed here because of the expense involved in securing permission to quote from them.

In addition to dressing up one's home with sight markers, it is also possible to dress up one's children, at little expense, in sweatshirts labeled "MARINELAND," "GRAND CANYON," "EXPO '70" and the like. I once saw a young lady in Paris wearing an English-language sweat-shirt that marked her off as something of an attraction in her own right: printed across the front was "My Name is Karen and I'm Horny." Even serious ladies' blouses are decorated with the names and images of attractions: the Egyptian pyramids, Big Ben, "ASPEN," "MIAMI BEACH" and the oversized signatures of famous designers.

Pictures of sights appear on calendars, kitchen aprons, ladies' blouses, water pitchers, men's ties, playing cards and other pieces of specialized domestic equipment. Recently, banks in urban areas in the United States have made available to their customers, in addition to brilliantly colored checks and checks with peace symbols, checks with pictures of local tourist attractions. Souvenirs are not restricted to two-dimensional imagery. There are also reduced, three-dimensional models of specific sights such as the gold and silver-colored miniature Eiffel Towers sold at concessions near the Tower and carried to all parts of the world by the individuals who buy them there. A resourceful student of mine made a living room lamp out of one of these little Eiffel Towers. There are ready made "Piggy" banks in the form of the Statue of Liberty, perfume bottles shaped like the Eiffel Tower and thermometers attached to models of the Washington Monument. Models of the United States Capitol Building are found in clear glass globes filled with an oily liquid and some white particulate matter which when agitated is alleged to simulate a snowstorm. Tiny copies of the Liberty Bell appear as decorative additions to adult wearing apparel on tie clips, earrings, bracelets, belt buckles, stick pins, watchfobs and money clips.

Blown-glass gondola effigies are generally accepted as representations of Venice. A certain type of shirt and a certain type of pants do not carry the name or the picture of the islands they represent, but they are known, nevertheless, as Hawaiian shirts and Bermuda shorts. Some young men on the West coast of the United States wear jackets of bright red, orange or yellow silk with a multicolored dragon and the word "Japan" embroidered on the back, the lettering of the word "Japan" simulating the brush strokes of Oriental characters. I think both Durkheim and the Australian peoples he studied would be astounded by the lengths to which we have carried our "totemic" symbolism. If it is argued that we do not hold our symbolism in the same respect and awe that an Australian holds his, my answer is: try to insult someone's Japan Jacket, or question his taste in wearing Bermuda shorts and Hawaiian shirts, or in decorating his homes with touristic heraldry. If questioned to his face along these lines, a person will behave as if his entire being has been thrown into the balance.

The same structures penetrate to a subtler level. At a "Tradin' Post" in the Rocky Mountains, a young lady explained to me that she was buying a cut and polished rock to send to her father in New York. Her gesture has the quality of a pun about it, and like all puns, it requires a certain understanding: the memory of the daughter's trip west, the association of rock and "Rocky." It is this understanding that makes of the rock a good gift for someone who might spurn a kewpie doll carrying a flag reading "Souvenir of Yellowstone", which was available in the same establishment. The kewpie doll requires less understanding from its recipient, while getting the same touristic message across as, for example, a bolt of Liberty Print paisley from London, a Swiss music box, an Australian boomerang, or a black-enameled gold necklace from Spain. These latter items, to serve as souvenirs, require that their receiver possess the knowledge that makes the connection between the object and its referent. In order to acquire this knowledge, it is necessary to cultivate what is called "taste." "Good taste" can generate entire environments: French Provincial, Early American, Danish Modern.

There are savants who can identify at a glance a suit of men's clothing as having been made and sold on Regent Street in London. This skill makes a souvenir of a sober suit just as the embroiderer of a Japan Jacket makes a most unsober suit into a souvenir. Of course,

Regent Street is not much of an attraction, but then neither is the skill required to turn one of its suits into a marker very common.


## MACROSTRUCTURAL SPURIOUSNESS

Spurious society is built up in this way on a domestic or microstructural level. Spuriousness drives everyone out of domestic and ethnic niches and minds into the modern world in search for a real experience: the Big Time. The individual then returns to a quotidian existence which is an increasingly complex elaboration of images of reality elsewhere, or an increasingly compelling reason to leave again to search for authenticity.

This was André Gide's point in his *Return of the Prodigal Son*, which ends in a conversation between the returned prodigal and his younger brother, who is about to leave to experience the world away from the domestic estate.

> *Younger Brother:* When you left home, did you feel you were doing wrong?
>
> *Prodigal Son:* No. I felt in myself something like an obligation to depart.
>
> *Younger Brother:* My brother! I am the same as you were when you left. Oh! say: did you not find anything disappointing along your route? All that I have a premonition of what is outside, of what is different from here, is it then only a mirage? All this anticipation I feel, is it only madness? . . . Why did you give up and return? Did you tire out?
>
> *Prodigal Son:* No. Not yet. But I doubted.
>
> *Younger Brother:* What do you mean?
>
> *Prodigal Son:* Doubted everything, myself; I wanted to stop, attach myself somewhere. . . . I feel it now: I faltered.

The Prodigal has difficulty expressing why he left home and why he returned. The conversation ends:

> *Younger Brother:* The wild pomegranate is of a bitterness almost disgusting; I feel, nevertheless, that if I were thirsty enough, I would bite into it.
>
> *Prodigal Son:* OK! Now I can tell you: it is *this thirst* in the desert I sought.

*Younger Brother:* A thirst that only this unsweetened fruit can quench—

*Prodigal Son:* Not exactly; but I learned to love the thirst.

*Younger Brother:* Do you know where to pick this fruit?

*Prodigal Son:* It is in a little abandoned orchard that one can reach before evening. No wall separates it from the desert any longer. A stream used to flow there; a few half-ripe fruits used to hang from its branches.

*Younger Brother:* What kind of fruits?

*Prodigal Son:* The same as in our garden, but wild.[1]

Today, Gide might have written: "the same as in our garden, but authentic."

If the individual does not bring home images of reality elsewhere, modern television programming will supply a bland, generalized stream of such imagery. But the dividing line between structure genuine and spurious in modern society is not the same as the line that divides micro- from macrostructure; that is, domestic life from the life of the entire society, or the image on the television set from the "reality" pictured there. It is possible for the individual to leave his everyday world in search of authentic experience only to find himself surrounded once again by spurious elements such as would occur, for example, in a trip to Disney World. Entire touristic communities and regions are now built up from spurious elements. The news that is transmitted worldwide is sometimes organized around touristic symbolism. There is a simple formula for this: "Here in the shadow of the Eiffel Tower, the peace talks began today in an atmosphere of . . ." Even the President of the United States lards his speeches with references to the Statue of Liberty, the Great Beauty of the Land, the Spirit of the People, etc. Even in the "ivory towers" of social science, the selection of topics for study, crime, the environment, the community, is based on the same underlying structure which generates other forms of touristic curiosity. The dialectics of authenticity lead to a progressive development of spurious structure, ever further removed from domestic life, as modern man is driven ever further in his quest for authentic values and his true self.

Modern technology makes possible the reduction of monumental attractions to the status of mere souvenirs, so the individual can feel that no matter how hard he tries to overcome it, he remains trapped in a spurious world:

NEW TOURIST TOWN BUYS HISTORIC SPAN

> Phoenix, Ariz., April 17 (Reuters)—London Bridge will be shipped to the United States later this year and re-erected at a resort town in southern Arizona. . . . The bridge, opened across the river Thames by King William the IV in 1831, is destined for Lake Havasu City, a community that does not appear on most maps. Millions of dollars are being spent on creating the resort town out of virgin desert along the banks of the Colorado River near Yuma, Ariz. . . . Frederick Schumacher, director of Lake Havasu City Development . . . said the bridge would be a top tourist attraction. . . . The bridge will be replaced in London by a modern, wider structure.[2]

Similar arrangements have brought a British church to Fulton, Missouri, where it now serves as a monument to Sir Winston Churchill, and the *Queen Mary* to Long Beach, where it has been converted into a kind of museum.

Absolutely spurious attractions are those like the "Matterhorn" at Disneyland and the "Belgian Village" at the recent New York World's Fair, built from scratch to be tourist attractions. A similar device is being proposed in Greece:

> Rhodes, Greece—Opinions on this verdant, 545-square-mile island 12 miles off the coast of Turkey are divided over whether or not to build a modern-day colossus, one that might resemble the great Colossus of Rhodes of antiquity that stood for 56 years as one of the Seven Wonders of the Ancient World. Those residents who favor the proposal to erect the statue admit frankly that their primary concern is to attract tourists, a matter that is of considerable importance to the economy of the island.[3]

Although unsuccessful, a most imaginative plan along these lines is the following one to build an entire spurious nation from scratch:

> A federal court has scuttled plans by two rival corporations to start a small but tax-free realm on two coral reefs eight miles offshore in the Atlantic near Miami. Louis M. Ray and Acme General Contractors, Inc., would have called their holiday resort "The Grand Capri Repub-

lic" and the Atlantic Development Corp. was going to use the name "Atlantis, Isle of Gold" for its projected independent country. The 5th U.S. Circuit Court of Appeals ruled yesterday that Triumph Reef and Long Reef are part of the continental shelf and subject to U.S. jurisdiction. Ray and Acme had spent $100,000 to build up the reefs in 1964 but Hurricane Betsy demolished the piled up sand and the reefs were once again under water.[4]

A spurious society is one that must be left behind in order to see a true sight. From the standpoint of the tourist, his own everyday life in the modern world is spurious—it begins to take on some of the negative attributes culture critics have claimed for it. And even the "high life" can take on a spurious quality if it is built out of borrowed and artificially constructed attractions. There is nothing better calculated to make an individual feel "out of place" than having his everyday life and his heightened experiences constructed from these spurious elements. The alienation of modern man, the work of making him feel that he does not belong, is accompanied by the double movement of the individual into new and foreign situations, and by moving attractions out of their original cultural contexts. Only the first kind of movement is ordinarily called "tourism", but the second qualifies equally as such from the standpoint of this perspective. Often, both the tourist and the attraction are "out of place," as would have occurred, for example, had Nikita Khrushchev been permitted to see the sights at Disneyland as he is reported to have requested on his first visit to the U.S.A. The construction, exchange and movement of attractions is a perfect index of modernization. It had its small beginnings at the dawn of civilization and cumulates progressively through history to the present time in national-level gift exchange, cultural borrowing, looting and purchase. The oldest civilization in the Western World has distributed obelisks by all these means. The Egyptian obelisk standing in Central Park in New York City came here as an alien, just as the tourist who glances up at it in a moment of silent identification is also an alien.

The displacement of the genuine attraction and authentic values out of everyday life is redoubled when details of other epochs and other cultures are borrowed, intermixed and expanded to become the immediate reality of modern man. Drive-in restaurants, gasoline stations and suburban housing developments are decorated after the fashion of little Dutch towns, Texas ranches, Aztec temples and the like. For two hundred thousand dollars, one can buy an "authentic" French country home on Philadelphia's Main Line. The modern world institutionalizes spuriousness in the values and material culture of entire wide areas of society. Puritans, liberals and snobs call it "tacky" when anyone can afford it and "pretentious" when it is dear. Pretension and tackiness generate the belief that somewhere, only not right here, not right now, perhaps just over there someplace, in another country, in another life-style, in another social class, perhaps, there is *genuine* society.[5] The United States makes the rest of the world seem authentic; California makes the rest of the United States seem authentic. The dialectic of authenticity is at the heart of the development of all modern social structure. It is manifest in concerns for ecology and front, in attacks on what is phony, pseudo, tacky, in bad taste, mere show, tawdry and gaudy. These concerns conserve a solidarity at the level of the total society, a collective agreement that reality and truth exist somewhere in society, and that we ought to be trying to find them and refine them.

# GENUINE STRUCTURE

Genuine structure is composed of the values and material culture manifest in the "true" sights. These true sights, real French country homes, actual Dutch towns, the Temple of the Moon at Teotihuacan, the Swiss Alps, are also the source of the spurious elements which are detached from and are mere copies or reminders of the genuine. The dividing line between structure genuine and spurious is the *realm of the commercial*. Spurious social relations and structural elements can be bought, sold, traded and distributed throughout the world. Modern economies are increasingly based on this exchange. The line is the same as the one between furniture and priceless antiques or between prostitution and "true" love which is supposed to be beyond price. It is also the same as the distinction that is commonly made between a gift that has been purchased, which is thought to be inferior, as opposed to one that has been made by the giver especially for the receiver. Marcel Mauss was the first to point out the moral impoverishment that is the result of the commercialization of exchange, but he was not sufficiently attentive to noncommercial exchanges in the modern world, and he was led to the conclusion that modernity is falling apart.[6] It is not possible simply to buy the right to see a true sight. The Golden Gate Bridge, the United States Capitol building and all the other genuine attractions must always appear as if they would continue to exist without the help of sightseers. No matter how much he might have desired to do so, Richard Nixon could not charge sightseers for the right to tour the White House.

At Disneyland and other such places where the tourist is made to pay for what he sees, the sight always seems to be faked up and "promoted." Often this is the case in fact:

> Lake Buena Vista, Fla., (NYT).—Out of the muck and matted tangle of cypress and palmetto trees, the stately spires of Cinderella's castle spring into the Florida sky, waiting to welcome a story-book princess and 10 million visitors a year. Walt Disney World, a monument in gingerbread to the creator of Mickey Mouse and a clutch of other childhood favorites, is taking shape in the interior of Florida, 16 miles southwest of Orlando. After eight years of planning, construction is under way in the biggest non-government project in the world. . . . The success of the Disney World will depend, however, on several factors apart from the public enthusiasm already set in motion by the popularity of its counterpart outside Los Angeles, Disneyland. A main one will be the health of the national economy. . . . A continuing sluggish economy could effectively shut it off from its customers if Americans are forced to curtail holiday travel. . . . But happy endings are a Disney trademark and backers of the $300 million development, scheduled for opening in October, are confident that the investment will be hugely profitable for the parent company, Walt Disney Productions and the state. Roy Disney, the 77-year-old board chairman of Walt Disney Productions, estimated in an interview here last week that the 37,500 acres of land purchased five years ago as the site for Disney World would now have a market value of $1 billion.[7]

Commercialization is pressing in on sightseeing from all sides. Still, at the heart of the act, the final contact between the tourist and a true attraction, such as the White House or the Grand Canyon, can be pure. The tourist pays for travel, food, hotels, motels, campground spaces, camping equipment, cameras, film, film processing, recreational vehicles, souvenirs, maps, guides, wash-and-wear clothing, packaged tours, traveler's checks and travel insurance, but they do not pay to see these sights. There are token charges at some, not all, museums. Where a substantial charge is levied, it is said to be a fee for a necessary related service, not for seeing the sight *per se*. For example, it does not cost to see Seattle from the "Space Needle" tower there. Rather, it costs to ride the elevator up to the observation platform. Once on the platform, the sightseer can stay as long as he wishes until closing time. This is a fine distinction to make, and it may not be important from the standpoint of common sense, but like many fine distinctions, it is a necessary one. A defining quality of a true attraction is its removal from the realm of the commercial where it is firmly anchored outside of historical time in the system of modern values.

It should go without saying that the authentic attraction itself cannot be purchased. Social attractions that have been purchased, such as the London Bridge in Arizona, and the ones that have been built up and promoted, such as Disney World, are not in and of themselves fake, of course. But because they represent the interests and values of only a small segment of society, a business or a community, they have little credibility as attractions and they seem to be expensive gimmicks more than true reflections of essential structures. Sightseeing in a fragmented and spurious society has the quality of picking over a random collection of tacky souvenirs inflated out of proportion. Some sightseeing in America has this quality. True attractions such as the Mona Lisa or Independence Hall are not for sale.

The commercial structure of authentic attractions and touristic experiences constitutes a total inversion of consumer behavior in the industrial world and the structure of commodities. In 1969, the state governments of the United States allocated an average of $600,000 each for the promotion of tourism. California, which ranks first on income derived from tourism, ranks forty-seventh in spending for its promotion. This is regarded as an anomalous fact in the travel industry, but the model presented here predicts it.[8] The cost of advertising is always hidden in the *price* of the industrial object, the commodity.

In the modern world, advertising an attraction or an experience, far from being a hidden cost, is the only source of commercial profits. Sightseers buy and take home an "advertisement" (marker or memory) for a "commodity" (sight—experience) which they leave behind for reuse by other tourists. Even the proprietors of commercialized pseudo-attractions are beginning to cash in on this structure. They once purchased advertising space. Now they sell bumper stickers, window decals, banners, and sweatshirts: "SEA LION CAVES ON THE OREGON COAST," "I VISITED GHOST TOWN USA," etc. The souvenir market, and by extension, the entire structure of everyday reality in the modern world, depends on the perpetuation of authentic attractions which themselves are not for sale.

## CONCLUSION

It is in the act of sightseeing that the representation of the true society is formulated and refined. But this act is neither continuous nor participated in by everyone. It is merely the moment of greatest intensity in the operation of tourist attractions on the touristic consciousness. The tourists return home carrying souvenirs and talking of their experiences, spreading, wherever they go, a vicarious experience of the sight. It is the vicarious representations that are general and constant. Without the slideshows, travel talks, magazines and other reminders, it would be almost impossible for the individual to represent to himself the differentiations of modern culture.

The price of this representation is very high. While the attraction is the more authentic, the memories and other souvenirs are more important in establishing society in consciousness. The society remains superior to the individual so long as the attraction remains superior to the souvenir. But the souvenir, because it is more immediate and intimate, constantly threatens the ascendancy of the attraction.

Roland Barthes has deciphered this relationship between the attraction and the souvenir:

> If . . . I take a walk in Spain, in the Basque country, I may well notice
> in the houses an architectural unity, a common style, which leads me to

acknowledge the Basque house as a definite ethnic product. However, I do not feel personally concerned, nor, so to speak, attacked by this unitary style: I see only too well that it was here before me, without me. It is a complex product which has its determinations at the level of a very wide history: it does not call out to me. . . .

Barthes goes on to describe his reaction to a town house built in the "Basque style" in Paris:

I feel as if I were personally receiving an imperious injunction to name this object a Basque chalet: or even better to see it as the very essence of *basquity*. This is because the concept appears to me in all its appropriative nature: it comes and seeks me out in order to oblige me to acknowledge the body of intentions which have motivated it and arranged it there as a signal of an individual history. . . . And this call, in order to be more imperious, has agreed to all manner of impoverishments: all that justified the [real] Basque house on the plane of technology—the barn, the outside stairs, the dove cote, etc.—has been dropped; there remains only a brief order, not to be disputed. And the Adhomination is so frank that I feel that this chalet has just been created on the spot, *for me*, like a magical object springing up in my present life without any trace of the history that has caused it.[9]

To prevent the souvenir from becoming elevated in importance to the point where it breaks its relationship with the attraction, it is always represented as a fallen object, as no substitute for the thing itself, as something fallen from its own naturalness, something with a name.

Similarly, the position of the person who stays at home in the modern world is morally inferior to that of a person who "gets out" often. Vicarious travel is freely permitted only to children and old folks. Anyone else may feel a need to justify saving picture postcards and filling scrapbooks with these and other souvenirs of sights he has not seen. Authentic experiences are believed to be available only to those moderns who try to break the bonds of their everyday existence and begin to "live."

Everyday life and its grinding familiarity stand in opposition to the many versions of the "high life" in the modern world. Everyday life threatens the solidarity of modernity by atomizing individuals and families into isolated local groupings which are not functionally or ideologically interrelated. But everyday life is composed of souvenirs of life elsewhere. In this way, modernity and the modern conscious-ness infiltrate everyday existence and, at the same time, subordinate it to life elsewhere. The dialectics of authenticity insure the alienation of modern man even within his domestic contexts. The more the indi-vidual sinks into everyday life, the more he is reminded of reality and authenticity elsewhere. This structure is, I think, the source of the social fiction that the individual's personal experience is the center of this, our most depersonalized historical epoch.

# 9

## On Theory, Methods
## and Applications

Too often in sociology, theoretical studies have little or no evident application to social problems while empirical studies of problems such as crime are not articulated to theory, depending for the most part on common sense categories to organize the ideas of the investigator. Sociological methodology is developed in a theoretical *and* empirical void as if independent from all constraint except its own internal logic. I want to try to counter this tendency toward fragmentation, at least in the context of my own study of tourism, by offering the following remarks on its theoretical and methodological implications and its possible applications. This is only a preliminary assessment. Though I have examined some of the implications that interest me, these are certainly not necessarily the most important ones.

## APPLICATIONS

Although not ordinarily perceived as such, every aspect of the cultural complex analyzed in this book has been subjected to some manipulation by a social group: historical societies, cultural commissions, acts of congress, the chamber of commerce, etc. The machinery of the social engineering that goes into the presentation of a "true" attraction tends to remain hidden from view because the work that goes into each presentation springs up spontaneously and seemingly independent of the movements behind the other attractions. These movements often begin when an old structure is slated for removal—a community leader points out its historical importance—and a group forms to try to save it. The best tourist I ever met, and one of the better men, the late Herb Eikenbary of Dayton, Ohio, a lawyer and world traveler, tried unsuccessfully to save the old jail in his town. He wrote:

> The Montgomery County Historical Society has ever sought to preserve, at least piecemeal, certain historic fragments of yesteryear whether same be in the form of an enchanted residence of Mid-Victorian vintage, or a marker, declaiming the site of an historic event. . . . Is there no demarcation, and no exception to the inviolate rule, that all must be turned into rubble, debris and waste? [The jail was torn down anyway.][1]

The question in the realm of tourism is not "Intervention, yes or no?" as it is in so many other areas of modern social life. Modern culture, as represented through the attractions, is already the product of intervention, but of an uncoordinated, "naturalistic" type which has little theoretical understanding of its own motives. For example, not even our old favorite, "the profit motive", operates unambiguously in the development of attractions. Some attractions are developed and maintained at great expense, though there are no economic returns. One of my main goals in writing this book was to clarify aspects of the structure underlying the many movements to develop local attractions so that this interesting form of social intervention can eventually be set on a scientific footing.

The development of an area for tourism has given rise to two new and distinctive political positions. A pro-tourist position is held by many planners of marginal economies who look to tourism as a new way of making money. An anti-tourist position is held by urban and modernized liberals and third world radicals who question the value of touristic development for the local people. They point out how tourism irreversibly alters local tradition, and the capital that is generated is siphoned off by the large corporations (the hotel chains and airlines) and returned to its point of origin in the rich countries and cities.

The pro-tourist position is sometimes so ill-conceived as to substantiate the anti-tourist position. The main mistake made by pro-tourist planners is they see tourism only in traditional economic terms as a new kind of *industry* (it is called "the tourist industry") and they try to build tourist factories, called "resorts" and "amusement parks," through which people are run assembly-line fashion and stripped of their money. Some Caribbean resorts come close to imprisoning their visitors by making the trip to town almost impossible to arrange or even more prohibitively expensive than the inflated charges for services within the resort compound. This kind of tourism is exploitative on both sides: the tourist gets little for his money and the local people do not see the money that is generated. In an excellent unpublished paper, Ruth C. Young calls this pattern "plantation tourism," and demonstrates empirically that it is found in societies with rigid, dualized class systems and already exploited peasant masses.

This kind of planning for touristic development errs by failing to take into account the degree to which tourism can grow and develop "naturally" within regional social structure. If the local people develop regional self-consciousness that transcends their immediate social situation and reflexive cultural structures, the tourists come in advance of the entrepreneurs, and a "cottage tourist industry" of the sort found in Ireland creates a more direct link between money from tourism and local economic development. I am suggesting, then, that the industrial or plantation version of tourism is economically short-sighted. Eventually, the capital that is generated by the natural growth tourism will exceed that of promoted, plantation tourism.

The difference I am highlighting here is the same as that between the now defunct Thomas Cook organization which pioneered highly controlled "packaged" tours in the nineteenth century, and the successful American Express Corporation which pioneered modern systems by which tourists could make use of existing social organization in their travels. At the end of the nineteenth century, William G. Fargo, one of the founders of AmExCo (then a freight company), observed correctly, "There is no profit in the tourist business *as conducted by* Thos. Cook and Son, and even if there were, this company would not undertake it."[2] Of course, the company eventually changed its position and devised highly innovative means by which modern, liberated tourists could make use of superior social organization at a higher system level than the organized tour. The most

important of these support systems is the one that is organized around
AmExCo's most profitable invention, the traveler's check, but the
same kind of thinking animates its other systems:

> The technique of the operation [at the 1933 Chicago's World's Fair]
> was for a railroad ticket agent to sell a traveler an order on American
> Express for one of its tours. On arriving in Chicago the tourist was
> directed to the American Express kiosk set up in the Union Station and
> manned by uniformed representatives. Here he exchanged his order
> for a strip of coupons. One of these paid his taxi to the assigned hotel;
> another paid for his room, and others were honored for meals and at the
> Fair. . . . The Fair venture paid off well. The gates were thrown open
> May 29, 1933, and by July 1 American Express had done more than
> $1,000,000 worth of business. During that summer the company hand-
> led 225,000 visitors to the Fair. The biggest day was Labor Day, 1933,
> when 5,100 people were serviced by American Express.[3]

It is clear from the population figures given in this early, simple
experiment that the growth potential of tourism making use of existing organization exceeds by far that kind of tourism which requires
the construction and promotion of a new resort or tour package for
each new batch of tourists.

The error of the anti-tourists is they tend to be one-sided and in
bad faith. They point out only the tawdry side of tourism and the
ways it can spoil the human community, while hiding from themselves the essentially touristic nature of their own cultural expeditions
to the "true" sights: their own favorite flower market in southern
France, for example, or their own favorite room in the National
Gallery. Anti-tourist positions can be reduced to a negative response
to the recent expansion of the tourist class to incorporate larger
numbers of different kinds of people. The anti-tourists are against
these other tourists spoiling their own touristic enjoyments which
they conceive in moralistic terms as a "right" to have a highly per-
sonalized and unimpeded access to culture and the modern social
reality.

The negative effects tourists can have on a community are sometimes lumped together under the generic term "Americanization":

Although it is further from the United States than it is from Mexico City (215 miles away), Tampico shows more traces of American influences than some border towns. . . . The sound of go-go has supplanted mariachi music in one of the many manifestations of the cultural "Americanization" of this bustling Gulf Coast metropolis. Indeed, Tampico only reverts to type as a true Mexican city in its unflagging fondness for fiestas and in the excitement of its marketplace.[4]

What is happening in Tampico is the emergence of a casual, outdoor, idling complex where strangers mingle together, rubbing elbows, while some agency lets loud music pour out into the public places where the mingling is occurring. This pattern was once restricted to festivals, beaches and amusement parks. It is not quite correct to call it "Americanization" because it is as noteworthy when it happens in North American cities as it is in Latin America and elsewhere. It can also be noted that a distaste for this phenomenon is far from universal. The urban ethnographer, Lyn Lofland, sees in it a sign of hope for a renewed solidarity among modern urbanites.[5] And at least one Marxist city planner, Henri Lefebvre, has arrived at a similar conclusion.[6]

There have been some recent efforts on the part of anti-tourists to realize their goals by counter-propaganda. For example, Oregon and Hawaii have mounted campaigns to discourage tourists:

Mayor Frank Fasi of Honolulu has urged the legislature to enact a hotel room tax, hoping to ease the tax burden of local residents. "We are fast becoming peasants in paradise," he said. The recent Rotary International convention brought 15,000 Rotarians to Honolulu, each spending from $50 to $90 a day. A group called the "Hawaii Residents Council" mailed mimeographed pleas to Rotarians urging them not to spend money here. "We are losing our shirts and souls to the soaring cost of living and the excessive greed that tourism brings," the leaflets said. "There is little in Hawaii that you cannot buy for less in your hometown."[7]

The two main strategies of anti-tourist campaigns involve (1) stating flatly that tourists are not wanted, and (2) publicizing negative attributes of the locality. Publicizing high prices for local goods and services, as the Hawaiians have done, is not effective because tourists expect to pay high prices, and the one thing they cannot buy in their home towns is their main motive for travel: the experience of being in Hawaii. Oregon publicizes her rain, California her earthquakes, and the major cities of the East, their crime. Even this approach is somewhat risky and it can backfire. Some tourists, as I have already indicated, come to see things like earthquakes and crime. Volcanic eruptions are enormously attractive, and some young people make the rounds of what is called "the revolution circuit." Even more dangerous from the standpoint of the anti-tourists, if the tourists ever suspect that the reason for the campaign against them is to preserve the natural, unspoiled, genuine, quality of local life and culture, the negative propaganda is immediately transformed into positive propaganda: everyone will want to be the first to see such a place. This seems to be happening in the Oregon case.

Both the pro-tourist position and the anti-tourist positions are ultimately based on the same fact: tourism has developed at a rate much faster than have its support institutions. For the last several years, in the month of August, there are several days during which every resort in the temperate climates in Europe, Africa, Asia and the Americas is filled in advance—the whole world is booked solid. This can be verified at any travel agency. Too many tourists are concentrated in insufficient facilities which are themselves unevenly distributed between the communities and regions of the world. Places with tourists have too many of them; places without have too few. This uneven distribution of the tourists is the basis of the politics of tourism.

Under conditions where there is too little to see and to do, the concentration of tourists around isolated attractions can be ugly and dehumanizing:

> Dagestan, a land of wild mountain beauty and exotic confusion of 32 languages and dialects, is stirring after long isolation and is moving to attract foreign tourists to diversify and stimulate its largely sheep and vineyard economy. . . . Travelers can drive for dozens of miles through the grassy plateaus and along mountain roads without seeing a single house or other sign of habitation. . . . An old shepherd, clad in flowing cape and a tall lambskin hat, turned slowly from his grazing flock as a bus stopped suddenly on a narrow, twisting dirt road. . . .

> The shepherd stared in bewilderment as a dozen shouting foreigners
> scurried from the bus with cameras and advanced on him with shutters
> clicking.[8]

The solution to Dagestan's problems, and the resolution of both
pro- and anti-tourist positions, is to increase the number of marked
attractions and support facilities for tourists on a worldwide base, so
tourists are more evenly diffused through world and local social
structure.

A neat solution to the problem of increasing both attractions and
facilities is provided in the following example from Yugoslavia:

> In Slovenia, in the mountainous north of Yugoslavia, a different kind of
> inn—the castle hotel—is attracting more and more foreign tourists.
> Old castles, mainly built on hills overlooking surrounding woods, have
> been outfitted as hotels with candlelight and romance atmosphere of
> past centuries—a combination of antique furniture and modern
> plumbing.[9]

In more developed areas, the typical pattern is a dual structure
there is the actual old castle and somewhere nearby, the "Castle
Hotel." In the United States, there are actual small towns and, for
tourists, at Disneyland, "Mainstreet U.S.A." In Hershey, Pennsylvania, there is a chocolate factory and a mocked-up display
chocolate-factory-for-tourists. In Lancaster County, Pennsylvania,
the home of the Amish plain folk, there are "authentic" restorations of
Amish Farms, Amish Villages and Old Covered Bridges. The one
room schoolhouses still in day-to-day operation in Lancaster county
are posted "No Trespassing TOURISTS" but there is also a listed
attraction: "One Room Schoolhouse as it existed for 93 years (life-size
figures depict lifelike animation of actual classroom activities)". (The
tourist puts a coin in a slot and peeks through the door to see a teacher
effigy make some teaching gestures while a boy pupil repeatedly dips
the braid of a girl pupil in his inkwell.) One also finds scattered
throughout this interesting area, as in the parking lot of the local
Howard Johnson's, realistically painted life-sized plastic replicas of a
family of plain folk: father, mother, child, horse and buggy.[10]

There seems to be almost no upper limit on how far a place can go
in transforming all its social, historical and natural elements into

tourist attractions. The case of Switzerland is most instructive: her mountains and lakes are not merely nature, but "scenery"; she has an elaborate transportation system for the exclusive use of sightseers; her national dish, fondue, is exclusively a party dish; her peasantry has obligingly continued to use picturesque outfits and equipment, Heidi and William Tell costumes, Alpine horns and oversized cowbells, long after other European peasants have abandoned their colorful ways; one of her main industries turns out what are two of the most stable souvenirs not merely of Switzerland but of Western Europe, music boxes and cuckoo clocks; her chalets are the model of mountain recreation homes throughout the Western world. Interestingly, and this is the point, Switzerland is rarely criticized for being "too touristy." Some of the most outspoken anti-tourists I know point to Switzerland as the model of what a modern nation should be.

There are two separate but related approaches, to the problem of tourism: (1) community planning for tourism in developed economies where there are too many tourists, and (2) the creation of new touristic facilities and interest in modernizing communities to draw some of the tourists out of the already overcrowded areas and to distribute the wealth more evenly.

## Community planning for tourism

Things that stand out from the others in their class for reasons of being foreign, old fashioned, weird or futuristic can be assembled on any local base, converting it into a place of touristic interest even for some of its local residents. The restored eighteenth- and nineteenth-century row houses of the "Society Hill" section of Philadelphia are admired by locals as well as visitors, as are the old Farmer's Market above the wharves in Seattle, the Italian market in the North End in Boston, Fisherman's Wharf in San Francisco and the quiet, high-speed subway in Montreal.

From the standpoint of the tourist, the movement of the edge of the tourist world always seems to be away from him. As each destination is reached, it is in a sense assimilated, becoming less foreign than the imagination held it to be. Then the frontier of the tourist's world recedes to his next destination. But tours are circular structures, and the last destination is the same as the point of origin: home. When the tourist returns home, if he is more careful in his observations than tourists need be, he can note certain developments: a resort being built somewhere nearby; the interest value of a quaint, local practice being discussed; an historic site being discovered and restored. Although it does not necessarily signal its arrival, the edge of the tourist world is in every tourist's town.

Planning the location of attractions and tourist support facilities in local communities can be made an integral part of other aspects of community planning. The principle of the arbitrariness of the authentic attraction assures that the touristic dimension of the modern community can be formed precisely according to the will of the people or lack thereof. Interventionist sight marking and guide writing can determine not merely the image of the community in the wider world but also the locations and proportional concentrations of the tourists within the community.

It should be noted that once a sight is sacralized, it is almost impossible to move it without desacralizing it, so the original location of any touristic element is also its final location. There is a plaque in the street in Florence where Girolamo Savonarola was burnt at the stake, and another in Paris where the Bastille once stood. It is not easy to move such items. It is easier to move the street out from under them. This contrasts sharply with industries and neighborhoods which are quite mobile by comparison. The original plasticity of the touristic aspects of community life, combined with their stability once established, suggests that *this* dimension, not neighborhoods and industry, should be planned first to provide an esthetic inner core around which the more flexible elements can be arranged.

The ultimate integration of tourism into the local community occurs when the local people discover the convenience and desirability of using facilities designed originally for tourists. I have noted some resourceful residents of big cities making constant use of guides such as *New York On Five Dollars a Day* in planning their own domestic travels, shopping trips, lunches downtown, evening entertainment and the like. Transportation systems can be designed so as to be convenient for both tourists and locals: inner city loop buses and "dime" shuttles stop at both the attractions and the department stores. Bridges and scenic roadways can and should be functional elements linking home and work, and, at the same time, attractions. Adult amusement parks such as Tivoli Gardens in Copenhagen and the one left over from the World's Fair in Seattle offer both high and popular culture at reasonable rates to both tourists and locals. Museum gift shops can function as souvenir stands and as little centers of do-it-yourself art and science education. As local food production, bakeries, fish market-restaurants and the like, become more pointedly developed for tourists, they can also provide locals with a more refined cuisine. I think that planning along these lines is the secret to Switzerland's success, and the success of "Chinatown" everywhere —outside of China, of course.

## The Development of Tourism in the Third World

The problem of modernizing areas seeking to attract tourists is not an absence of sights. Rather, it is the lack of a fully developed system of sight *markers* with worldwide extension. One way of overcoming this is elaborately contrived advertising to build up some consciousness of the place; another involves an effort to attract nontourist visitors, mainly businessmen, without ever suggesting that they need be full-time sightseers. The idea here seems to be to recruit a small army that will re-deploy itself worldwide and spread the word. In the meantime, the sight marking process or modernization of the place can keep pace with and adapt itself to the interests of the growing number of tourists. This seems to be the underlying plan of an East African nation that offers her untamed charms to visiting business-men:

> Add to the animal life, wide, sunlit plains, deep tropical forests, towering mountains, and the very source of the mighty river Nile, and then for good measure add the vast roads in East Africa, plentiful air services, both international and domestic, modern hotels and friendly service, and you can see where the confidence of Uganda's recently formed Tourist Board comes from. But best of all, why not come and see for yourself? A working holiday in Uganda would let you research the prospects in your particular field. And with modern hotels and efficient administration, you would surely find time to relax and dis-cover the excitement and charm that the country has to offer. Re-member Uganda is only a few hours away by jet.[11]

What Uganda is attempting is to develop an experimental, pre-touristic relationship with a specialized segment of the middle class requiring somewhat less differentiated facilities than would be the case if they attempted a broader sweep. Other nations are not so selective in their choice of a special segment. Some third world countries willingly accept, even encourage, visits not merely from businessmen but from hippies and others who are sometimes seen as "undesirables":

> Katmandu, Nepal (AP)—For the hippie set, there's no high like getting high in the high Himalayas. At a time when Laos has grown disenchanted with the flower power folk and Thailand will not let them in without a bath and a haircut, and Japan requires a bond of $250 as proof of financial stability, the tiny kingdom of Nepal looms as the last stronghold of hospitality for the great unwashed.[12]

Malawi's approach is calculated but practical:

> Blantyre, Malawi—Malawi, a poor black nation that is more concerned with economic development than ideology, is making a determined effort to get the tourist business of South Africa, the citadel of apartheid, or racial separation. . . . The international unpopularity of South Africa and Rhodesia is expected to help Malawi in her drive to reach this goal. South Africans and Rhodesians cannot obtain visas to some African countries and Europe is a long way to go for a vacation.[13]

This pattern of a phase of experimental contact with a special population of businessmen, hippies and Afrikaaners in the early stages of the development of third world tourism appears to be widespread and functional. When the Afrikaaners pull out of Malawi, they can be replaced by a more differentiated middle-class population if the institutions of tourism are sufficiently elaborated during the original occupation. American troops served a similar purpose in the Southeast Asian capitals officially designated Rest and Relaxation centers for soldiers on leave from Vietnam.

The original tourist populations, being new at travel themselves, or for some reason desperate for travel, are more likely than the seasoned tourist to tolerate the experiences associated with serious errors in service production. In this regard, hippies seem to function worldwide as the shocktroops of mass tourism. They opened up Mexico in the 1960's and are now concentrating almost all their energies on the overland route from Western Europe to India, finding the communities, cafés and hostelries that can handle the traffic. They teach the service personnel the language of tourism, which is Partial English.[14] Interestingly, when hippies continue coming to a place once they have already been followed in by the straight tourists, they may find that its character has changed and they are not welcome in their old haunts.

> The town [San Miguel Allende, Mexico] was designated a national monument to preserve its colonial atmosphere, and the building code is rigidly enforced. A luxury hotel is being built by Cantinflas, the Mexican movie star, but the Government is closely scrutinizing the architect's plans. . . . To write of San Miguel Allende and ignore its hippies would be to give a false picture of the town. The Mexican equivalent for the word hippie is "exhistentsialist," [sic] but it is a hard word for a Mexican to handle, even in his own language, so he just says "hippie" and calls this place "Hippiecuaro," the "cuaro" being Taras-can Indian for "place of." . . . Periodically, the town police stage house-cleanings. The last batch of deportees numbered 22 of the more pronounced hippie types. . . . At times, local police take it on them-selves to clip hippie hair arbitrarily, and at least one shearing session was publicized in the United States press.[15]

This unfortunate situation can be avoided when hippies are suc-cessfully integrated into the local area as one of the sights to be seen there by the straight tourists. So far, however, this transformation is limited to the developed areas where new sights are more easily and rapidly integrated. San Francisco and Amsterdam's hippie quarters provide examples. When integration does not occur, after the tourist hotel has been completed, as in San Miguel, the original marriage of convenience between the hippies and the rising tourist town is dissol-ved in divorce. I am not entirely certain of this, but the precise referent of the term "hippie" may be a tourist who comes to town but does not leave after a few days, or of his own accord.

## Conclusion

Social structures developed for tourism have the capacity to ser-vice populations which are larger than the resident population, some-times quite a bit larger. The island of Majorca, which has a resident population of 380,000, hosts more than two million tourists annually.[16] In 1967, the Soviet Union reported hosting 1.8 million tourists while sending 1.5 million Russians abroad.[17] When compared with Majorca, there is some room for development. Over 1.5 million tourists requested tickets to see the 1970 Passion Play at Oberammergau.[18] Swiss ski lifts can accomodate 260,000 riders every hour.[19] The Kennedy Space Center averaged 152,000 visitors a month in 1969. On a busy day in the same year 33,000 visitors were counted.[20] In 1968, Yosemite hosted 1.1 million campers (overnight visitors, not merely visitors passing through).[21] The National Forests in California registered 41 million visitors in 1968, according to the National Forest Service.[22] In 1969, 1.3 million tourists went to Greece and stayed in 108,000 extra beds available to them there.[23] A radio news reporter claims: "Turnout for Expo '70 (in Japan) is light. 257,000 visitors on the first day was below expectations . . ." These figures reflect capacities to handle nonresident populations which would exceed most communities' and institutions' needs if most communities and institutions were developed for tourism. The figures are also a sign that modern social structure, through the institutionalization of tourism, is naturally adapting itself to the problem of "overpopulation."

## METHODS

Among the many products of industrial society are some historically new and rather sharply felt forms of alienation. No one could adjust very well to the kinds of work created by industrialization. Difficulties resulting from cultural and class dislocations and mixed loyalties made it hard for industrial man to live day-to-day without considerable confusion and self-doubt. Psychoanalysis appeared in this context, offering some ingenious ways of adjusting individuals to fit into industrial reality, into communities and families much altered by industrial processes. In the modern world, ethnography and general systems approaches are growing alongside of psychoanalysis in response to a new set of problems: namely, the difficulties entire groups of men, families, ethnicities and communities are experiencing as they attempt to adapt themselves as totalities to the modernization process.

I think that ethnography will eventually occupy a position in the modern world similar to the one occupied by psychoanalysis in the industrial world. Ethnography has always dealt with social totalities, and it has always attempted to discover the *meaning* of the relationships between the parts of society. One is reminded that Erving Goffman began his important research on the structure of face-to-face interaction with an ethnography of a rural community: "For a year he resided on one of the smaller of the Shetland Isles while he gathered material for a dissertation on that community . . ."[24] Of course, newer and more powerful techniques of ethnographic analysis such as the societal and community comparisons pioneered by Murdock and Redfield must eventually replace the case study if we are to follow up Goffman's example and continue the analysis of the social structure of modernity and the meaning of modern life. All this was stated more or less as I am stating it here twenty years ago by Everett C. Hughes:

> Redfield's work is, more than any other that I know, a continuation and a further development of the urban versus primitive, folk, or rural made by so many of the precursors of modern social science. . . . There are, however, certain dificulties involved in carrying their work [Redfield's and Singer's] further. One of them is methodological. Redfield's *The Little Community* bears the subtitle "Viewpoints for the Study of the Human Whole." It is much easier, in practice, to study a little community as a whole than to study a great civilization, with its immense cities and its great systems of technique, thought, institutions, and arts, as a whole. . . . I want . . . to make clear the direction of the wind I am stirring up. The Redfield and Singer enterprise is moving in the direction in which we need to go; I only wish to say that to get full benefit of it will require ingenious, brilliant, and although I hate the thought, massive attacks upon the problems of method which are involved.[25]

The method I devised for this study, that of following the tourists, I see as a provisional, comparative approach. The tourists had already launched the "massive attack" on modernity Hughes called for. On the other hand, they obviously offered little in the way of control over variables that is necessary for hypothesis testing. I had to secure every finding under much more evidence than would have been necessary had I based the study on a random sample and constructed measures of the study variables. I was willing to sacrifice scientific efficiency in this case, however, as I was suspicious from the beginning (and the study confirmed my suspicions) that the tourists are way out ahead of the sociologists and anthropologists in their attempt to reconstruct modern social structure: they are certainly better financed and better organized, and there are more of them. Some of them are borrowing ethnographic techniques and adapting them to their purposes in travel writing. Interestingly, a tourist's report filed from Shetland Isles, the place where Erving Goffman gathered data for his dissertation, is organized entirely around the categories of traditional ethnography. The usual advice for prospective visitors is swept aside in a casual, offhand way ("Shetland is hardly for swingers") and the writer gets down to the hard business of ethnographic description:[26]

PREHISTORY:

Occupied by crofter-fishermen since the Neolithic period, Shetland boasts that it contains more prehistoric sites to the square mile than any other country in Britain. Pictish brochs—mysterious stone towers originally 30 to 40 feet high—can be clambered over throughout the island. . .

CULTURE HISTORY:

One is never allowed to forget that Shetlanders—with their own ponies, dogs, language, sheep, sweaters, festivals and history—consider their islands Viking territory.

CEREMONY AND RITUAL:

One Viking tradition has endured, and Shetlanders recommend it as their spectacle of the year. It is the winter fire festival of Up-Helly-Aa, based on ritual fires and feasting marking the time when Norsemen of old celebrated the end of the Yule Holidays by begging the sun to come back.

COTTAGE INDUSTRY AND ECONOMY:

In the knitwear shops of Lerwick's Commercial Street, appropriately enough the town's one shopping street, local women deposit their handiwork wrapped in brown paper, and the shopper can buy a soft, warm sweater, in natural, undyed shades or in a delicate, heathery color, for $5.

LANGUAGE:

It is impossible to spend more than a few hours in Shetland without learning at least one word of Shetlandic—"peerie." "Peerie"—what the ponies, dogs and sheep are—means little and, like the rest of the Shetlandic vocabulary, it is salted casually through otherwise normal English conversation.

COOKING:

In Shetland, one munches homemade Scottish scones and oatcakes at bed-and-breakfast houses.

GAMES:

One plays British Monopoly in pounds for Fleet Street & Marylebone Station, instead of Park Place and Boardwalk.

COSMOLOGY:

The Shetlander, who shares 60 degrees latitude with the southern tip of Greenland, with the northern half of Hudson Bay and with Helsinki, Leningrad and vast stretches of Siberia, is accustomed to being seen in an unusual light—that of the midnight sun.

The writer wants to impress on us that Shetland Isle is an interesting and worthwhile place for tourists to visit, and she believes that a report on aspects of its social structure and culture is a means of producing that impression.

The tour is the only unit of social organization in the modern world that is both suffused with cultural imagery and absolutely detached from surrounding culture. The tourists, drawing upon their collective experiences of other societies, are attempting to construct a world which is complete and total in and of itself, in short, a world which has the same qualities as the ones we have claimed for "primitive isolates." A tour encircles the life of the tourist while he is away from home, determining what he eats, and when and where he eats and sleeps, the kinds of services he may and may not obtain, where he goes and what he does and sees there, and who he does and sees things with. The tourist world is expanding but as it expands, it also tends toward closure and completeness. Tourism is *economic* (entire nations such as the Bahamas are economically dependent on it), and it is *cultural* and *historical*. Quasi-*religious* and *psychological* factors may enter into the motivation to become a tourist. *Language* separates tourists from locals as does the use of special *social establishments*: hotels, restaurants, and guides.[27] Tourism exhibits its own emerging *class structure*, first class, tourist class and economy class, to which even "classless" societies subordinate themselves. The inaugural Moscow to Montreal Aeroflot flight had "first" and "tourists class" accommodations. There are *laws* and *norms* that apply only to tourist and others which tourists are permitted to disobey.[28]

Although there is a great deal to be learned about this emerging structure by following the tourists, the sociologists and anthropologists have for their part not neglected it entirely. It has recently become possible to construct a model of a modern community from touristic establishments and relationships that have been the subject of ethnographic reports properly so called. The "community" includes: members of the *leisure class* as analyzed by Thorstein Veblen;[29] *hotels* and *trailer camps* as studied by Norman Hayner;[30] Roebuck and Spray's *cocktail lounge*,[31] Cavan's *bar*,[32] Richard's *tavern*,[33] Gottlieb's *tavern*,[34] and Melendy's *saloon*;[35] Fred Davis' *taxi cab company*;[36] Cuber's *amusement park*;[37] Whyte's *restaurant*;[38] Moore's *dance ball*[39] and Howard Becker's *dance band*.[40] Perhaps these elements would be concentrated in a city in an area Anselm Strauss described as "attracting and controlling the movements of the tourist when he reaches the city."[41] And perhaps, too, this area would be characterized by the kind of minor difficulties arising out of culture contact which Edward T. Hall has described so well.[42]

The sociologist and the tourist stare at each other across the human community, each one copying the methods of the other as he attempts to synthesize modern and traditional elements in a new holistic understanding of the human community and its place in the modern world. While both touristic and ethnographic methods are unrefined and inexact and far from having reached their final form, they are nevertheless beginning to produce some interesting preliminary results. These results augment the existing scientific literature on development and modernization and can be summarized as follows.

The literature on development and modernization has stressed the movement of traditional people away from their agricultural roots and into cities where, only half assimilated, they become some of the better-known "social problems." At the same time, changes in traditional communities have been documented, especially successes and failures at "modernization." The perspective employed in this study, that of the tourist-ethnographer, focuses on a complex of countertendencies for traditional folks to dramatize their backwardness as a way of fitting themselves in the total design of modern society as attractions. As modern ideas and institutions increase their sphere of influence, a mobile international middle class, spearheaded by tourists and ethnographers, is widening its base of operations into areas of the world that long remained outside the mainstream of development. This process is accompanied by the social production of highly fictionalized versions of everyday life of traditional peoples, a museumization of their quaintness. It is here in this other change, paralleling the great technological innovations that flow in the opposite direction, that some new and unstudied problems are appearing: the moderns' nervous concern for the authenticity of their touristic experience; the traditional folks' difficulty in attempting to live someone else's version of their life; the replacement of the specialized perspectives of the ethnologist, the art historian, the urban planner and the critic, for the general point of view of the tourist in the organization of modern towns, museums, displays and drama. The common goal of both ethnography and tourism is to determine the point at which forced traditionalism ceases to base itself on the truths of day-to-day existence and begins to crystallize as a survival strategy, a cultural service stop for modern man.

## Conclusion

It is necessary, in conclusion, to note that tourism is different from ethnography, and perhaps this is the secret of its success, because it is not conscious of its aims. The tourist remains mystified as to his true motives, his role in the construction of modernity. He thinks he is going out for his own enjoyment. We have always reserved our finest mystification for the act of dutifully paying respect to society and its works. The ethnographer is not, or ought not be, mystified as to his true motives or taken in by the grandeur of his undertaking. He must simply set about the task of making the social world more understandable than it was before he began to study it, hopeful that his theory and methods will help him to accomplish this task, knowledgeable that there are no guarantees that this will be the result.

One is reminded of Auguste Comte's idea of a sociology-religion (with sociologist priests), the queen of the sciences, taking as its domain all of social life including the other fields of study that evolved earlier. Sociologists are somewhat embarrassed by this grandiose scheme and they tend to shy away from it. Sociology did not even try to form itself according to Comte's vision. Tourism did. Of course, Comte assumed that the super-sociology he envisioned would be rational as well as spiritual, clear-cut as well as comprehensive. Tourism and the modern consciousness have only gropingly and inexactly realized his program.


## THEORY

Every study owes something to the theory that produces its particular viewpoint, that animates the inquiry and the handling of evidence; namely, a return to the theory and a clarification and modification thereof in terms of any new findings that have been produced. The analysis of tourism presented here was based on *social structural differentiation* and, I think, it has enriched that variable. I have attempted to incorporate Erving Goffman's front vs. back distinction into differentiation, to link it up to Marxist and semiotic theory, and to ethnomethodological studies of behavior. I have concentrated on a special type of differentiation especially prevalent in tourist settings, a duplication of structure, which is the basis for what I have termed the dialectics of authenticity. When something is doubled, there is always the question of which side is the true or original side, or the authentic representation.

Before moving to specific conceptual reformulations, it is appropriate to remark that this study is almost unique in its selection of tourism as a topic, but it is not at all unique in its use of the differentiation variable. It is only a limited contribution to a growing body of theory. Interestingly, although it was a sociologist, Émile Durkheim, who originally formulated the differentiation variable (as "organic solidarity") and applied it to the analysis of social systems, sociologists have not, for the most part, taken up his suggestion, so the approach has been refined in the other social sciences. The anthropologist, Leslie White, offers the explanation that sociology is culture-bound and, at the same time, underscores the importance of differentiation to anthropology:

> Culture became differentiated as soon as it appeared. Ever since the earliest days of human history local groups of people have been distinguished from one another by differences in speech, custom, belief, and costume, insofar as any was worn. We may believe, also, that man has always been aware of these differences that set his own group apart from others. Thus we might say that, in a sense, mankind has always been culture conscious. . . . In comparatively recent times the new sciences of sociology and social psychology worked out general principles of a science of social behavior, but these were assumed to be common to all mankind and so could not account for cultural differences among tribes and nations. Social interaction is a universal process; conflict, co-operation, accommodation, the four wishes, etc., are worldwide; they might account for cultural uniformities, but not differences. True, these sciences did not address themselves to the problem of cultural variation; they were limited almost entirely to the framework of one culture, Western civilization. But when one turned to the question of cultural differences among peoples, it was found that sociology and social psychology had virtually nothing to offer.[43]

It seems to me that Leslie White has not gone far enough. He assumes (this is the central bias of anthropology) cultural homogeneity *within* a single culture even as he correctly points out heterogeneity across cultures. All cultures, especially modernized ones, but also including the simpler ones, are internally differentiated. Some sociologists are beginning to design their researches around this differentiation with the result that their work immediately takes on the appearance of being engaged with the contemporary social reality. There are some topics that are impossible to comprehend unless research is so designed. Bennett Berger, for example, bases his excellent analysis of popular culture and youth culture in American Society on their internal differentiations. Berger has concluded that "a society highly differentiated on the level of social structure but homogeneous on the level of culture . . . is emptied of its cultural meaning."[44] On a similar note, the linguist, William Labov, has criticized linguistic theories that are based on the assumption of a homogeneous speech community, and he has designed his own studies of English around its internal differentiations that correspond to the social differentiations between groups, regions, situations, and classes.[45]

Frank W. Young has gone the furthest in providing both sophisticated conception and measurement of social structural differentiation. In his writings and research reports. which are too diverse to be summarized here, he has systematically developed a model of community and regional development within which differentiation is the key variable. ("Structural differentiation is not a synonym for development, but it implies or correlates what many people conceive development to be.")[46] Young has made explicit the logic of his deduction of structural differentiation from Durkheim's organic solidarity and he has linked his revised definition to semiotics which he calls "structural symbolics." ("Differentiation is defined as the number of specialized social symbols maintained by a given system.") He understands the symbol to be operating at the level of myth and institution not merely as it is understood by the Symbolic Interactionists to be operating at the level of words and gestures. Finally, Young and his associates have successfully measured social structural differentiation at the community and regional level and in different cultural contexts, and they have found that it predicts the variation of other indices of modernization. ("The typical mode of measurement . . . is a Guttman scale of community institutions or, sometimes, a count of such institutions.")

I was aware of this approach to social structure before I began my own study of tourism; it was helpful to me and my findings support it in all but a few particulars. The most important qualification of Young's paradigm that emerges from this research is an altered view of high levels of structural differentiation. Young has suggested that differentiation is a limitless growth dimension. The picture that results from his conception is an inexorable movement of all areas in the direction of a global, urban-industrial complex. ("Some communities, nations, regions etc., are more differentiated than others and the rate of change varies." This differentiation is a "continuing and universal fact.") The alternative picture emerging from this study of tourism suggests that a qualitative change in social structure occurs as differentiation passes a certain point.

As urban-industrial society develops, it seems to arrive at a point beyond which it can go no further: it runs out of resources, gets hemmed in or absorbed by other regions, or it is rendered obsolete by superior organization elsewhere. If it continues to differentiate beyond this point, it turns in on itself. Each earlier differentiation develops a reflexive self-consciousness at the group level. Factories construct models of themselves just beside themselves for use by tourists. Automobiles (sports cars) and bridges split into dual functions, as transportation devices and as touristic experiences. The human group itself becomes conscious of itself as the source of the fulfillment of the human potential and arbitrary, intentional groupings appear and experimentally vary the theme of fulfillment. Entire nations are becoming aware of their internal, cultural elements, not in terms of industrial functions, but as attractions for tourists from other countries. The results are often quite striking. A United States Travel Service poster aimed at encouraging Europeans to visit the U.S.A. appears as a farrago of words, fancifully lettered, which I have reproduced *in toto*. Here is our official version of our contribution to international culture:

> Supermarket, Niagara Falls, Ranch, Weekend, A-OK, Drugstores, Cowboy, Hot Dog, Musicals, Jeep, Snack Bar, Jazz, Grand Canyon, Cola, Bar B-Que, Pop, On the Rocks, Rodeo, Chewing Gum.

Every tourist attraction analyzed in this study is an example of this new kind of involuted differentiation. It is possible now, I think, to clarify two important terms: *Industrial society* is that kind of society that develops in a cumulative, unidimensional, growth sequence, by simply adding on new elements—a new factory, population growth, a new social class, for example. Frank Young's paradigm is still the best for explicating the development of industrial structure and its rural hinterland. *Postindustrial* or *modern society* is the coming to consciousness of industrial society, the result of industrial society's turning in on itself, searching for its own strengths and weaknesses and elaborating itself internally. The growth of tourism is the central index of modernization so defined.

## The End of the Tourist World

One might legitimately ask just how far modernization has progressed and follow it out to its furthest limits by following the tourists out to theirs. The frontiers of world tourism are the same as the frontiers of the expansion of the modern consciousness with terminal destinations for each found throughout the colonial, ex-colonial, and future-colonial world where raw materials for industry and exotic flora, fauna, and peoples are found in conglomeration. The tourist world has also been established *beyond* the frontiers of existing society, or at least beyond the edges of the Third World. A *paradise* is a traditional type of tourist community, a kind of last resort, which has as its defining characteristic its location not merely outside the physical borders of urban industrial society, but just beyond the border of peasant and plantation society as well. This touristic version of the folk-urban continuum figures in the following bird's-eye view of an island that has a paradise on its southwest coast.

> St. Lucia today has three faces. One is modern, having grown out of tourism and mass real estate developments that have created a burgeoning resort strip in the island's northwest. The island's second face is one of fertile mountainous land that is well watered and richly cultivated. Morne Gimie rises 3,000 feet in the center, forested by a whopping 160 inches of rainfall, and valleys knifing off in all directions are carpeted with thousands of acres of bananas. Barefoot women trudge, balancing stems of bananas on their heads. The banks of broad, shallow rivers are white with clothes spread to dry, while women wash more in the stream. Banana boats are loaded at efficient, stark docks by women in ant-like lines. . . . Then there is the third face of St. Lucia, the one bejeweling the south end of the west coast. Here, one finds bays and peaks and harbors and forts that have made St. Lucia a yachtsman's delight for generations. . . . Gros Piton and Petit Piton are 2,000-foot spires of scrub-covered rock rising steeply from the sea. Viewed from the land they are fascinating; from the sea, mesmerizing. Immediately to their north sits the town of Soufrière, named for the steaming mass of sulfurous rock and volcanic spewings. Public mineral baths here date from Napoleon's era and are still in use. . . . The hotels along the northwest coast of the island provide the typical chic Caribbean holiday—bamboo bars under palms along magnificent beaches.[47]

These idyllic places where, we are told, characters like Fletcher Christian, Paul Gauguin, Greek shipping magnates, ex-Nazi officials, anthropologists, and "beautiful people" hang out are physically removed from our humdrum, workaday world, even when they are linked to this world by teletype to the stock exchange and by airstrips for private jet aircraft. The separation of paradise from already established matrices of social institutions is the mark of viable social structure. It suggests that tourism is the cutting edge of the worldwide expansion of modernity.

Representative contact where articulate members of the most socially influential class are found in remote, isolated, relatively autonomous communities is an inversion (or an "in version") of the folk-urban continuum: the movement and transformation being from urban to folk. Interestingly, modern society's return to nature is as unidimensional as Redfield hypothesized its earlier development in the opposite direction was. Wherever resorts are found, in no matter what remote area, they are assembled from the same social establishments. There are areas of the world, however, where the social and geographical terrain is rugged and the resort necessarily adapts, taking on a regional aspect as its establishments fit themselves into a distinctive local landscape. In one of the frontiers of the tourist world, this process of fitting-in has apparently resulted in some limits' being placed on paradisical qualities:

> Hangora, Easter Island—Easter Island, which until recently was scarcely more accessible than the South Pole, has thrown open its shores to the foreign tourist, provided he is well-heeled both as to bank account and shoes. . . . The Chilean Government, which owns Easter Island, is bringing a prefabricated hotel from the United States for erection on Easter Island. It is scheduled to open in August. A New York travel agency, Lindblad Tours, even has a permanent representative living on Easter Island. He is Mark Gross of Hempstead, L. I., who is settled on Easter Island with his wife and baby daughter. The main attraction of Easter Island is, of course, its archaeology . . . . The mystery of the statues and the more recent history of civil wars and ritual cannibalism appeal not only to archeologists but to tourists. . . . Despite these attractions and the new weekly jet flight to the island, there are virtually no tourists here. The Chilean Government operates

the only hotel on the island, which is neither cheap nor comfortable. It consists of several rows of tent barracks covered by corrugated metal roofs. Common bathroom facilities are a quarter of a mile away from the camp and do not offer hot water. The tourist has difficulty getting to the bathroom through the mud when it rains. The prices for drinks, which are rationed, are staggering, and a couple sharing one of the tents pays $40 a day. While the island's lobsters are very good, the tourist must do without butter, eggs, and many other things. Unless he brings his own toilet soap he will have to make do with Rinso. . . . "We not only have one of the world's most expensive hotels," Mayor Alfonso Rapu said of the tent camp, "but also one on the most uncomfortable. We call it the concentration camp. . . ." There are no vehicles for rent, even bicycles. Consequently, the tourist is almost wholly reliant on the Lindblad Travel Agency for any form of transportation, which costs $12 per person a day, plus a 17 percent tax.

"Things are high," Mr. Gross said, "but I think it's better that way. No one here is anxious to see hippies and such on the island."[48]

I have quoted this account at length because the writer provides us with a rare description of a resort under construction, and modern values in their most rugged form. The evident attitude of the writer of the report can be discounted. There are some tourists who would regard the accommodations offered as being "for the tourists," and who would push on to still more undeveloped delights. The fervor behind touristic efforts to transcend existing social structural arrangement can match any other form of fervor.

The hotel-bar-beach communities established on the islands of the Caribbean constitute the upper outer limit of world tourism and Easter Island approaches the lower outer limit. As the writer of the account of Easter Island indicates, however, Easter Island is not quite The Lower Limit. Antarctica is.

Palmer Station, Antarctica—Two thousand American scientists and Navy personnel of Operation Deep Freeze spend the six months of each austral summer, when it is winter in the United States, conducting experiments and busily provisioning bases for the six months of cold, 24-hour, winter darkness ahead. Why, they wonder, would civilians spend up to $5,000 each and come 12,000 miles from the United States to spend a night out in a white-out, travel in below zero temperatures and lean into 50-mile-an-hour winds? The reason is, apparently, to be the first on their block to have visited Antarctica. Armed with Nikons, fur hats planted atop their gray hair and Dramamine in their parka pockets, tourists are advancing in successive waves toward the icy shoreline. . . . What a visitor actually gets to see in Antarctica on one of these cruises depends on precisely the same raw elements that cost Scott his life more than 50 years ago: Weather . . . This is not a hotel-motel nightlife country, and once you've gone up alongside a round and roaring (but relatively harmless) Weddell seal to have your picture taken, there's not much else to do but climb back into the landing craft, head to the ship and hang over the rail waiting for the next piece of geography to appear.[49]

This kind of place, if there are any others like it, is the actual frontier of world tourism. Adventuresome tourists visit even though no regular tourist community has yet been established.

Perhaps I have stopped short of my mark. Although tourists adopt the rhetoric of adventure, they are never independent of a social arrangement wherein a host organizes the experiences of a sightseeing guest. And this arrangement, minus the usual support establishments, is found everywhere.

A veteran Canadian flier has something to offer to the man who has seen and done just about everything—a trip to the North Pole. For $2,500, Weldy Phipps, a World War II ace and one of the Arctic's best-known airmen, will drop straight down on the pole itself, a travel service he hopes to start this year and have in full operation by 1972. From casual discussions about the project, Phipps already has received some 150 inquires from potential customers. "There's an old fellow in Nova Scotia who wants to go," said Phipps. "He's retired, he's got the $2,500, he's always wanted to go, so he's saying 'What the hell. I'll never get another chance.' " The flier reckons he'll have to set up a main staging camp plus a landing strip at the pole, with shelters at both sites. "It won't be good enough to land eight or ten miles away and tell the fare-paying passenger, 'It's over there somewhere,' " said Phipps. "It has to be fair ball. If people are paying $2,500 to go to the North Pole, then that's where we have to take them."[50]

It is an interesting characteristic of the tourist world that the tourists themselves believe that it has no end, that there is always some new frontier. A dispute arose over the tourists' rights to visit the scientific facilities in Antarctica:

(T)he United States and the U.S.S.R. have signed a treaty recognising Antarctica as a no-man's-land and barring all military activity here —and tourists, accordingly, have, or ought to have, at least *some* rights. One can imagine this sort of dispute arising 50 years from now *on the moon*. (emphasis supplied)[51]

A major dilemma today is whether the preindustrial areas, and the areas outside of existing society, will choose to enter the modern world on the bottom rung of development and undergo their own industrialization, or whether they will jump ahead of this dirty phase of development and fit themselves into modernity as attractions. Neither alternative is especially desirable. If a group avoids industrialization as it modernizes, it may end up spending all of its time wondering if it is real or not—that seems to be the price for rapid advancement in the modern world. A somewhat better ending might be the one outlined in the section on "Applications": a simultaneous development of industrial social structure *and* modern self-consciousness so the industrial structures are realized as attractions even as they are first coming into existence. Some of the crimes, the rape of nature, for example, committed in the name of industrialization might be avoided, and so might some of the crimes committed for the sake of tourism.

# Notes

## INTRODUCTION

1. An important exception to this is the work of Everett C. Hughes. Hughes began his distinguished studies of occupations with research on realtors, and he has studied doctors and other high status occupations. See his *The Sociological Eye: Selected Papers on Work, Self, and the Study of Society*, 2 vols. (Chicago: Aldine, 1971).

2. Daniel J. Boorstin, *The Image: A Guide to Pseudo-Events in America* (New York: Harper & Row, 1961), pp. 87–88.

3. Claude Lévi-Strauss, *Tristes Tropiques*, trans. John Russell (New York: Atheneum, 1968), p. 17.

4. Mark Twain ridiculed this rhetoric as it applied to religious attractions but was happily taken in by it when it applied to social attractions. "But isn't this relic matter a little overdone? We find a piece of the true cross in every old church we go into, and some of the nails that held it together. I would not like to be positive, but I think we have seen as much as a keg of these nails." *The Innocents Abroad or the New Pilgrim's Progress*. (New York: New American Library, 1966), pp. 119–20.

5. Reported in *The New York Times*, September 17, 1972, sect. 4, p. 4.

6. Reported in the *Contra Costa County* [California] *Times: "The Green Sheet*," July 18, 1972, p. 10A.

## CHAPTER ONE

1. Marx may not be completely alone in this. Some would argue that Rousseau's *Social Contract* and other political writings inspired the French Revolution, and one finds in his *Oeuvres Complètes*, vol. III (Paris: Gallimard, 1964), specific blueprints for the organization of two states: "Projet de Constitution pour la Corse," pp. 901–50, and "Considérations sur le Gouvernement de Pologne et sur sa Réformation Projetée," pp. 953–1041. Along these lines it is worthwhile to recall that when Fidel Castro arrived victorious in Havana, he carried in his jacket pocket not the *Manifesto* but the *Social Contract*.

2. While I know this to be widespread from firsthand acquaintance with teachers and students so inclined, I know of no study or analysis of it. It is my own impression that the radicalization of marginal colleges and universities in the United States during the past decade results from the "dumping" of Ph.D.'s trained in the mainstream during the latter part of the 1960's. As the post-World War II "baby boom" crested through the colleges, there were insufficient facilities and teachers for them. The response of the institutions was disorganized, and after some initial build-up to meet the problem, as the population levels began to stabilize, there was much discussion of "cutbacks," and of the "overproduction of Ph.D.'s." Interestingly, there has been no discussion of using the new, broader manpower base to strengthen the institutions. The new talent, in fact, is increasingly treated as a "problem," and the procedures used in the hiring and advancement of new Ph.D.'s and assistant professors during the early 1970's often bordered on cruelty. Many new academics are going to teach at the kind of college that had previously made do with less-qualified teachers. It appears that a strengthening of the institutions on the periphery is occurring as a part of the same process that is weakening the institutions in the mainstream, all without conscious planning, and with an interesting twist: the experience of being turned out of the mainstream has, in many instances, produced powerful revolutionary sentiments in new academics all across the land, and these sentiments are, for the first time, finding an audience among the "left-behinds." The so-called marginal colleges are becoming centers of a new intellectual ferment with (so far) unspecified potential and direction.

3. G. F. Hegel, *The Phenomenology of Mind*, trans. J. B. Baillie (London: Allen and Unwin, 1910, rev. ed., 1931).

4. Cited in Wilhelm Windelband, *A History of Philosophy*. vol. 2 (New York: Harper & Row, 1958), p. 641.

5. For a discussion of the ideology of Boston-based Progressive Laborites, see Barrie Thorne, "Resisting the Draft: An Ethnography of the Draft

Resistance Movement," an unpublished Ph.D. dissertation, Brandeis University, 1971.

6. Karl Marx, *Capital*. vol. 1 (Moscow: Progress Publishers, 1965), p. 74.

7. Lake Park, Florida: Addco Industries, Inc., n.d.

8. Emile Durkheim, *The Elementary Forms of the Religious Life*, trans. J. W. Swain (New York: Free Press, 1965), p. 264.

9. For a discussion of the relationship of social life to fictional accounts of it, see Juliet Flower MacCannell, "Fiction and the Social Order," *Diacritics* 5, no. 1 (1975), pp. 7–16.

10. The term "experience" is scattered in the writings on the avant-garde of the human sciences. There is little systematic effort to define this term. (Notable exceptions include Erving Goffman's recent *Frame Analysis: An Essay on the Organization of Experience* [New York: Harper & Row, 1974] and R. D. Laing's popular *The Politics of Experience* [New York: Ballantine, 1967].) In current discourse, scientific and otherwise, one finds the assumption that everyone knows and agrees about what "experience" means, even though this assumption could not be further from the truth.

11. Ibid., p. 41.

12. H. Marshall McLuhan has argued, and gained much agreement, that the media are entirely responsible for the construction of cultural images. This radical position probably accords the media too much primacy and independence. See his popular *Understanding Media: The Extensions of Man* (New York: McGraw-Hill, 1964).

13. Howard Becker has published an article, "Art as Collective Action," *American Sociological Review* 39, no. 6 (December 1974), pp. 767–76, in which he makes the point that many individuals cooperate to produce culture. He does not treat art and other cultural productions as models for the organization of our modern society and experience. His sociology remains centered on the individual even after the discussion of "cooperation" and the like. Erving Goffman has opened the door to understanding the structure of modern society with his dramaturgical studies of modern life, but he arbitrarily restricts his analysis to the individual and situational level. Goffman uses cultural models (dramatic devices, social fictions, etiquette) as his tools—he does not treat them as part of his subject matter. For example, in a somewhat overstated disclaimer, Goffman writes: "I make no claim whatsoever to be talking about the core matters of sociology—social organization and structure. . . . I personally hold society to be first in every way and any individual's current involvements to be second; this report deals only with matters that are second." *Frame Analysis*, p. 13.

14. See, for example, his *Leçon Inaugurale* published in English as *The Scope of Anthropology*, trans. S. O. Paul, and R. A. Paul (London: Cape, 1967).

15. It can be noted that electronically mediated experience is de-ritualized to some degree. As compared to *live experience*, electronically mediated experiences separate the performers from the audience and the members of the audience from each other. Because the audience need not get itself "up" for the experience, it can avoid taking a role in the experience, and if the media lull their audience to sleep in this way, they cannot play an important part in the emergence of modern civilization. There are signs that television is retreating into a position fully subordinate to everyday life, a kind of self-censuring "Muzak" background noise for domestic settings: the "talk shows" only go so far as to bring the living room into the living room; the "soaps" bring the kitchen into the kitchen.

16. Suggested by Virginia McCloskey, who attributes the remark on the moon landing to Margaret Mead.

17. The philandering professor anti-hero in Alison Lurie's novel, *The War Between the Tates* (New York: Random House, 1974), tried to bridge the gap to his graduate-student girlfriend in this way.

18. Reported to me by Barry Alpher, who has done linguistic fieldwork among the Australians.

19. Max Weber, *Gesammelte Aufsätz zur Wissenschaftslehre*. (Tübingen: Mohr, 1922), p. 204. Cited in M. Merleau-Ponty, *The Primacy of Perception*, ed. J. M. Edie (Evanston, Ill.: Northwestern University Press, 1964), p. 205. This passage also appears, translated somewhat differently, in Weber's *The Protestant Ethic and the Spirit of Capitalism*, trans. Talcott Parsons (New York: Scribner's, 1958), p. 182.

20. Lewis Mumford, *The Conduct of Life* (New York: Harcourt Brace Jovanovich, 1970), p. 209.

21. Edward Sapir, *Culture, Language, and Personality*, ed. D. G. Mandelbaum (Berkeley: University of California Press, 1961), p. 92.

## CHAPTER TWO

1. Detailed microstudies of social structure are provided by Edward T. Hall, *The Hidden Dimension* (Garden City, N. Y.: Anchor Books, 1969), and Robert Sommer, *Personal Space: The Behavioral Basis of Design* (Englewood Cliffs, N. J.: Prentice-Hall, 1969).

2. See Erving Goffman, *Relations in Public: Microstudies of the Public Order* (New York: Basic Books, 1971) and *Behavior in Public Places: Notes on the Social Organization of Gatherings* (New York: Free Press, 1963).

3. *The New York Times*, June 30, 1969, p. 1.

4. Ibid., May 22, 1967, p. 39.

5. Goffman, *Relations in Public*, p. 62.

6. Ibid., p. 63.

7. Emile Durkheim, *The Rules of Sociological Method*. trans. S. A. Solovay and J. H. Mueller (New York: Free Press, 1938), p.30.

8. Walter Benjamin, *Illuminations*, ed. Hannah Arendt, trans. Harry Zohn (New York: Schocken, 1969), pp. 223–24.

9. Karl Baedeker, *Paris and Environs*, 14th rev. ed. (Leipzig: Karl Baedeker, Publisher, 1900), pp. xxix–xxx.

10. *The Sociology of Georg Simmel*, ed. and trans. Kurt H. Wolff (Glencoe, Ill.: Free Press, 1950), p. 410.

11. See Simmel's essay on "The Stranger," ibid. pp. 402–8.

12. *The New York Times*, April 12, 1970, p. 34.

13. From my field notes.

14. Paris: *International Herald Tribune*, March 26, 1971, p. 7.

15. Interestingly, behavior *for* tourists is only felt to be degrading by members of already exploited minorities. Middle-class hippies and radicals seem to enjoy working in front of the camera. Perhaps the leaders of exploited minorities teach noncooperation with tourists because this is one of the only areas in which members of these minorities can dramatize self-determination.

16. Paul Hoffman. "Hippie's Hangout Draws Tourists," *The New York Times*, June 5, 1967, p. 43.

17. Irwin M. Chapman. "Visit to Two Russian Towns," *The New York Times*, February 23, 1969, sect. 10, p. 29.

18. News release dated April 27, 1970 from "Operation New Birmingham," a civic group, quoted in "Images of America: Racial Feeling Remains Strong in the Cities," *The New York Times*, May 24, 1970, p. 64.

19. "For Tourists Who Want to See All," *International Herald Tribune*, November 4, 1970.

# CHAPTER THREE

1. Roland Barthes, *Mythologies* (Paris: Editions du Seuil, 1957). Barthes wrote this book between 1954 and 1956. Selections from it are published in English as *Mythologies*, trans. Annette Lavers (New York: Hill and Wang, 1972).

2. H. Marshall McLuhan, *The Mechanical Bride* (New York: Vanguard, 1951).

3. See his discussion of method in his *Le cru et le cuit* (Paris: Librarie Plon, 1964). This work appears in English translation as *The Raw and the Cooked* (New York: Harper & Row, 1968).

4. *New York City* (New York: Michelin Tire Corporation, 1968), p. 95.

5. Alden Hatch, *American Express: A Century of Service* (Garden City, N. Y.: Doubleday, 1950), pp. 109–10.

6. See his *Illuminations*, ed. Hannah Arendt, trans. Harry Zohn (New York: Schocken, 1969), p. 266.

7. Other guides consulted: Paul Joanne, *Paris: Ses environs et l'exposition* (Paris: Librarie Hachette et Cie, 1900); Henry Haynie, *Paris, Past and Present* (New York: Frederick A. Stokes, 1902); Katherine S. and Gilbert S. Mac-Quoid, *In Paris: A Handbook For Visitors to Paris in the Year 1900* (Boston: L. C. Page, 1900).

8. The elevated tone of the Baedeker guides has been subjected to much ridicule. See, for example, Daniel J. Boorstin, *The Image: A Guide to Pseudo-Events in America.* (New York: Harper & Row, 1961), pp. 104–6. Boorstin concentrates his criticism on the person of Karl Baedeker. For a fictional account that focuses on the users of Baedeker's guides, see Thomas Pynchon's novel *V.* (New York: Bantam Books, 1963), pp. 58–65.

9. Of course, no amount of methodological caution can place this type of analysis above criticism. There is no case of a sociologist suggesting an historical reading of social facts which has not been faulted. History in its plentitude always proffers negative evidence. Perhaps someone will take the pains to point out that the *entire* relationship I am trying to establish between tourism and modernity is false because sightseeing is very old and modernity is not. Sightseeing predates modernity, I want to be the first to say, in the same way that capitalism predates Protestantism. But this is not the point. Premodern tourists were not socially organized as they are today. Sightseeing, before about seventy-five years ago, was mainly speculative and individualistic. It was not a central and essential feature of the structure of society.

10. In selecting work displays from among the social attractions for special attention, I am guided equally by traditional sociological concerns and by the empirical requirements of my study. In his *Division of Labor in Society* (Glencoe, Ill.: Free Press, 1947), Durkheim suggests that the solidarity of our current societies is based on a progressive repartition of tasks so that the growth of the society requires increased cooperation among members. Durkheim describes sexual and economic differences but, for illustration, he refers most often to occupational specialization. Marx also located the relationship of men and their work at the center of his study of structural change. Max Weber took as his central question in his study of Protestantism: What could possibly compel men to work as hard and as long as they do under the régime of modern capitalism? And academic sociology in the United States has provided more and better descriptions of work and work settings than of any

other aspect of modern society. Chicago sociology treats what Everett C. Hughes has called the "universal drama of work" as its analytical and empirical foundation—according to work arrangements, status not unlike that accorded kinship systems by anthropologists.

11. In *The Presentation of Self in Everyday Life* (Garden City, N. Y.: Doubleday, 1959), Erving Goffman has gone one step further to suggest that the most essential elements of a social display *must* be omitted in order for it to appear to be real.

12. In Diderot, d'Alembert, et al., *Encyclopedia: Selections*, trans. Nellie S. Hoyt and Thomas Cassirer (Indianapolis: Bobbs-Merrill, 1965), p. 141.

13. For an elaboration of the concept, see Harold Garfinkel, "The Conditions of Successful Degradation Ceremonies," *American Journal of Sociology*, 61 (March 1956), pp. 420–24.

14. Mark Twain, *The Innocents Abroad or The New Pilgrim's Progress* (New York: New American Library, 1966), p. 97.

15. I am indebted here to a paper (unpublished) by Judith Kinman.

16. Patrick Nolan has suggested to me that killing is a low-status occupation and middle-class individuals may stay away from it because they risk being mistakenly identified with it. Members of the upper classes (who are not threatened) and of the lower classes (who have nothing to lose) are more likely to enjoy a beheading, etc., according to this idea.

17. Joan Paulson, "In the Footsteps of Jean Valjean," *The New York Times*, May 17, 1970, travel sect., p. 5.

## CHAPTER FOUR

1. The classic statements here are those of George Brown Goode, the enthusiastic first Secretary of the United States National Museum. Some of his papers and addresses are reproduced in early issues of the *Memoirs of the Smithsonian Institution*. For a more recent statement see Hiroshi Daifuku, "The Museum and the Visitor," chap. 5 of *Museums and Monuments Vol. 9, The Organization of Museums: Practical Advice*. (Paris: United Nations Educational, Scientific and Cultural Organization, 1960), pp. 73–80. Daifuku writes:

> Applied museography, the use of museums and exhibits to help people to assimilate new values, has not yet been fully developed. For example, cause and effect correlations based upon scientific and pragmatic observation are a product of a particular culture and must be explained to people having entirely different modes of thought. Among many folk societies the failure of crops, desiccation of pasture lands, poverty, sickness and other serious difficulties are often ascribed to the effects of witchcraft, failure to observe proper rituals, the malignant attention of some deity, etc. . . .

Exhibitions presenting in summary form a sequence showing the land with adequate cover, the changes which resulted from overgrazing, and explaining a programme for the reduction of herds with possibly the introduction of new breeds, and the resulting restoration of plant cover would help bring people to understand the problem and the suggested cure. At the same time it would introduce them to one of the methods of evaluating phenomena which has been essential to the development of contemporary science. (pp. 78–79.)

2. Douglas A. Allen, "The Museum and its Functions," ibid., chap. 1 p. 13.

3. Thomas R. Adam, *The Civic Value of Museums* (American Association for Adult Education, 1937), pp. 2, 8.

4. Alma S. Wittlin, *Museums in Search of a Useable Future* (Cambridge, Mass.: M.I.T. Press, 1970), p. 209.

5. "A Trip to Niagara Falls," *Harpers Weekly*, October 2, 1858, quoted in *The American Heritage Book of Natural Wonders* (New York: McGraw-Hill, 1963), p. 121.

6. William R. Catton, Jr., *From Animistic to Naturalistic Sociology* (New York: McGraw-Hill, 1966), pp. 185–86. Professor Catton provides evidence that Samuel A. Stouffer's theory of mobility (*American Sociological Review*, 5 [December 1940], p. 867) does not predict the travel patterns of visitors to national parks. That is, Catton finds attractiveness and distance (i.e., intervening alternative destinations) are not strongly inversely associated in his study of tourists. Similarly, Catton finds that Zipf's model (which attributes attraction to population size) is not adequate when the average daily number of park visits is equated with "population" of the destination. Catton's hypothesis is that people are attracted to the parks by their beauty.

7. César Graña, *Fact and Symbol* (New York: Oxford University Press, 1971), p. 98.

8. H. H. Frese, *Anthropology and the Public: The Role of Museums*, Ministerie van Onderwijs, Kunsten en Wetenschappen, Mededelingen van het Rijksmuseum voor Volkenkunde, Leiden, No. 14 (Leiden: Brill, 1960), pp. 124–25.

9. Georges-Henri Rivière (Director, International Council of Museums), "Conclusion," *Museums and Monuments Vol. 9*, pp. 187–88.

10. *International Herald Tribune*, January 29, 1971, p. 16.

11. Theodora Kroeber, *Ishi in Two Worlds: A Biography of the Last Wild Indian in North America* (Berkeley: University of California Press, 1961), pp. 129–34. It should be noted that a better solution than Waterman's was eventually found: Ishi held office hours in an upstairs room of the museum with Kroeber as an interpreter.

12. *International Herald Tribune*, December 19, 1970, p. 14.

13. The difficult case of the railroad locomotive should be mentioned here. Locomotives are important tourist attractions but they are exactly of a size that makes the decision as to whether they should be museumized (inside) or monumentalized (outside) difficult. At the inventor's park in downtown Dayton, Ohio, where the Wright Brothers' Workshop has been reconstructed, there are also some interesting locomotives displayed indoors, but they are cracking the foundations of the buildings they are in. The largest locomotive in the USA and perhaps the world, "Big Boy," on display in Cheyenne, Wyoming, is outside—in a park, of course. The Leland Stanford, Jr. Museum in Palo Alto, California was itself built around a locomotive but at some point it was decided to remove the display, and new bricks in the side of the building in the exact shape of an old steam engine, mark the place where it was removed through the wall to a siding constructed there for that purpose. [Explained to me in 1963 by Hal Glicksman who was then Assistant Curator of the Leland Stanford, Jr. Museum.]

14. *Philadelphia Evening Bulletin*, October 13, 1969, p. 4.

15. *The New York Times Magazine*, March 16, 1969, p. 16.

## CHAPTER FIVE

1. Erving Goffman, *The Presentation of Self in Everyday Life* (Garden City, N. Y.: Doubleday, 1959), pp. 144–45.

2. M. Mintz, "Cancer Link Possible in Food Tinting," *International Herald Tribune*. I regret I have lost the citation of my clipping.

3. Anonymous, "Dear Mom and All Mothers," *Tiohero 5* (Ithaca, N. Y.: Glad Day Press, n.d.), pp. 32–33.

4. Margaret Mead, *Male and Female* (New York: Mentor, 1955), p. 31.

5. Goffman, *Presentation of Self*, p. 247.

6. A. Young, "Travels in France" in vol. 19 of *The World's Greatest Books*, eds. Lord Northcliffe (Alfred Harmsworth) and S. S. McClure (n.p.: McKinlay, Stone and Mackenzie, 1910), p. 332.

7. E. Pearson, "Discovering an Undiscovered Town in Southern Spain," *The New York Times*, June 6, 1969, sect. 10, p. 29.

8. Advertisement for Swissair in *The New York Times*, April 19, 1970, sect. 10, p. 42.

9. A. Keller, "He Said: 'Tourists Never Take the Mail Boat'—That Clinched It," *The New York Times*, May 24, 1970, sect. 10, p. 24.

10. I. H. Gordon, "The Space Center Is Open to Visitors Even in a Crisis," *The New York Times*, May 3, 1970, sect. 10.

11. J. Sjöby, "Dining Out: International Fare in Danish Restaurant."

*International Herald Tribune,* February 26, 1970, p. 5.

12. Daniel J. Boorstin, *The Image: A Guide to Pseudo-Events In America* (New York: Harper & Row, 1961), pp. 77–117.

13. Thorstein Veblen, *The Theory of the Leisure Class* (New York: New American Library, 1963), pp. 41–60.

14. Mark Twain, *The Innocents Abroad or The New Pilgrim's Progress* (New York: New American Library, 1966).

15. Boorstin, *The Image,* p. 99.

16. Ibid., p. 114 (my emphasis).

17. Ibid., p. 85.

18. B. Thompson, "Hustled, Harried—But Happy," *The New York Times,* August 16, 1970, sect. 10, p. 3.

19. J. Goodman, "Hitting the 'Freebee' Jackpot Without Trying—in Las Vegas," *The New York Times,* January 25, 1970, sect. 10, p. 11.

20. For a discussion of this aspect of the intellectual approach to tourism, see O. Burgelin, "Le Tourisme jugé," in *Vacances et tourisme,* a special edition of *Communications,* no. 10, 1967, pp. 65–97.

21. Claude Lévi-Strauss, *Tristes Tropiques,* trans. John Russel (New York: Atheneum, 1968), p. 17.

## CHAPTER SIX

1. Charles Dickens, *American Notes* and *Pictures from Italy* (London: J. M. Dent, 1931), p. 255.

2. Reported in *The New York Times,* August 14, 1967, p. 3.

3. Mark Twain, *The Innocents Abroad or The New Pilgrim's Progress* (New York: New American Library, 1966), pp. 136–37.

4. Ibid., p. 137.

5. Reported in *Philadelphia Evening Bulletin,* November 17, 1969, p. 3.

6. No author, date, copyright, publisher, or pagination. This piece of information was sent to me by Frank W. Young.

7. William R. Catton, Jr., *From Animistic to Naturalistic Sociology* (New York: McGraw-Hill, 1966), p. 191.

8. Susan Marsh, "Come See Your Car Crushed," *The New York Times,* October 26, 1969, sect. 10, part 2, p. 12.

9. *The New York Times,* October 12, 1969, p. 41.

10. Time-Life Books advertising flyer—no copyright, no author, no date.

11. This fraud is discussed by Otto Kurz in his excellent study, *Fakes,* 2nd ed., rev. and enlarged (New York: Dover, 1967), p. 45.

12. Herbert R. Lottman, "Walking Through Masterpieces In Low Countries," *The New York Times,* May 24, 1970, sect. 10, part 2, p. 7.

13. See P. Francastel, "Problèmes de la sociologie de l'art," in Georges Gurvitch, *Traité de sociologie*, vol. 2, p. 284. (Cited in Olivier Burgelin, "Le Tourisme jugé," *Communications*, no. 10, 1967, p. 69.)

14. Twain, *Innocents Abroad*, p. 83.

15. *The Anglo-American Guide to Exhibition Paris, 1900* (London: Heinemann, 1900), p. 357.

16. Marilyn Stout, "In Vermont: You'll Wonder Where the Billboards Went," *The New York Times*, May 31, 1970, sect. 10, part 2, p. 3.

17. Maxine Molyneux, "At Risk: The Look of London." *International Herald Tribune*, November 25, 1970, p. 16.

18. Twain, *Innocents Abroad*, p. 91.

19. Ibid., p. 101.

20. Suggested by Iles Minoff.

## CHAPTER SEVEN

1. Katherine S. and Gilbert S. MacQuoid, *In Paris: A Handbook for Visitors to Paris in the Year 1900* (Boston: L. C. Page, 1900), p. 61.

2. Reported by Joe Hitt.

3. Reported by Juliet Flower MacCannell, who also helped me to reconstruct the logic.

4. *The New York Times*, November 5, 1969, p. 3.

5. Ibid., April 12, 1970, sect. 10, part 1, p. 1.

6. *International Herald Tribune*, April 20, 1968, p. 4.

7. *The New York Times*, August 19, 1969, p. 65.

## CHAPTER EIGHT

1. This is translated from André Gide, *Retour de l'enfant prodigue* (Paris: Librairie Gallimard, 1929) pp. 228–33.

2. *International Herald Tribune*, April 18, 1968, p. 1.

3. *The New York Times*, July 12, 1970, sect. 10, p. 9.

4. *Philadelphia Evening Bulletin*, January 23, 1970, p. 12.

5. The French, who have as much society as anyone else, nevertheless used "La vie est ailleurs" as one of their slogans in their abortive May revolution in 1968. Radicals are especially attached to the idea of the true society.

6. Marcel Mauss, *The Gift* (New York: Norton, 1967), pp. 63ff.

7. Jon Nordheimer, "Florida Disney World to Open This Year," *International Herald Tribune*, January 2, 1971, p. 12.

8. See the report in *ASTA Travel News,* Official Publication of the American Society of Travel Agents, Inc. (April 1970) p. 13.

9. Roland Barthes, *Mythologies* (New York: Hill and Wang, 1972), pp. 124–25.


## CHAPTER NINE

1. "H. M. Eikenbary Noted Dayton Lawyer Dies," *Journal Herald* (Dayton, Ohio) September 21, 1974, p. 1.

2. Alden Hatch, *American Express: A Century of Service* (Garden City, N. Y.: Doubleday, 1950), p. 105.

3. Ibid., p. 169.

4. Jack McDonald, "Americanization of Tampico Has A Go-Go Beat," *The New York Times,* March 8, 1970, sect. 10, p. 38.

5. Lyn H. Lofland, *A World of Strangers: Order and Action in Urban Public Space* (New York: Basic Books, 1973).

6. Henri Lefebvre, *Everyday Life in the Modern World* (New York: Harper & Row, 1971). See especially his remarks on "Urban reform and revolution," and on "The festival rediscovered," pp. 205–6.

7. *The New York Times,* June 8, 1969, p. 96.

8. Raymond H. Anderson, "A Soviet Republic Seeking Tourists," *The New York Times,* May 28, 1967, p. 13.

9. Carl Buchalla, "Yugoslav Costs Are Still Low," *The New York Times,* February 23, 1969, sect. 10, p. 25.

10. I am indebted to John Hostetler for having given me a guided tour of the Amish.

11. From an advertisement in *The New York Times,* February 22, 1970, p. 48.

12. *The New York Times,* September 15, 1968, p. 29.

13. Charles Mohr, "Malawi Seeking Tourist Business," *The New York Times,* April 26, 1970, p. 7.

14. A Turkish respondent of mine, whose job it is to divert tourists off the main thoroughfares of Istanbul to a backstreet leather coat factory, described the language he uses in his work as "Tarzan English, you know, the kind one reads in comic books."

15. Jack McDonald, "Hippies Get in the Artists' Hair In Mexico's San Miguel Allende," *The New York Times,* January 25, 1970, sect. 10, p. 5.

16. Reported in ibid., April 23, 1967, p. 5.

17. *International Herald Tribune,* April 18, 1968, p. 12.

18. *The New York Times,* April 26, 1970, sect. 10, p. 1.

19. Ibid., May 3, 1970, sect. 10.

20. Ibid., May 3, 1970, sect. 10.

21. Ibid., May 3, 1970, sect. 10, p. 1.

22. Ibid., November 2, 1969, p. 34.

23. Ibid., February 22, 1970, sect. 10, p. 26.

24. Erving Goffman, *The Presentation of Self in Everyday Life* (Garden City, N. Y.: Doubleday, 1959), p. iii.

25. Everett C. Hughes, *The Sociological Eye*, vol. 1 (Chicago: Aldine, 1971), pp. 110–11.

26. Barbara Bell, "All Aboard for Talob, Muckle Flugga, Yell, Unst, Etc.," *The New York Times*, August 24, 1969, sect. 10, p. 27. All citations are from p. 27.

27. The Berlitz version of a foreign language is the functional equivalent of a multilingual waiter or bellhop for tourists who use a class of establish- ments lacking multilingual personnel.

28. Tourists can ignore parking regulations in all of Bozeman, Montana and parts of Paris. Apparently they were once able to break the curfew regulations in Haiti. See *New York Christian Herald Book of the Rulers of the World at Home: How They Look and How They Live* (New York: Louis Klopsch, 1899), p. 248. However, on the negative side, tourists must submit to search of body and belongings and sometimes to quarantine and fumigation.

Jean-Jacques Rousseau was quarantined:

> It was the time of the plague at Messina. The English fleet, which had anchored there, inspected the felucca on which I was. On arriving at Genoa, therefore, after a long and tiresome voyage, we were subjected to a quarantine of twenty-one days. . . . I was led into a large two-storied building, absolutely bare, in which I found neither window nor table nor bed nor chair, not even a stool to sit on, nor a bundle of hay on which to lie. They brought me my cloak, my travelling bag, and my two trunks; the great doors with their huge locks were shut upon me. . . .

*The Confessions of Jean-Jacques Rousseau,* translated and with an introduction by J. M. Cohen (Middlesex, England: Penguin Books, 1953), p. 278.

Charles Dickens was quarantined:

> This wool of ours had come originally from some place in the East. It was recognized as Eastern produce, the moment we entered the harbour. Accord- ingly, the gay little Sunday boats, full of holiday people, which had come off to greet us, were warned away by the authorities; we were declared in quarantine; and a great flag was solemnly run up to the masthead on the wharf to make it known to all the town. It was a very hot day indeed. We were unshaved, unwashed, undressed, unfed, and could hardly enjoy the absurdity of lying blistering in a lazy harbour, with the town looking on from a respectful distance, all manner of whiskered men in cocked hats discussing our fate at a remote

guardhouse, with gestures (we looked very hárd at them through telescopes) expressive of a week's detention at least. . . .

Charles Dickens, *American Notes* and *Pictures From Italy* (London: J. M. Dent, 1931), p. 304.

Mark Twain was fumigated:

> When we walked ashore, a party of policemen (people whose cocked hats and showy uniforms would shame the finest uniform in the military service of the United States) put us in a little stone cell and locked us in. We had the whole passenger list for company, but their room would have been preferable, for there was no light, there were no windows, no ventilation. It was close and hot. We were much crowded. It was the Black Hole of Calcutta on a small scale. Presently a smoke rose about our feet—a smoke that smelled of all the dead things of earth, of all the putrefaction and corruption imaginable. We were there five minutes, and when we got out it was hard to tell which of us carried the vilest fragrance. These miserable outcasts called that "fumigating" us, and the term was a tame one indeed.

Mark Twain, *The Innocents Abroad or The New Pilgrim's Progress* (New York: New American Library, 1966), pp. 142–143.

29. In *The Theory of the Leisure Class* (New York: New American Library, 1953).

30. Norman S. Hayner, "Hotel Life and Personality," *The American Journal of Sociology*, 33 (March 1928), pp. 784 –95.

31. J. Roebuck and S. Lee Spray, "The Cocktail Lounge: A Study of Hetero-sexual Relations in a Public Organization," *American Journal of Sociology*, 72 (January 1967), pp. 338–95.

32. Sherri Cavan, *Liquor License: An Ethnography of Bar Behavior* (Chicago: Aldine, 1966).

33. Cora E. Richards, "City Taverns," *Human Organization*, 22 (January 1964), pp. 260–68.

34. David Gottlieb, "The Neighborhood Tavern and the Cocktail Lounge—A Study of Class Differences," *American Journal of Sociology*, 62 (May 1957), pp. 559–62.

35. Royal L. Melendy, "The Saloon in Chicago," *American Journal of Sociology*, 6 (November 1900), pp. 289–306.

36. Fred Davis, "The Cab Driver and His Fare: Facets of a Fleeting Relationship," *American Journal of Sociology*, 65 (September 1959), pp. 158–65.

37. John F. Cuber, "Patrons of Amusement Parks," *Sociology and Social Research*, 24 (September, 1939), pp. 63–68.

38. William Foote Whyte, "The Social Structure of the Restaurant," *American Journal of Sociology*, 54 (January 1949), pp. 302–10.

39. Elon H. Moore, "Public Dance Halls in a Small City," *Sociology and Social Research*, 14 (January 1930), pp. 256–64.

40. Howard S. Becker, *Outsiders: Studies in the Sociology of Deviance* (New York: Free Press, 1963), pp. 79–120.

41. Anselm L. Strauss, *Mirrors and Masks: The Search for Identity* (San Francisco: Sociology Press, 1969), p. 159.

42. Edward T. Hall, *The Silent Language* (Garden City, N. Y.: Doubleday, Inc., 1959).

43. Leslie A. White, *The Science of Culture* (New York: Farrar, Straus and Giroux, 1969), pp. xvii–xviii.

44. Bennett Berger, "On the Youthfulness of Youth Cultures," in *Life Styles: Diversity in American Culture*, eds. S. Feldman and G. Thielbar (Boston: Little Brown, 1975), pp. 281–97. The quote is from p. 296.

45. See, for example, Labov's *Sociolinguistic Patterns* (Philadelphia: University of Pennsylvania Press, 1972), pp. 44, 186–87, 191, 192.

46. Frank W. Young and Ruth C. Young, *Comparative Studies of Community Growth*, Rural Sociological Society Monograph no. 2 (Morgantown: West Virginia University Press, 1973). All quotes are from pp. 1–13.

47. *The New York Times*, January 18, 1970, p. 17.

48. Malcolm W. Browne, "Tourists are Sought by Easter Island," *The New York Times*, May 24, 1970, p. 29.

49. Arturo Gonzalez, Jr., "Tourists Are Getting a Foothold on the Antarctic Wasteland," *The New York Times*, August 23, 1970, sect. 10, p. 3.

50. *International Herald Tribune*, March 22, 1971.

51. P. J. Laine, "In the Antarctic, the Visitors are Giving the Admiral Fits," *International Herald Tribune*, April 26, 1971, p. 6.

# Index